The politics of foreign aid in India

The politics of foreign aid in India

P. J. Eldridge

MA (Oxon), PhD (London)
Lecturer in Political Science at the University of Tasmania

London School of Economics and Political Science

Weidenfeld and Nicolson
5 Winsley Street London W1

SBN 297 17862 8
Printed in Great Britain by
Lowe & Brydone (Printers) Ltd., London

Contents

A*

List of tables

Abbreviations

AMOCO	American International Oil Company
AICC	All India Congress Committee
AOC	Assam Oil Company
CPI	Communist Party of India
DLF	Development Loan Fund
G of I	Government of India
IBRD	International Bank for Reconstruction and Development
ICICI	Industrial Credit and Investment Corporation of India
IDA	International Development Association
IFC	Industrial Finance Corporation
IISCO	Indian Iron and Steel Company
IOC	Indian Oil Company
ISCON	Indian Steel Works Construction Company Limited London
NIOC	National Iranian Oil Company
ONGC	Oil and Natural Gas Commission (G of I)
OPEC	Oil Prices Enquiry Committee
PL 480	Public Law 480
SVOC	Standard Vacuum Oil Company
TISCO	Tata Iron and Steel Company
UNCTAD	United Nations Conference on Trade and Development
USAID	United States Agency for International Development

Preface

This work is the result of several years of study, initiated at the London School of Economics and completed in India and Australia. Aid to India is viewed primarily in an international relations context rather than in terms of its impact on economic development, though of necessity a fair amount of economic data is presented to assist in evaluation of political issues. Comprehensive data is presented up to 1965, although much additional data is included for the most recent years. In my judgment it would be an unnecessarily laborious task to bring all the figures completely up to date, since this would not significantly alter the general conclusions. A more important problem, however, has been to relate major changes during the last two or three years in the overall political and administrative framework within which aid operates to the basic trends observed during the earlier period. The most striking changes are outlined in the Introduction, and at various points throughout the tensions between earlier and later trends are made apparent. The reader is therefore asked to relate particular propositions to their various time periods, though these latter each contain counter-trends and are in many cases overlapping. Despite these difficulties, I have succeeded in arriving at certain broad conclusions concerning the political impact of aid on India, on the basis of which a few general prescriptions are offered for the future. These latter can be no more than tentative, since the whole system of foreign aid relationships is now very much in transition and the diversity of pressures bearing upon them is very considerable.

It is hoped that this book will fill a certain gap. Most studies which deal with foreign aid tend to cover several countries at once. They tend also to look mainly at the objectives of donor countries and institutions, analysing the reactions of recipients in terms of these objectives. Various works have attempted to analyse the economic impact of aid, but serious difficulties are encountered in attempting to isolate the aid factor from other economic variables and in the process one is again likely to analyse a country's pattern of development in terms of donor objectives. Studies which compare various recipient countries seem automatically to produce a methodological distortion whereby donors' interpretations are established as the common factor. Naturally, aid-givers are primarily concerned to know how far their objectives are being achieved, but self-interest as well as altruism requires that the perspective be reversed, which is what I have endeavoured to do. So far as India is concerned, whilst several useful studies of aid and development problems have been made at the local level, little attention has been paid to the 'macro' political level. The main weight of this study, therefore, is on the Indian view of its own political interest with regard to aid. Following an initial statement of the various patterns of aid established by different countries and institutions, and an analysis of the main trends of policy development in Russia and America, Indian attitudes are broken down at various levels of responsibility and awareness and in relation to specific issues. Interactions are observed through a number of specific situations and finally evaluated in the Conclusion.

This work should properly be preceded by an earlier volume analysing the diversity of pressures at work in relation to Indian economic development and planning. It is only possible to give references, and some prior knowledge of India's political and economic problems, and the debate which surrounds them, must be assumed. From India's standpoint aid will then properly be viewed as one important and complex piece in a much larger jigsaw. Whereas donors look on aid as an important instrument of policy, for India it is a question of obtaining the right type of aid on the best possible terms in order to assist existing policy objectives. A wide variety of permutations has in fact proved possible, but viewed in this light it is easy to see why the Indian government has been anxious to confine discussion within a technical and administrative framework and why the intrusion of ideology has been so much resented. Fortunately for India, the global balance of interests on the subcontinent has tended to neutralise the major Cold War influences.

India's planners are acutely conscious of a dilemma which does not seem consistently apparent to aid-givers. In accepting aid it is hoped to build an economy sufficiently strong within a reasonable period of time to have no need of aid. In the short run, however, substantial funds will be needed. They therefore seek the type of aid which will help them achieve this goal of independence. In fact a cycle of frustration sets in as the debt burden mounts and as donors fail to see tangible results. A serious rethinking is necessary if the present mood of disillusion is to be overcome and aid programmes are to continue on a constructive basis.

It is necessary for foreign aid, especially Western aid, to acquire, or at least re-acquire legitimacy in a changed context. When this has been achieved, proper areas of responsibility will be apparent and there will be much less scope for mutual recriminations. Notions of 'pay-off' are not very meaningful as they stand, in the same way as expectations of gratitude have been predictably disappointed. In both cases aid is only one of many factors that may influence Indian opinion towards particular countries, whilst the specific contribution of aid to development is not easily identifiable. The better approach, in my view, is for aid-givers to recognise India's sovereign right to formulate its own goals and to select those goals which they think are worth backing, leaving aside other areas until firm agreement can be reached. This is probably the real secret behind the success of Soviet aid, besides its contribution to the achievement of national economic sovereignty. Of course, the West is more concerned with problems of overall balance, which would make such a strategy harder to define, whilst the private sector, both domestic and foreign, must also be fitted into the picture. Nonetheless, if certain firm bases of agreement could be established, a greater spirit of expertise and professionalism could then be fostered, with a far more dynamic and uninhibited dialogue occurring over the whole field of development and planning. As things stand, the interaction between general antipathies and particular programmes–and vice versa–has been uncertain, confusing and unprofitable.

Although Indian attitudes are often ambivalent and irritating to the Western mind, they nevertheless have their own system of logic. I have tried to identify and convey something very complex and in many ways intangible. A more formal sociological approach might well extract data from this analysis for a study in non-communication. The layman may find the well-known analogy between an irresistible force and an immoveable object equally useful. My arguments must necessarily rest on a cautiously attained and somewhat delicate balance. Whether I have reached the correct conclusions or not, I hope to have made some fresh approach to a subject that has become rather stale, but which is still in fact very important.

The whole system of aid has developed piecemeal in response to successive pressures and is a far more subtle process than many Westerners, 'liberal' or otherwise, are prepared to credit. A distinct air of unreality permeates much of the discussion which surrounds it. One assumption after another has proved untenable and matters are now in an unhealthy state of drift. I have stated more problems than answers, which must of course be developed by actors close to the scene of operations, having greater access to information than I can hope to possess. This work will have achieved its objective, therefore, if it in any way contributes towards inducing ideological self-doubt amongst planners and opinion-formers, at whatever point they fit into the total equation.

P. J. ELDRIDGE

Hobart, Tasmania
April, 1968

Acknowledgments

Research for this work has been conducted over six years, initially within the Department of International Relations, London School of Economics, under the guidance of Professor G. Goodwin, and then privately in Australia, subsequent to my appointment to a lectureship in the University of Tasmania in August 1964.

Sources include Lok Sabha Debates, the United States Congressional Record and Hearings etc., Indian Five Year Plans, Reserve Bank reports and numerous other official reports, press reports, books, articles, etc.

Three field trips were made to India in August 1964, in January-February 1966 and in September-October 1967. For the second visit warm thanks are due to the Social Science Research Council of Australia and for the second and third trips to the University of Tasmania for provision of funds. Work was mainly conducted in New Delhi, but also in Bombay and Calcutta. Assistance is appreciated from many academic acquaintances in the Institute of Economic Growth, University of Delhi, the Economics Departments of the Universities of Bombay, Calcutta and Jadavpur (where the help of Dr Raj Vasil and others in the International Relations Department is also much appreciated) and the Indian Institute of International Studies, Sapru House, New Delhi. An extensive range of interviews was conducted in India with officials of the government of India, including the Planning Commission, the Ministries of Finance (Department of Economic Affairs), Petroleum and Chemicals, Food and Agriculture, Steel and Mines; also with officials of foreign embassies and high commissions, officials of the United States Agency for International Development, the Ford and Rockefeller Foundations and the World Bank, with politicians, journalists, representatives of business, both Indian and foreign, and with officials of semi-government agencies connected with the private sector. The extent of assistance is too great to be fully acknowledged, but appreciation is nonetheless real. However, I would especially mention Shri Tarlok Singh, a senior member of the Planning Commission until 1967, and now engaged in research at Sapru House, for much interest, help and criticism, and also Sir James Plimsoll, formerly Australian high commissioner in India, for much encouragement and interest.

Acknowledgments are made to the Indian Institute of Public Opinion for permission to reproduce their polls, and the director, Shri E. da Costa for assistance in interpretation. Thanks are also due to Shri Dilip Mukerjee, economic editor of *The Statesman*, Calcutta, for access to his personal collection of press cuttings, and to the Federation of Indian Chambers of Commerce and Industry for access to material. Thanks are due to the director and staff at Chatham House, London, for extensive use of press cuttings and other material. Appreciation is also expressed to the library staffs at the United States embassy, London; India House, London; Indian School of International Studies, New Delhi; the National Library, Canberra and the University of Tasmania, Hobart. Assistance and interest from the academic and research staff of the International Relations Department, Australian National University, Canberra is also appreciated. Sincere thanks are given to my friends and colleagues in the Political Science Department, University of Tasmania, for encouragement and support, and especially to Dr S. V. Rao for valuable criticism.

Warmest acknowledgments are due to Professor G. Goodwin for constant criticism, encouragement and advice, though responsibility for presentation of data, arguments and conclusions is entirely my own.

Finally, deepest gratitude is due to my wife for her patience and strength, sustained over a long period of time.

Chapter 1

Introduction

The primary object of this work is to study the political relationships between India and foreign donors arising from aid programmes. These relationships are viewed in a global setting, the relative impact of aid programmes being analysed against a background of ideological conflict, albeit diminishing in recent years. Areas of conflict are identified and their overall weight assessed, whilst the politics of aid administration are seen as an important part of the total equation. The borderline between 'economic' and 'political' issues is indistinct, but analysis of the former is only undertaken within the wider framework of the latter. In this context, economic data presented in chapter 2 serve to identify differences of emphasis by various donors, providing points of reference for issues considered subsequently, but especially in Part 2. Whilst the overall objective is to arrive at a meaningful definition of relationships, purposes and priorities, the main weight of analysis is placed on the Indian viewpoint. Her reactions to various policies and methods adopted by donor countries and institutions are extensively analysed at governmental level. An attempt is also made to assess the general effect of aid programmes in shaping Indian public opinion towards aid-supplying countries. My general conclusion is that despite some measure of mutual interest, there are important differences of emphasis and viewpoint between India and the donor countries, especially Western countries. Where donor objectives remain unfulfilled, this may be due to failures in communication or because these objectives are in need of redefinition, or even because they are meaningless. Some possible remedies are suggested in the concluding chapter.

The term 'aid' may cause confusion. I have been obliged to use it somewhat loosely. Some people would only class outright gifts as aid, whereas in fact the major part of what is called aid is in the form of loans. However, loans which are granted on better than commercial terms may legitimately be defined as aid, depending on individual judgments. Though the official Indian sources used do in fact classify all loans and grants from foreign donors as 'external assistance', close scrutiny of many agreements will explain why so often Indians obstinately refuse to be grateful, to the chagrin of public opinion in the West. For stylistic reasons the term 'aid' is used to cover loans and grants, but the above qualifications must always be borne in mind. A further point is that aid is normally associated with governments and international institutions. In India's case a significant proportion of foreign assistance is channelled to the private sector, directly or indirectly.

The period covered is from independence in 1947 to the present day. In fact, no significant aid appeared in India until the beginning of the First Five Year Plan in 1951, but some prior account is taken of the evolution of attitudes in America and Russia. Large scale aid does not make its appearance until the Second Plan beginning in 1956. In the early post-independence years India's foreign currency position was strong, as large sterling balances had been accumulated during the second world war and afterwards. The First Plan was largely concerned with agriculture and the establishment of basic 'infrastructure' such as power, irrigation, transport, communications, education, etc. The Second Plan however called for a massive effort on the industrial front, demanding a large increase in imports. Poor harvests from 1956-8 (plus a too large dose of deficit financing) upset the Plan's financial balance, and India suddenly found herself requesting large sums of aid to avert a foreign exchange crisis. This crisis has deepened ever since. On both sides the adjustments were painful. India was unwilling to sacrifice either the freedom in international diplomacy which she had asserted during the earlier period or her economic sovereignty on the domestic front. On the Western side aid commitments on an unprecedented scale occasioned a massive debate on objectives and priorities. A large number of propositions established in this work apply especially to the period approximately 1956-64, during which a modus vivendi was so painfully built up. Later events have called for yet more painful readjustments.

The central themes which I am concerned to develop may be summarised as follows:

1. India has for most of the period considered maintained initiative with regard to definition of basic objectives and priorities of foreign aid and the framework within which it has operated, although some modification of this proposition is necessary for the latter period. This has been due to her tight system of planning, authoritative allocation of priorities and firm statement of principles, coupled with a general acquiescence and adjustment by the main donors who, despite many tensions, have been prepared to take a broad conception of their interests in India.

2. Though considerable areas of mutual interest between India and

foreign donors can be shown to exist, basic emphases and definition of issues are widely different. Whereas the latter view economic aid against the background of wider policy objectives, India is more concerned to integrate it within the framework of her own development plans. Aid is thus viewed in a narrower context and this is demonstrated by the nature of issues where conflict arises. Aid is not isolated as a specific issue in India as in the United States, attitudes being reactive rather than positive. Assertions of national sovereignty are emphasised, but despite the extent of India's dependence, she has yet to evolve an adequate philosophy of foreign aid on her own account.

3. Ideological objectives and issues connected with aid are more important to donor countries, especially the United States, than to India, her policy-makers and planners being generally concerned to contain issues of conflict within a narrow technical and economic framework. Ideological conflict takes most concrete shape in the debate over the proper roles of public and private sectors.

4. Whilst India is concerned that global rivalries between the West and the Soviet bloc should not impinge on her, their existence has notably increased her bargaining power with regard to aid. Conversely, their diminution makes her position weaker. In this respect India's efforts to reduce Cold War conflict may be seen in a more generous light than is customary in the West. Perhaps at the same time she has had hopes that coexistence would increase resources for development aid.

5. Attempts to link aid with foreign policy or military quid pro quos have been almost entirely unsuccessful.

6. Despite an initially competitive approach between America and Russia an area of mutual interest, served by aid programmes, can be shown to exist. Different emphases in their respective types of aid serve to support the overall balance of Indian economic development. Growth and stability in India, besides assisting international stability, will also provide a huge potential market.

7. Aid has played a growing part in influencing Indian popular attitudes towards donor countries, though issues affecting national sovereignty and prestige have been still more powerful in this respect.

Having stated the main lines of discussion, it is necessary to draw attention to certain related themes which cannot be covered adequately in this work. Research in these fields could provide further valuable evidence. At the same time certain limitations must be observed. Aid relates to wide questions of international diplomacy, economic issues at both practical and theoretical levels, internal Indian politics, philosophical aspects of

Indian political thought on such issues as socialism, communism, democracy, etc., basic social structure of Indian society and finally administrative structure. The problem is to keep a sense of perspective and yet not lose sight of the central themes. It is necessary to assume broad knowledge of Indian economic and political questions which are necessarily woven into the main discussion. References are given throughout, which to some extent covers the difficulty.

The impact of aid in a straight economic sense is not considered though this clearly must have great long-term significance in determining the pattern of internal politics. This would involve a major study of the Indian economy, entailing great difficulties in isolating the aid factor and in correlating patterns of economic and political development.

A study of the role of foreign experts would provide evidence at a more 'grass roots' level. However, many projects would need to be analysed, special factors being carefully isolated, to establish useful conclusions. A study of cultural and educational programmes could also provide valuable information.

The question of aid is in many respects a very sensitive one. Questions of gratitude, dependence, obligation and sovereignty are involved. Since such questions obviously touch on aspects of psychology, the problems may only be stated briefly if subjective judgments are to be avoided. At the same time existence of such factors cannot objectively be ignored.

Aid negotiations are clearly subject to substantial secrecy. Also, the extent of secret operations by donor countries in India cannot be adequately assessed, though one would not wish to be unduly cryptic. In the case of the Soviet Union, speculation is rendered more difficult by the paucity of English language sources from Russia itself.

Other than limited reference to the Ford and Rockefeller Foundations, the operations of private agencies have been omitted. This does not spring from any intention to discount their economic usefulness but from the fact that their activities do not significantly relate to the central themes discussed. Similar considerations apply to United Nations aid, which–though operating over a wide field–has succeeded in acquiring an almost wholly non-political character.

In the past year very important developments have taken place in India which throw the whole future of foreign aid into the melting pot. The general elections in February 1967 showed a massive swing against the ruling Congress party. At the Centre only a thin overall majority was retained, while eight states fell into the hands of non-Congress majorities. Except in Madras, won by the Dravida Munnetra Kazagham (DMK) mainly on the linguistic issue, these states are ruled by coalitions of varying degrees of stability, sometimes including both extreme Right and Left parties. Since the elections, India's largest state of Uttar Pradesh and the new state of Haryana, created from the division of Punjab, have lost their Congress majorities through defections. Without going into the complexities of the situation, donor countries must now deal with a far weaker central government of the Indian union. This may be seen from the fact that the Fourth Five Year Plan, due to start in 1966, has been shelved until 1969 at least and there is now a serious question whether planning on the previous model will ever again be resumed. This is due in part to a reaction against socialist-type planning with a heavy industry bias in the context of massive food crisis, and in part to sheer lack of resources, especially foreign exchange. Efforts must now be concentrated on agriculture and its related 'infrastructure', resting content with consolidation of existing industrial projects.

Aid has been geared to the requirements of the Five Year Plans and institutionalised within this framework. Although allocations to the states were always decided as much by a system of political horse-trading as by objective investment criteria, the existence of the Plans did at least provide common points of reference and even some sense of common purpose, the mechanisms of the Congress Party being available to work out a rough consensus. Whilst the traditional aid negotiating patterns continue, the priorities are now less clearly stated, giving the donors far more freedom of manoeuvre though at the same time rendering the bargaining process far more uncertain. The states also have far greater manoeuvrability and already there are signs that foreigners are willing to negotiate with them as well as with Delhi, a process that must weaken India's bargaining power. To date, however, this trend is mainly confined to the field of private investment.

The present work is divided into two parts, followed by the Conclusion. Part 1 deals with basic economic characteristics of aid supplied to India, followed by an analysis of American and Soviet objectives. Part 2 deals with the political impact of aid on India. Chapter 5, which may be regarded as the key chapter, defines basic principles and priorities applied by India in the acceptance of aid, identifies the main areas of conflict between her and the donors and assesses the political significance of aid programmes at governmental, parliamentary and popular levels (the main weight being placed on government).

The remaining chapters in Part 2 deal with aid in specific contexts, Indian policy objectives being demonstrated through a process of interaction. The various elements of conflict are assembled in a state of dynamic tension in the Conclusion.

A word of warning is necessary. Many shades of opinion will be brought to light and many strands of policy identified. Some of these may appear irrational, but in dealing with a subject of this nature irrationalities to some extent constitute evidence. Though much dry material must be dealt with, the topic even has its humorous side. The ideas and opinions presented must therefore not necessarily be taken as my own. I have tried to bring out the many varied and fascinating aspects of the discussion, but style can sometimes be misleading when one endeavours to act as interpreter. For instance, in chapter 3, I try to show the sheer confusion of much of the debate in the United States over foreign aid. Yet in my view this must be looked at with some degree of sympathy. One is viewing the evolution of policy with hindsight and the sheer magnitude of the task was not immediately appreciated, though the rapid adaptation of American thinking was in many ways remarkable. At the same time, India is only one country amongst many which receives American aid, although she is the largest single recipient of purely economic aid. Again, in chapter 4 it has been my intention to attack some of the more cryptic views of Soviet aid. In the process I may appear to be taking a somewhat cryptic view myself. A further point, which applies especially to the latter part of chapter 5, is that when dealing with non-government expressions of opinion, some degree of arbitrariness is unavoidable, though every attempt has been made to select the widest cross-section of views. On the whole I have played the role of interpreter though comments are periodically interspersed, either directly or implicitly. My own views are generally reserved for the Conclusion.

Part 1

Foreign donors: methods and objectives

Note

1 lakh = 100,000
1 crore = 10,000,000

Data concerning external financial assistance in chapter 2 and in subsequent chapters is stated mainly in terms of rupees. Exchange values should be computed at rates prevailing before rupee devaluation in May 1966–i.e. \$1 = Rs 4.76, \$2.1 = Rs 10, \$2.1 m = Rs 1 crore.

Sterling devaluation in November 1967 must also be taken into account.

Chapter 2

Economic data

In this chapter I shall provide some outline economic data with a view to defining the prime characteristics associated with assistance provided by various donor countries and institutions. This data is in no sense comprehensive, my aim being to indicate a few simple points of reference which may assist in uderstanding the more complex political analysis which follows. Although data is given here concerning all donors, large and small, only the United States, the Soviet Union and to a lesser extent Britain, West Germany and the World Bank are discussed at any length in the main body of the work. Nevertheless, information concerning the smaller donors may easily be related by the reader to the subsequent general discussion.

India naturally seeks the best terms available when negotiating aid agreements. In this context grants are obviously more advantageous than loans, though against this some sense of inhibition against receiving grant aid has been felt on political grounds. Donors have in any case steadily increased the proportion of their loan aid. In assessing the value of loan aid to India, interest rates and repayment periods are the most important factors. Also, the extent to which aid is tied to purchases in the country of origin, to particular projects or to both, affects the pattern of India's development and the debt burden she must carry. At a higher policy level there have been differences between India and certain donors as to the size and direction of her Plans and the proper allocation of resources between public and private sectors. Data concerning types of aid provided, overall terms of such aid, allocations to various purposes and between public and private sectors are given separately in this chapter for each country and institution, concluding with a brief comparison of Soviet and American terms of aid.[1] It is not intended to suggest that some kind of merit scale can be drawn up on this basis, but by reference to subsequent analysis, especially in chapter 5, it can be seen more easily which types of aid are most likely to achieve harmonious political relations with India. It is recognised that wider considerations may override this particular objective, desirable as it may be; but at least some yardstick is given by which to make political judgments.

With regard to comparisons of overall magnitudes, both in terms of total aid and in terms of relative allocations by type and purpose, the reader is referred to appendix no 1, where further comparisons are also given concerning distribution of aid between public and private sectors and the extent to which different donors' aid is tied to projects.

Table 1
percentage distribution by purpose of authorised American Aid (excluding third country currency assistance) to 31 March 1965

purpose	per cent	purpose	per cent
railways	3.8	steel, iron ore	1.8
power, irrigation	7.0	1951 wheat loan, PL 480,665 food and commodity assistance	55.9
transport, communications	1.1	grants for technical assistance in health, agricultural, social, educational, etc. fields	5.3
industrial development	25.0		

America's primary contribution has thus been in the provision of food assistance, though counterpart funds so created are used largely for development purposes by agreement with the Indian government. The political aspects of this type of aid are considered in chapter 6, but in broad economic terms American food aid supplies a vital deficiency, at the same time helping to maintain a degree of price stability–a fact of no mean political significance in itself. However, in spite of a widespread image to the contrary, the United States has provided a significant proportion of its aid to India's industrial development (26.8 per cent including steel and iron ore) apart from 'infrastructure' projects.* These latter constitute 17.2 per cent of the total, of which 5.3 per cent is devoted to grants for a wide variety of technical assistance projects. In view of the widely held opinion that the United States tends to spread its aid 'thin' over a wide range of projects with little 'impact' value, the relatively low percentage spent on small technical assistance projects should be noted, though the actual number of such projects is considerable.

As between various types of aid, assistance was divided in the following proportion up to 31 March 1965: Loans 41.8 per cent (repayable in dollars 31 per cent: repayable in rupees–10.8 per cent); Grants 5.9 per cent: PL 480, 665 and Third Country Currency assistance–52.3 per cent. The main sources of loans have been the Export-Import Bank, the

*I use this term in its purely descriptive sense to refer to public utilities–specifically transport, communications, harbour development, irrigation, power and also technical, educational and social services.

Development Loan Fund–replaced in 1961 by the Agency for International Development–and a variety of programmes, such as the Indo-American Technical Cooperation Programme, Surplus Agricultural Commodities Programme, President's Asian Development Fund, etc. Until 1961, apart from Eximbank loans, loans were normally repayable in rupees. In that year loans from the newly-created AID became repayable in dollars. Compensation was made, however, by a considerable easing in loan terms. Since the inception of American aid, loan terms have shown considerable variation, though on closer analysis a discernible pattern emerges. Eximbank loans show a range of interest rates from 5.25–6 per cent, most commonly 5.75 per cent. Repayment periods normally range from thirteen to sixteen years with grace periods averaging three to four years. In the case of DLF loans a clear pattern was established whereby infrastructure projects such as power, irrigation and railway development receive loans at 3.5 per cent, compared with 5.5–5.75 per cent for loans towards industrial development and non-infrastructure imports. Loans to government lending institutions carry 5 per cent interest charge. DLF 'infrastructure' loan repayment period was normally twenty years, but sometimes fifteen, whereas other loans were in the range of ten to fifteen years. AID loans showed a marked fall in interest rates. The same distinction between categories has been maintained, 'infrastructure' projects carrying only a ¾ per cent credit charge and a repayment period of forty years, with ten years grace period, whereas other projects, in addition to the credit charge pay rupee interest charges to the Indian government (though this is only an accounting factor in the case of public sector enterprises) ranging from 2.75–5 per cent, while repayment periods range from twelve to sixteen years with only short grace periods in the region of eighteen months. Loan terms for PL 480 counterpart funds vary from rates of 3–5 per cent over forty year periods, with four-year grace periods. Whilst early loans were more often repayable in rupees, the future trend will be towards dollar repayments.

Excluding PL 480 assistance, the United States has given 47.7 per cent of its aid in 'non-project' form, and has provided 71.3 per cent of all non-project aid made available to India until the end of 1964 (See appendix no 1, table 10). Apart from one Eximbank credit in 1958, all non-project assistance has been provided subsequent to 1961, thus indicating a significant policy departure during this later period.

Overall contribution of the United States to the public and private sectors is indicated in table 2. A clear pattern is established whereby public sector loans are favoured for 'infrastructure' projects and private sector loans for industrial development, including the steel industry, though this pattern represents at least approximately the distribution of ownership between the two sectors within India.

Table 2
percentage US Aid. allocation by purpose between public and private sectors

	public sector		private sector	
purposes	authorised	utilised	authorised	utilised
railways	100.0	100.0	5.5	8.9
power, irrigation	94.5	91.1	5.5	8.9
transport, communications	79.3	79.3	20.7	20.7
steel, iron ore	35.4	34.0	64.6	66.0
industrial development	23.3	24.6	76.7	75.4

A preliminary overall view of American aid establishes the broad nature of its objectives and methods, and with certain limitations, assistance has been provided to every major sector of the Indian economy. It is clear from the wide range of technical assistance provided in the educational, health, training and social service spheres that a real attempt has been made to adopt a 'micro' as well as a 'macro' approach to India's development problems. This has frequently led to the observation that American aid is too diffuse to make any strong political impact. Besides being a somewhat unsophisticated political judgment, the preceding statistical analysis would seem to disprove the contention in that over 80 per cent of aid has been concentrated on food aid and industrial development, with perhaps only 10 per cent concentrated on technical assistance.

Only subjectively can it be asserted that steel mills make a greater 'impact' than food aid, though the opinion is widely held; but at least the preceding analysis establishes a definite identity and pattern to American aid. Similarly it weakens, without entirely disproving the cruder prejudices about lack of American support for industrialisation and the public sector.

The United Kingdom

British aid is overwhelmingly (99.5 per cent) in loan form. The small balance of grant aid is devoted to technical and training assistance.

Interest rates have been tied to the rates applicable to loans from the British Consolidated Fund, which in turn varies with Bank Rate. In practice this means a rate in the region of 5–6.5 per cent. However, during the Third Plan, repayment periods have been extended to twenty-five years and since 1963 interest has been waived for the first seven years, making an effective interest rate in the region of 3½ per cent.

British aid has been allocated to Steel (21 per cent) (the Durgapur project receiving the overwhelming bulk of this aid)–Industrial Development (78.5 per cent) and technical and training assistance (0.5 per cent). The major industrial projects assisted by Britain, other than Durgapur, have been an oil pipeline in Assam for Oil India Ltd, a Heavy Electrical Plant at Bhopal, a fertiliser plant at Nahorkatiya (Assam) and equipment for Hindustan Cables Ltd. Otherwise British aid in this category is somewhat hard to identify. However the bulk of aid clearly goes to the public sector.

Substantial emphasis is placed on 'non-project' assistance, constituting 34.3 per cent of total British aid (appendix no 1, table 10), thus providing balance of payments support at a time when this is becoming increasingly vital to the efficient operation of Indian Industry. A further quantum of aid is provided within broad categories of machinery, equipment, etc. while some has been allotted to 'British orientated' enterprises under the so-called 'kipping loans'.[2] Nevertheless sufficient emphasis is placed on a few major projects–outstandingly the Durgapur steel mill–thus giving British aid a clear identity.

West Germany

West German aid has also been almost wholly (99.5 per cent) in loan form. Loan terms have varied from 3–6.75 per cent though the majority of loans are in the region of 5.5 per cent. No clear pattern is discernible, though one may note some easing of terms during the Third Plan. Repayment periods for loans other than Rourkela refinance loans vary from twelve to twenty-five years, the normal period being twenty years, though twenty-five year terms have become more common during the Third Plan. Some pressure has been placed on West Germany to ease its repayment terms and this has had some marginal effect.

Authorised West German aid has been allocated in the following proportions: steel 41.2 per cent; industrial development 58.2 per cent; technical assistance 0.6 per cent. Steel loans have been concentrated entirely on the Rourkela project. Loans in the industrial sector have been made for the development of fertiliser, power and electrical equipment, mining, shipbuilding and for the capitalisation of government lending institutions. Technical assistance has been concentrated on four projects, of which the first two received the bulk of funds. These are 1. The Indian Institute of Technology at Madras; 2. A prototype production cum training centre at Okhla; 3. A Joint Advisory mixed farming project in Himachal Pradesh and 4. A joint seismic survey during 1960-3. This distribution illustrates the strong emphasis placed by the German Federal Republic on development of technical and managerial skills as a necessary prerequisite for the industrialisation of an underdeveloped economy and may reasonably be related to the emphasis, noted elsewhere, given to German control of enterprises, at least for a long initial period.

The majority of West German aid (71.6 per cent) is directed towards specific projects. However, a significant proportion (17.4 per cent) is in non-project form, whilst the remaining 11 per cent is best classified as 'semi-project' (appendix no 1, table 10).

Assistance to steel is 100 per cent in the public sector, though there was an initial intention on the German side for the Rourkela project to be at least partially in the private sector. The allocation to each sector of industrial development loans cannot be determined since these are tabulated in official statistics as general credits (Public/Private) (see appendix no 1, table 9).

German assistance is heavily identified with the Rourkela steel project and generally with heavy industrial development. Loans emphasis is basically, though not rigidly, commercial. While Germany has been anxious to participate in the development of the private sector, the distribution of her aid shows a substantial willingness to cooperate with public sector enterprises.

Other non-Communist donors

Of the remaining non-Communist donor countries, the most striking distinction lies between Australia, Canada, New Zealand and Norway on the one hand, and the rest. Denmark and Sweden constitute an intermediate category, but otherwise aid from countries in this group, other than those mentioned, has taken the form of loans on more or less strictly commercial terms, with a clear emphasis on promotion of exports by the donors. In this latter group repayment periods are generally between ten to fifteen years, with interest rates in the region of 5–6 per cent. The most notable of the minor donors are France, Japan and Italy, all of which operate chiefly through suppliers' credits financed through a complex of banking systems. A wide variety of machinery and equipment has been purchased from these three sources. In the case of Japan the outstanding projects are in the spheres of iron ore, textile machinery, fertiliser and power equipment. Perhaps of long-term importance will be the four demonstration farms established since 1962, aimed at experimentation with Japanese intensive agricultural methods in Indian conditions. All but a small fraction of Japanese aid is in the form of loans. Japan does not claim that her participation in India's development constitutes aid but is rather an expression of mutual interest, which helps the promotion of Japanese trade. Furthermore she claims that she cannot afford to give aid on terms much easier than normal commercial terms.[3] Information is not adequate to determine allocation to public and private sectors, but the majority would appear to have gone to the public sector.

Italian aid is concentrated mainly in the oil distribution and exploration fields, the outstanding projects being the Barauni-Kanpur and Barauni-Calcutta refined oil product pipelines. 9.3 per cent of Italian loans are 'non-project'. Assistance is on a 100 per cent loan basis. Due to the government's classification of the oil industry under the 1956 Industrial Policy Resolution, Italian aid is of necessity directed primarily towards the public sector.

French aid is almost entirely on a loan basis, apart from a minute fraction devoted towards somewhat disparate forms of technical assistance. Loans have been made towards industrial machinery, chemical plants, power equipment, machine tools and aircraft, but perhaps the best known French assisted project is the oil exploration joint venture with the government of India in the Jaisalmer region of Rajasthan, as yet unsuccessful. There is wide distribution between public and private sectors, though information is inadequate. One may reasonably conclude that the French government is non-dogmatic on this issue, being mainly interested in the trading aspects involved. French aid is 100 per cent project-orientated, though as in many other cases, this is misleading since credits are authorised in advance, their allocation being worked out subsequently.

Austria, Belgium, Netherlands and Switzerland have all provided small loans towards India's industrial development. Other than fractional amounts, loans constitute the total sum of aid from these sources. Loans are on generally commercial terms with interest rates in the region of 6 per cent and repayment periods rarely exceeding ten years. Loans are project-oriented except in the case of Netherlands, which provides 59.5 per cent of its aid in 'non-project' form, the highest proportion of any donor.

Denmark has made one loan of Rs 10.3 million, repayable in rupees, which are then allocated to mutually agreed projects. The second loan of Rs 13.8 million is at 4 per cent over twenty years with a five and a half year grace period, repayable in foreign currency. Thus Danish terms are distinctly easier than those of most Western minor donors.

Swedish aid is divided almost equally between grants (Rs 20.9 million) and loans (Rs 22.1 million), although the latter remain unutilised to date. Loan terms are generous, 2 per cent over twenty years with a five year grace period.

Canadian aid in many ways contains some of the most liberal features of all donor countries. 74.3 per cent of aid is in the form of grants. The loan component only appears during the Third Plan, when it was felt that the degree of aid now required by India was beyond the scope of Canada to provide in grant form. Loans from Export Credits Insurance Corporation of Canada bear interest rates of 6 per cent over periods ranging from fourteen and a half to twenty years with grace periods of three to five years. However, there are now signs of Canada's loan terms easing with the signing in 1964 of two development loans totalling Rs 6.6 crores at 0.75 per cent over fifty years with a ten year grace period.

Table 3
percentage purposewise distribution of Canadian Aid by Purpose (to 31 March 1965)

railways	11.0	agriculture, commodity assistance	29.0
power, irrigation	28.3	technical assistance, education, health, etc.	0.5
industry	29.5	steel	0.5
transport, communications	1.2		

The majority of aid is thus devoted to 'infrastructure' aspects of the economy though 30 per cent is allocated to industry, a proportion very similar to that of the United States.

96.8 per cent of loans authorised have been channelled to the public sector; though the precise amount cannot be determined, it is reasonable to assume that a substantial proportion of grants went also to the public sector.

All but a minute fraction of Canadian aid is project-oriented. In view of the high proportion of grant aid this factor loses much of its significance, since grants are almost always in kind or services. Nevertheless, this is perhaps the only feature of Canadian aid that has been less than liberal.

The most notable feature of Australian aid is that it has been in 100 per cent grant form and has been directed mainly towards the public sector. This latter feature stems not so much from any conscious policy but from the miscellaneous nature of Australian aid, whereby a wide variety of material, equipment, expertise, etc. is provided on a somewhat ad hoc basis, according to availability and demand. Gifts to the value of Rs 60.67 million–28.5 per cent of total aid–have been in the form of wheat and flour, electrolytic copper, sulphate of ammonia and skimmed milk powder which have been sold in the Indian market with the proceeds generating counterpart funds to be used for mutually agreed projects. Australian aid is 100 per cent project-oriented, though this stems directly from the grant form of aid.

New Zealand aid is likewise in 100 per cent grant form. Out of total aid of Rs 37.74 million, 38.9 per cent is devoted to one project, the All India Institute of Medical Sciences, 5.6 per cent to technical assistance and the vast bulk of the remainder to Milk and Dairy Farming schemes. New Zealand aid is 100 per cent project-oriented and would appear to be mainly in the public sector.

Norwegian aid is 100 per cent grant aid and is directed exclusively to fishing projects in Kerala, Mysore and Madras, though health and education projects have been operated conjointly with these schemes.[4]

The Soviet Union

The pattern of Soviet aid is basically clear-cut. Aid is almost 100 per cent in loan form and 100 per cent project-oriented. All loans bear interest at 2.5 per cent with repayment over twelve years, except for a credit for the manufacture of drugs, which is repayable over seven years. Loans are repayable in rupees which are used for purchases of Indian goods. Indian officials appreciate this method since it provides India with the means of repayments. The true foreign exchange significance of this 'trade and aid' method can only be determined according to whether goods exported to the Soviet Union could have earned foreign currency elsewhere or in fact constitute additional exports.[5] On this point there is little hard evidence, but much speculation.

Allocation of Soviet aid for various purposes is given in table 4. 66.3 per cent of contracts placed up to 31 March 1965 were allotted to five projects–the Bhilai steel mill, the oil and natural gas exploration programme in Gujerat and elsewhere, the Barauni and Koyali refineries

Table 4
distribution of Soviet Aid by purpose (to 31st March 1965)

steel*	40.0	heavy machine building	7.2
oil, gas	19.1	heavy electricals plant	4.9
power	18.1	drugs project	3.1
coal mining	6.5	miscellaneous	1.1

*Refers only to Bhilai project-Bokaro project, agreed in January 1965, will substantially increase the percentage allocated to steel

and the Ranchi Heavy Machine Building plant. Concentration on a few outstanding projects gives a very high impact value to Soviet aid, and this concentration will be further marked when the Bokaro project is fully operational.

The only assistance in the sphere of agriculture has been a grant of Rs 7.9 million for the Central Mechanised Farm at Suratgarh (Rajasthan), intended to act as a 'demonstration' project.

Aid is 100 per cent in the public sector, although there has been some willingness to invest in joint collaboration projects with the Indian private sector.[6]

Loans are 100 per cent project-oriented, though it might perhaps be argued that since Soviet aid is supplied in such a form as to stimulate trade, indirectly India's general purchasing capacity for Soviet components and materials is enhanced.

Other Communist countries

Rumania, Poland and Czechoslovakia follow the Soviet pattern closely, aid being concentrated on a few projects in the sphere of industrial development. In the former case aid is directed 100 per cent to the Guahati oil refinery project.[7] The Polish emphasis on coal mining and power projects is very marked. The Czech contribution is somewhat more diverse, the largest single project being the machine tool foundry forge project at Ranchi, in association with the Soviet Union; considerable emphasis is also placed on power projects.

Rumania's loan is at 2.5 per cent over seven years. The Polish and Czech loans are both divided into two credit agreements, both bearing interest at 2.5 per cent, but for each country the first credit is repayable over eight years compared with twelve for the second. For all three countries loans are repayable in rupees, thus stimulating trade in line with the Soviet pattern.

Rumanian and Polish aid is directed 100 per cent to the public sector, though Czechoslovakia channels a proportion of loans to the private sector —the exact proportion being unidentifiable.

For all three countries, aid is 100 per cent project-oriented. Of the three, only Czechoslovakia provides technical assistance, Rs 6 million being supplied to assist the Machine Tools Technology and Design Institute at Bangalore.

Aid from Yugoslavia is 100 per cent in loan form, with interest rates at 3 per cent, varying repayment periods negotiable with each contract and loans repayable in rupees. Aid is distributed in the following proportions:

Import of ships, 47 per cent; power, 32 per cent; Rajasthan Iron Works, + 16.9 per cent; miscellaneous, 4.1 per cent. Thus, as with other Communist countries, Yugoslav aid is substantially concentrated on a few projects. Loans are 100 per cent project-oriented and predominantly in the public sector, though 17.6 per cent is allotted to the private sector.

The World Bank

Apart from a fractional amount (devoted to surveys of a possible second Hooghly river crossing in Calcutta and a coal transport survey) all World Bank assistance is in the form of loans. Interest rates vary from 4–6 per cent in the public sector with repayment periods ranging from seven to twenty-five years (though only in two cases less than fifteen years) while for the private sector interest rates have varied from 4.5 to 6 per cent with repayment periods ranging from ten to twenty years, though in only two out of thirteen private sector loans up to 31 December 1964 were loans extended for longer than fifteen years.

Distribution of World Bank loans for various purposes is shown in table 5.

Table 5
distribution of IBRD loans by Purpose (to 31st March 1965)

purpose	authorised	utilised
railways	44.6	50.2
power, irrigation	10.8	12.0
port developments	7.6	5.7
transport, communications	0.7	0.8
agricultural development	0.8	0.9
industrial development	14.7	9.3
steel	20.8	21.1
total	100.0	100.0

The emphasis on railway development is very marked. Although World Bank aid has been primarily directed towards 'infrastructure' development, 35.5 per cent of loans authorised have been in the industrial and steel sectors.

The World Bank is often viewed as being in opposition to the development of Indian public enterprise; although this is partially true, it is important to qualify this view correctly. Overall, up to 31 March 1965, 61.7 per cent of IBRD loans went to the public sector and 38.3 per cent to the private sector.

Table 6 indicates how loans earmarked for various purposes have been distributed between public and private sectors.

Table 6
percentage IBRD Aid allocation by Purpose between public and private sectors (to 31st March 1965)

purpose	public sector	private sector
railways	100.0	–
power, irrigation	74.3	25.7
transport, communications	100.0	–
port development	100.0	--
industrial development	–	100.0
agricultural development	100.0	–
steel, iron ore	–	100.0

The IBRD distinction between 'infrastructure' and other projects is thus more rigid than that of America, the latter having allowed at least a minority proportion of aid within the steel and industrial development categories to the public sector. Only in the case of irrigation and power is aid divided between private and public sectors. This suggests that the IBRD is non-dogmatic with regard to ownership within 'infrastructure' categories.

Distribution of public and private sector loans respectively according to purpose is shown in table 7.

The high importance attached to railways is again apparent. 100 per cent of public sector loans are for 'infrastructure' purposes and 92.8 per cent of authorised private sector loans are for 'non-infrastructure' purposes.

Table 7
percentage IBRD Aid allocation by Purpose within public and private sectors (to 31st March 1965)

purpose	public sector		private sector	
	authorised	utilised	authorised	utilised
railways	72.3	75.5	–	–
power, irrigation	13.0	13.4	7.2	9.2
transport, communications	1.1	1.1	–	–
port development	12.3	8.6	–	–
agriculture	1.4	1.4	–	–
industry	–	–	38.5	27.8
steel	–	–	54.3	63.0
total	100.0	100.0	100.0	100.0

IBRD aid is still 100 per cent project-oriented, though the fact that such aid represents free foreign exchange softens the severity of this policy very considerably.

The International Development Association

The IDA made its appearance as a separate branch of the World Bank during the Third Plan. Its terms are markedly easier than those of the IBRD, with loans at .75 per cent service charge only, repayable over fifty years with ten years moratorium.

In other respects, however, IDA aid follows the IBRD pattern. Aid is 100 per cent in loan form and 100 per cent project-oriented.

Distribution of IDA loans by purpose is given in table 8.

Table 8
percentage distribution of IDA loans by Purpose (to 31st March 1965)

purpose	authorised	utilised
railways	26.7	37.3
power, irrigation	11.5	5.1
transport, communications	27.8	30.3
port development	3.7	1.2
industry	18.6	11.9
agriculture	11.7	14.2
total	100.0	100.0

Significant differences compared with the IBRD are 1. The higher percentage devoted to 'infrastructure' projects; 2. The much greater weight given to forms of transport other than railways; 3. The absence of assistance to the steel industry; 4. The higher percentage devoted to agriculture–reflecting the greater emphasis placed on this objective lately both by India and the leading Western donors.

Distribution between public and private sectors follows even more rigidly the IBRD distinction between infrastructure and non-infrastructure projects. In this case the distinction is maintained 100 per cent.

IDA aid may thus be seen as complementary to IBRD aid, in fact reflecting the close institutional relationship. The significant difference lies in the vastly easier terms on which loans are provided.

At one time it seemed likely that the IDA pattern would take precedence over the traditional IBRD pattern. During the Third Plan period up to 31 March 1965, IDA loans constituted 73.4 per cent of total IBRD-IDA loans authorised and 52 per cent of loans utilised. This pattern reflected growing awareness of India's external debt burden and indeed the World Bank authorities have been active in the 'Aid India' Consortium to promote such an awareness. Assistance on more generous terms was encouraged and this was to a considerable extent forthcoming during the Third Plan. The atmosphere surrounding aid, however, has again become more stringent and the IDA concept has lost ground, while its funds have diminished correspondingly.

The United Nations

United Nations aid is 100 per cent in grant form and 100 per cent specific and project-oriented. Aid is directed primarily towards training, research, education, health and social services. It is very substantially directed towards the public sector, though the exact distribution cannot be gauged.

United Nations aid is divided into three categories: 1. Expanded Programme of Technical Assistance; 2. Aid from the United Nations Special Fund, which special UN agencies acting as executors, which constitutes the bulk of aid; 3. Direct aid from particular UN agencies. Equipment is provided along with UN experts and provision is made for training of Indians both in India and abroad under all three categories. In the second category, 33.3 per cent of total aid was devoted to equipment, though it may be calculated that the proportion would be much less in the other two categories. This illustrates the substantial qualitative difference between UN aid and aid from all other sources, the bias in this case being very clearly towards, training, education and demonstration.

The Ford and Rockefeller foundations

Aid from these private foundations [8] differ qualitatively from that of other donors. On the one hand their assistance is quantitatively large enough to distinguish them from other voluntary agencies and place them alongside the minor country donors, but on the other hand by virtue of being private organisations far greater independence and unorthodoxy is possible. The bias of both organisations is towards education and research. A survey of projects supported shows a great diffusion and the initial impression is of a somewhat ad hoc approach. However, both organisations, especially Ford, explain their philosophy as being the selection of projects to break through specific 'bottlenecks' by initiating research surveys, educational institutes, planning bodies, etc. which it is hoped will have a 'catalyst' effect. Examples of such projects, in varying degrees successful, are the Calcutta Metropolitan Planning Organisation (Ford), designed to replan that city, realising that its efficient functioning plays a crucial role in India's whole development programme; the Indian Institute of Public Administration (Ford and Rockefeller), intended to study administrative bottlenecks in India's planning; the Ministry of Agriculture Postgraduate Agricultural Research Institute (Rockefeller), which has performed important work in demonstrating possibilities of growing improved hybrid strains of grain and sorghum, the foundation technique being to buy land and demonstrate possibilities itself rather than operating indirectly through the government. The work of the two Foundations has undoubtedly had great influence on the development of the concept of intensive agriculture schemes now operating in selected areas in each state.

In terms of politics, the two foundations are often seen as at least indirect extensions of the United States government, expressing similar ideological views and aims. The foundations naturally object to this view and it seems clear that a reasonably distinctive philosophy is discernible. However, it seems also reasonable to argue that they can approach delicate questions, reaching to the heart of India's social and economic problems, which governments fear to approach. The United States government have, until very recently, shown a total unwillingness to touch anything to do with population control, whereas the Ford Foundation, through the establishment of its Programme of Demonstration and Training in Population Statistics, has done much to persuade the government of India to tackle the administrative problems involved. It is uncertain exactly what part of the foundation played in encouraging the new birth control programme instituted in 1965, but the catalyst theory must at least be credited with some measure of success.

Thus, although the foundations must keep basically within the framework of India's planning system, they are in a better position than governments or official agencies, first to initiate schemes and ideas of their own, secondly to persuade the Indian government to give some particular emphasis it would not have spontaneously shown, and thirdly to refuse Indian requests for particular forms of aid without political embarrassment.[9]

Conclusion

In this brief survey comparisons have been avoided, as has the question of efficacy of various types of aid. However, insofar as comparisons between aid programmes are made, with a view to making political judgments, some final economic comparisons must be attempted. I shall confine such comparison to the United States and the Soviet Union, since Cold War considerations inevitably play their part in this analysis.

Appendix no. 1 (table 1) shows that America has provided some five and a half times the quantum of aid authorised over the period under review, and some eight times the quantum of aid utilised, as compared with the Soviet Union. Furthermore, she has provided a greater amount of aid for all purposes, including industrial development, other than steel.

A comparison of aid terms over the whole period would appear clearly favourable to the United States. Up to the end of the Second Plan, Russia's interest rates were lower, but at the same time American repayment periods were longer and a significant proportion of her aid took the form of grants. During the Third Plan, most American dollar loans have carried a far lower interest rate and enjoyed very long repayment periods.[10] Against this, however, must be set the very important fact of Soviet loans being repayable in rupees. With regard to distribution between public and private sectors, the Soviet Union leads only slightly in percentage contributions of authorised foreign currency loans to the public sector (28.5 per cent against 27.4 per cent; See appendix no. 1, table 9). If grants and rupee loans are taken into account the United States has a clear lead. However, table 9 shows Russia having a substantial advantage in quantum of public sector loans provided for steel and industrial development, which has gained her special prestige and goodwill.

Table 9
American and Soviet contribution to public sector steel and industrial development (to 31st March 1965) (Crores of Rupees)

	loans authorised	loans utilised
United States	171.9	140.9
Soviet Union	484.2	244.0

Evidence is provided subsequently[11] to suggest that economic aid is a factor which significantly affects Indian public opinion in its attitude to particular countries, though foreign policy and defence factors appear more important. At the top governmental level, certainly, aid is a strong opinion-forming factor. At all levels, however, it will appear subsequently that there is no necessary correlation between statistics and political judgments. These latter are affected as much, if not more, by factors such as policy considerations believed to lie behind aid-giving activities, the degree of harmonisation between aid and the general objectives of Indian planning, as well as the donor's style of aid-giving, which is in fact part of overall diplomatic style.

Finally, it must be remembered that the direction and rate of growth of the Indian economy is the factor that will have the most profound long-term effect on Indian politics and therefore upon her external relationships. Short-term political effects of foreign aid must therefore be viewed against this long-term background.

Chapter 3

The development of American aid policy in India

It is intended in this chapter to analyse the development of American aid policy towards India. It must be stressed here, as elsewhere, that aid should be regarded as a tool of diplomacy, as part of a total political and economic relationship between countries, and not in isolation. At the same time India is one of many recipients of American aid and as such is subject to general fluctuations in American policy. However, I hope to show that the American aid relationship with India has certain special political characteristics, based on that country's high status in American diplomatic and ideological priorities.

American aid policy has developed in a somewhat piece-meal fashion rather than as a process of deliberate planning, as can be seen by studying the subject from two viewpoints. First, an approximate chronological outline will be offered, followed by a more general comparative analysis at the level of conflicting ideas.

The former approach has the disadvantage of a certain degree of arbitrariness, since the various cross-currents of opinion do not neatly fall into chronological categories. However, for purposes of analysis, four time periods may conveniently be distinguished within the overall period of this study, each dominated by reasonably well-defined policy issues and priorities, though of course counter-trends are to be found at every stage.

Early Period: Limited Involvement

The first period lasts from approximatley 1949 to 1954, beginning with the enunciation of the 'Point Four Programme' by President Truman in January 1949[1] and ending with the inception of Soviet aid in 1954. This declaration may be regarded as the first official recognition of the need to assist Asia's development,[2] yet at this time the magnitude of her economic problems was only dimly apprehended. The 'Point Four' concept appears to have been based on two assumptions: 1. That technical aid was the chief deficiency experienced by developing countries and that direct capital aid was therefore unnecessary, except to supplement technical aid; 2. Efforts should be concentrated on attracting private foreign capital rather than relying on direct government aid. To this end, technical assistance would provide a basis, while foreign capital would bring further managerial skills and technical 'know-how'.[3] It can reasonably be argued that these assumptions were unduly influenced by the experience of Marshall aid, which had produced substantial results in a short period. The distinction between rebuilding the war-damaged but advanced economy of Europe and developing backward and traditionalist societies to the point of self-sustaining economic growth was not properly appreciated. In the latter case a dynamic public sector is generally regarded as necessary to provide the basis for private investment. The 'laissez-faire' climate of opinion then prevailing in the American Congress would almost certainly have rendered this approach unacceptable. At the same time, the political implications of emphasising private foreign capital as the best means of development seem to have remained largely unrecognised, even by 'liberal' economists such as W. Malenbaum.[4] Whilst in theory emphasis was placed on the right of newly independent countries to choose their own political and economic systems, it is clear that the consensus of official opinion assumed the American free-enterprise model as the proper objective for developing countries to pursue. Little comprehension was displayed of Asian sentiment towards foreign capital and capitalism generally as manifestations of imperialism, nor of the passions excited by experience of colonial rule and the struggle for national independence. Nor was it appreciated that indigeneous cultural and social influences in this region are predominantly collectivist rather than individualist.

From these hesitant beginnings America's aid effort has grown to its present high level, while the scope of debate and policy alternatives at both theoretical and practical levels has been widened to an extent that would appear unrecognisable within the framework of assumptions here stated. There is good evidence that the Point Four Programme, in spite of the dramatic nature of its announcement, was the result of no clear policy formulation[5] and was based on nothing more specific than vague humanitarian sentiment and a dim recognition of the existence of Asia, a recognition that was soon to become far sharper with the Communist takeover in China. The economic assumptions behind the programme were only elicited in subsequent elaborations by official spokesmen, and in the early years the aid programme moved forward more as a response to events than as a deliberate process of policy formation. Serious theoretical analysis of the scope and objectives of aid policy was only to emerge with the commencement of Soviet aid on a large scale.

Indo-American relations during this period were at a formative stage. India was anxious to assert her independence in matters of foreign policy, but as is shown by her action in joining the Commonwealth,[6] there was no intention at the top level of defining India's attitudes in consistently anti-Western terms. The United States was not seen generally as a colonialist power and as Nehru frequently acknowledged, Indian political thinking was considerably influenced by American liberal and democratic ideas.[7] During his visit to the United States in 1949 the two countries seemed to have achieved some reasonable degree of mutual sympathy in general outlook on world affairs, though this was soon to change with the emergence of the People's Republic of China and the outbreak of the Korean War.[8] Large-scale aid commitments did not result, however, first because India's development plans had yet to take shape, and secondly because (as already indicated) American thinking on this subject was still at the most tentative stage. Only a few voices criticised the inadequacies of the 'Point Four' approach, and still fewer appreciated the significance of India in this context. Of these the most notable was Senator Hubert Humphrey, who specifically urged the dangers of forgetting India in the light of events in China. These had occurred, he argued, because the West had ignored awakening Chinese nationalism and the need for economic development. The same thing would occur in India unless her aspirations for better living standards were supported with aid on the scale of the Marshall Plan.[9] Even here a false analogy with Europe was used, but at least the magnitude of financial assistance requirements was recognised.

Cold War Tensions

The first substantial outflow of American aid to India occurred in 1951,[10] when large quantities of wheat and rice were shipped to meet famine conditions arising from the monsoon failure of the previous year. Unfortunately the shipments were preceded by a bitter and lengthy debate in Congress,[11] which took place in the context of strained foreign policy relations, caused by India's recognition of Communist China and her active mediatory role in the Korean War. As the first of its kind, the debate was instructive. Humanitarian concern for India's plight coupled with fears of dangers to its infant democracy were the dominant themes, yet the political impact of aid eventually sent was considerably diminished by the bitter opposition expressed in some quarters against India's foreign and other policies, and the extreme length of the debate. An emergency request was received in February 1951, but the necessary legislation was not completed until 15 June of that year. The critics seemed to show little appreciation of India's concern to establish her newly won independence and sovereignty in the conduct of foreign policy. One issue in the debate particularly illustrates this. It was noted that India had placed an embargo on the export of certain materials relevant to military purposes.[12] Of particular interest to the United States was monazite sand, which contains thorium—vital to America's atomic energy programme. Monazite sand is found in great abundance in India, especially in the south, but only in negligible quantities in the United States. The only other source of supply was stated to be Brazil, which has relatively small deposits. Apart from a quantity of monazite believed to have been exported to France in 1946, India had only exported a very small quantity to a few American manufacturers of gas mantles for the Indian market, who had in fact embargoed sales to India for the purpose of bringing pressure on her to lift the ban. As a result of Indian protests, the State Department had forced the lifting of the embargo by threatening reprisals to the manufacturers. The State Department was strongly lobbied to put pressure on India, but this lobby was resisted on the grounds that such pressure smacked of colonialism. It was also alleged that beryl, a material on India's embargo list, was embargoed from export by Brazil on 16 January, 1951.[13] This was believed to have been the result of a visit by the chairman of the Indian Board of Atomic Research, H. J. Bhabha. It was therefore demanded that the Wheat Loan be made conditional on India allowing export of monazite and beryl materials and on the granting of rights to explore and develop uranium deposits in India. Only after a House-Senate conference was specific reference to these and other materials excluded. A general formula was agreed which laid down that: '. . . The Administrator is directed and instructed that in his negotiations with the government of India he shall, so far as practicable and possible, obtain for the United States the immediate and continuing transfer of substantial quantities of such materials, particularly those found to be strategic or critical.'[14] Thus it was agreed that India should pay part of the cost of food shipments by export of materials in short supply in the United States. Repayments have in fact been rescheduled to commence in 1986. The importance of Indian materials to America's nuclear programme would therefore appear to be remote, and more narrow manufacturing interests may be presumed to have influenced the debate. However, sufficient heat was produced to effect a House-Senate deadlock and the strength of feeling in Congress on this issue at that time must accordingly be recognised. Although the matter was not eventually pressed, a principle had been attached to an aid bill which constituted a challenge to India's concept of sovereignty, forshadowing subsequent conflicts.

The Indo-US Technical Cooperation Programme,[15] established in 1951, provided the first institutional arrangement for American aid to India. This development was strongly influenced by Chester Bowles and Sherman Cooper and gave expression to the emphasis on technical know-how indicated by the Point Four approach. Apart from the Wheat Loan, only technical assistance projects under this programme were forthcoming during the First Plan period. The Wheat Loan debate worsened already strained relations, in spite of the eventual extent of assistance. Following this, India's mediatory policies in Korea and Indo-China came into increasing conflict with the Dulles policy of ideological polarisation and massive military containment of Communism. Mr Dulles's general obsession with pacts, and above all his insistence on fostering Pakistan membership of SEATO on what appeared to India as purely ideological grounds, bred violent and continued resentment. Pakistan's motives were viewed as primarily anti-Indian and opportunistic, and the supply of F-84 jets in particular was viewed as a dangerous distortion of the power-balance on the subcontinent.[16] A further issue related to Portugal's membership of NATO and what was seen as an ideological interpretation of the Goa issue by the United States.[17]

The second period, from approximatley 1954 to 1958, witnessed the lowest level of Indo-American relations. Opposition to neutralism reached its highest point in the United States Congress and this was accompanied by strong hostility towards the type of socialist economic policy laid down in India's Industrial Policy Resolution of 1956 (See appendix No. 2). India's alleged prevarications during the Hungarian uprising in that year further exacerbated relations. The incursion of Soviet aid on a substantial scale thus came at the worst possible time, but in spite of the strong hostility this excited, it undoubtedly had a catalytic effect in bringing about a drastic reappraisal of both the size and conception of American aid in India and from 1956 onwards American aid became much more substantial

'Liberalism': Stalemate

The Soviet Sputnik space-launching heralded an era of nuclear stalemate, a consequent thawing of the Cold War and a closer attention by both the United States and the Soviet Union to the interests of the 'non-aligned' nations. It is against this background that the steady improvement in Indo-American relations from about 1958 onward must be viewed, marking the beginning of the third period, lasting until approximately

1962-3. At the same time the acute foreign exchange crisis of 1957-8 involving urgent appeals by Indian ministers to America and the World Bank[18] produced the growth of a strong pro-India lobby in Congress and the Administration. This was spearheaded by such personalities as the former ambassadors Bowles and Cooper, Professor J. K. Galbraith, later appointed as ambassador to India, and Senators Kennedy, Kefauver, Humphrey, Mansfield and Fulbright. An outstanding achievement by this group was the establishment in August 1958 of the World Bank Consortium for India and Pakistan to study India's development needs and plans and to coordinate the annual allocation of funds by donor countries. World Bank opinion and influence have thus become crucial for the realisation of India's economic objectives. With the election of J. F. Kennedy as President in 1960 the views of this group became dominant, a fact which was reflected in massive aid increases to India. During this period questions of public enterprise, socialist planning and non-alignment in external affairs were treated with greater flexibility. There was a steady diminution in hostility towards Soviet aid and involvement in India. Above all, India was recognised as a key Asian country, in whose stability and growth the West had a prime interest, transcending differences of policy and outlook. The approach thus became far more pragmatic in all respects. However, it must be noted that the Kennedy 'liberal' view failed to achieve complete acceptance, and even before the President's death reassertions of more rigid ideological attitudes found voice with growing effect. Increasing difficulty was encountered in steering the foreign aid programme through Congress. In a vain attempt to placate the conservatives the Clay Committee was appointed to study the aid programme. After a lightning world tour the committee produced a report[19] which consisted of a series of dogmatic assertions based on unexamined assumptions. Of these the most significant for India was the statement

> . . . We believe the United States should not aid a foreign government in projects establishing government-owned industrial commercial enterprises which compete with existing private endeavours. While we realise that in aiding foreign countries we cannot insist upon the establishment of our own economic system . . . the observation of countless instances of politically-operated, heavily subsidised and carefully protected inefficient state enterprises in less developed countries makes us gravely doubt the value of such undertakings in the economic lives of these nations. Countries which would take this route should realise that

while the United States will not intervene in their affairs to impose its own economic system, they too lack the right to intervene in our national pocketbook for aid to enterprises which only increase their costs of government and the foreign assistance burden they are asking us to carry.[20]

These arguments provide a good case for rejecting public sector projects which are uneconomic, but the tone of the statement scarcely gave confidence that individual projects were to be examined on their merits. The Clay Report was crucial in causing the rejection of the Bokaro steel project by the House of Representatives on 22 August, 1963,[21] which resulted in Mr Nehru withdrawing India's request. In India the report played an important part in dashing hopes that had been built up under the Kennedy 'new order',[22] of weakening the prestige of the 'liberals'[23] and of hardening the image of American policies as ideologically predetermined.

Effect of the Indo-Chinese Border Dispute

The transition to the fourth period commenced with the Chinese border incursions in 1962, which produced a complex variety of influences on Indo-American relations. The manifest effects on the American side were the raising of India's strategic importance and the dispatch of substantial emergency military assistance, normal economic aid being maintained at its existing high level. The United States predictably recognised the need to support India in repelling Communist aggression, but there is some evidence of disagreement between the two countries as to the extent of the Chinese threat.[24] The extent of military aid, particularly in the field of aircraft and radar equipment, was therefore disappointing from the Indian viewpoint. Although the quantity was substantial it was insufficient to offset the hostility engendered by the more substantial and continuing military aid to Pakistan over a longer period of time. Differing estimates of Indian military requirements led India to negotiate substantial arms deals with the Soviet Union,[25] causing some controversy with the United States, particularly with regard to jet aircraft. Although objections were raised to the mixing of Soviet and Western weapons systems,[26] there was considerably less objection on the American side than might have been expected. With regard to general economic aid the official view had changed at least to a neutral and in many respects friendly position. The primary emphasis of the Kennedy administration was that India should make economic progress by the best available means. To the extent that Soviet aid assisted this objective, simultaneously relieving the United States of some financial burden, the administration was favourable, despite some residual Congressional hostility. Averell Harriman went so far as to emphasise the need for India to maintain good relations with the Soviet Union, claiming that this was equally to America's interest.[27] This seems to reflect her strategy of encouraging the Moscow-Peking ideological split, there being a general assumption that the Chinese border incursions had drawn India closer to the Western camp. Though gratification was doubtless felt in certain quarters at the disorganisation of India's philosophy of 'peaceful non-alignment', official spokesmen were careful to avoid statements that might embarrass her in this respect.

On the Indian side, there has been a continuing re-evaluation of foreign policy assumptions,[28] of which the outstanding feature has been the emphasis on acquiring military power. Continued improvement in American Soviet relations has allowed India to maintain at least the outward form of non-alignment and a reasonable degree of diplomatic independence has in fact been maintained; but the emphasis is now far more on the protection of immediate vital interests than on playing the role of world mediator.

Disenchantment and Reappraisal

President Johnson at his inauguration[29] made only passing reference to foreign aid, but there was hope that the general lines of Kennedy's policies would be maintained. In spite of substantial changes of personnel in key administration positions, so far as India was concerned the appointment of Chester Bowles as ambassador in Delhi for the second time seemed to augur well for the continuation of Kennedy's 'liberal' aid policies. The appointment of John P. Lewis as Director of AID in New Delhi in 1965 would seem to have reinforced this impression. However, President Johnson lacks Kennedy's strong commitment to and involvement in the problems of India, and the quality of relationship between the two countries has thus been altered little by little. The strong Congressional pro-India lobby has lost its coherence, and though India's views still carry weight she is clearly not accorded the vital status in American world strategy she enjoyed under the Kennedy administration.

Beginning with the Bell Mission Report on behalf of the World Bank in August 1964,[30] India has come under increasing pressure to revise her economic policies. The United States government and the Bank would appear to be acting in conjunction, in view of the parallel lines on which their policies have run, though some principle of division of labour no doubt exists. The Bank has always been in a stronger position to press its advice, in view of its international character. It would now appear, however, that the United States government is losing many of its inhibitions and formulating far more active and positive views as to the needs and defects of the Indian economy, being prepared to suffer some political opprobrium in return for greater involvement in solving the more intractable economic problems. This tougher attitude partly reflects the character of President Johnson, though many observers would argue that Kennedy also was becoming restless with India's slow progress. However, the main cause has been the growing weakness of the Indian economy and a combination of external and internal factors that have reduced her bargaining power. The war with Pakistan during August and September 1965 caused the United States and most donor countries to suspend all aid to both countries. When the fighting ceased America did not resume aid, except for some emergency food shipments, until April 1966. Even the Tashkent Agreement did not prove sufficient to allow the resumption of aid on the original terms. The United States has been particularly anxious to shift the emphasis of Indian planning towards agriculture. This does not imply hostility to industrialisation, but rather a view that existing projects should be consolidated before too many new large-scale projects are undertaken. The Draft Outline of the Fourth Plan[31] substantially reflected such a new emphasis on agriculture, providing for intensive 'demonstration' projects in every state and a fertiliser production target of 3.35 million tons by 1971 compared with an estimated output for 1965 of 1.05 million tons.[32] Although America insisted on such a balance of priorities, it is clear that India was moving in this direction of her own accord, with Lal Bahadur Shastri acting as prime mover. Certainly, however, realisation of increasing dependence on American aid as a result of a series of monsoon failures, the foreign exchange crisis and the war with Pakistan have given a still sharper urgency to the massive debate on food problems now being waged in India. Dependence is further increased by the new emphasis on agriculture, in view of Russia's both practical and ideological inability to assist substantially in this sphere.[33] The importance of fertiliser production has persuaded the government to sanction new ventures in the private sector with majority foreign capital, mainly American, together with internal relaxation of controls over the industry.[34] This was a dramatic move indeed, since fertiliser development was laid down by the 1956 Industrial Policy Resolution as predominantly the preserve of the public sector, while in any case majority foreign ownership is sanctioned only in exceptional circumstances.[35] These decisions were an important factor in the resignation in December 1965 of T. T. Krishnamachari, Minister of Finance, and a strong opponent of the new American pressures. Pressure has been further directed towards liberalisation of the economy, particularly with regard to the complex licencing procedures, held to be a major deterrent to the attraction of foreign capital. The rigidity of the procedures has been justified in terms of acute foreign exchange shortage, to which the whole of Indian economic policy is increasingly geared. This has naturally produced the criticism from the private sector, both domestic and foreign, that this shortage is caused primarily by the emphasis on gigantic public sector industrial enterprises, which view is generally backed by the United States and the World Bank. During 1965 and early 1966 intense pressure was built up from both sources, especially the Bank, for rupee devaluation, as a measure of economic reality and as an inducement to liberalisation. This was strongly resisted and rumours repeatedly denied. Pressure was reduced for two or three months in deference to Indian sovereignty until the decision to devalue was suddenly announced in May 1966.[36] President Johnson's known impatience with the Kashmir dispute, and with the arms buildup on the subcontinent that this entails, has created a further source of tension. The extent of American pressure in this context is not known, but one may assume that it is considerable.[37] There have also been some undertones of conflict over the Vietnam issue, reminiscent of the Dulles period. The United States seemed to be asking at one stage for some token commitment in Vietnam by India,[38] but this pressure appears to have been successfully withstood for the present. India's silence on this issue, however, seems uncharacteristic in the light of her earlier foreign policy philosophies.

It is as yet too early to say whether American aid policy in India is about to take some radically new turn, but there are signs that a new 'hard line' is emerging and the United States will expect to take a far more active part in formulating domestic policies. This new approach might well be described as one of 'payment by results'. In many respects the policies urged might widely be regarded as progressive and beneficial. However, the new approach can only be regarded as a substantial challenge to India's national sovereignty, hitherto defended so successfully. The proposed Indo-American Foundation, for instance, appears to be based on the concept of joint planning in key aspects of the economy, notably agriculture and education.[39] This would appear to depart from the established system of donor countries dovetailing their aid with Indian Plan priorities, and will presumably entail a sharper and more continuous questioning of those priorities.

Against this outline chronological background, it is now necessary to attempt a classification of the main strands of opinion in America, official and otherwise, into a few manageable categories, to trace the development of ideas and to consider changes in direction and emphasis in American economic assistance towards India.

Idealism

The first question is the extent to which influential opinion favours the concept of aid in any form; and here there is an obvious conflict of views. To state the antithesis in its extreme form, there is on the one hand the humanitarian, idealistic viewpoint, as opposed to that section of opinion which has consistently regarded all forms of foreign aid as a waste of taxpayers' money. The former viewpoint has been well stated in the words of President Truman in his 'Point Four' speech. 'Democracy alone can provide the vitalising force to stir the peoples of the world into triumphant action, not only against their human oppressors but also against ancient enemies–hunger, misery and despair.' [40] Or again, in the words of President Eisenhower in his address to the Indian Parliament on 10 December 1959,

> I come here representing a nation that wants not an acre of other people's land; that seeks no control of another people's government; that pursues no programme of expansion in commerce or politics or power of any sort at other people's expense. It is a nation ready to cooperate towards achievement of mankind's deep eternal aspirations for peace and freedom.[41]

Such sentiments are easily dismissed as either propaganda or as a merely naive desire to 'do good', not based on any understanding of economic realities. However, it would be unrealistic and mistaken to underestimate the influence of idealism in shaping America's aid policies, as can be seen from the millions of dollars poured out on aid programmes where the political returns are indeed doubtful. President Johnson has stated the case very simply thus:

> Friendly cynics and fierce enemies alike often underestimate or ignore the strong thread of moral purpose which runs through the fabric of American history. Of course, our security and welfare shape our policies. But much of the energy of our efforts has come from moral purposes. It is right that the strong should help the weak defend their freedom. It is right that the wealthy should help the poor emerge from their hunger.[42]

Aid is Defence?

The one argument which is consistently advanced in favour of economic aid programmes, particularly in India's case, is that Communism will be resisted by rising living standards. This was always the first 'practical' argument advanced by Kennedy, Humphrey and others whose humanitarianism was never in doubt, to convince more sceptical opinion. There are dangers in combining the humanitarian and anti-Communist approaches. Chester Bowles, for instance, argues strongly that India will only be convinced of American sincerity if humanitarian ideals are followed for their own sake and that the problem of poverty exists irrespective of the existence of Communism.[43] Adlai Stevenson has reiterated the same theme.[44] Eugene Black, former director of the World Bank, has argued that more is needed than loans, grants and technical expertise, though these are vital. The West '. . . must be willing to work side by side with these people and make common cause with them . . . nor is it enough to talk about an integration of political aims and ideals between the West and those parts of the world; there will be no such integration unless it grows out of a long period of constructive contact in tasks of common interest.'[45] The political dangers of such involvement apply in at least equal measure to humanitarians as to more narrowly interested parties. However, neither the practical nor the intellectual influence of the humanitarian school of thought may be easily discounted in any realistic assessment of American ideas.

At the other end of the political spectrum are the consistent and implacable opponents of all foreign aid programmes, especially to neutralist and socialist-sympathising countries such as India. Notable protagonists of this group have been Senators Ellender, Bridges, Knowland, Hickenlooper, Welker, Jenner, Maybank, Kersten and Representative Passman. These Congressmen have provided a mighty flow of information and statistics to support their cause.[46] Although persistent, their influence has been rather limited for most of the period. More recently, however, the trend of opinion has moved in their direction.

The majority viewpoint has ranged across a broad spectrum between the two extremes. There seems to exist an overall disposition in favour of helping developing countries, but at the same time this must be in America's interest and must be done in such a way as to bring maximum political benefits. The relevant questions in this context are 1. The political objectives of aid; 2. Countries to which such aid should be given; 3. The quantum and form in which aid should be given.

The first two questions are clearly related. As already stated, the most consistent and emphatic argument produced in favour of aid is that of promoting democracy and resisting Communism. This argument is advanced more vigorously in the case of India than any other country. From the viewpoint of her geographical position, size of population and political influence in the Asian region, she has naturally been seen as vital to American global interests. Whilst at the height of the Dulles era these were viewed crudely in terms of ideology and power, a more broad-based view has subsequently emerged of India as essential to world order and stability. In more idealistic moments concentration of large American resources in India has been justified by the objective of making her a 'showpiece of democracy'. Despite such periodic extravagances, however, the belief is deep-rooted that the success or failure of India's development plans provides a crucial test as to whether economic progress can be achieved within the framework of democratic institutions.[47] Nor is this simply an ideological view, for it is held that failure and instability in India would encourage instability throughout the region, thus threatening the delicate balance of coexistence created by the United States-Soviet nuclear stalemate and mutal fear of China. This analysis has led to a more sophisticated appraisal of American interests, whereby India's stability and independence, for which rapid economic growth is essential, are viewed as supreme goals in themselves as long as political or economic methods adopted can generally be maintained within a democratic framework.[48] This in turn has led to a reappraisal of attitudes towards the role of Soviet aid in India and towards policies of socialism and neutralism.

Reaction to Soviet Aid

The emergence of Soviet aid has had mixed results. It eventually forced a total re-examination of American aid policy, especially marked in India's case, in which the dimensions of the 'Point Four' programme were seen as quite inadequate. As already seen, it eventually altered American attitudes to Soviet aid fundamentally. Initially, however, Soviet intervention produced a temporary paralysis in American thinking, in which fear became the dominant element.[49] Some statements by Kruschev at the time lent colour to these fears. A Special Survey prepared for the Senate in 1957 quotes some of these statements in its first chapter: 'We recognise the necessity for the revolutionary transformation of capitalist society into socialist society . . . the fact that we support peaceful coexistence does not mean that one can relax in the struggle against bourgeois ideology. . . . It is quite likely that the forms of the transition to socialism will become more variegated.'[50] The Survey declared that prudence required the United States to interpret the Soviet economic offensive '. . . in the light of declared long-term aims, though other secondary aims can be shown to exist. . . . The Cold War is still on. The present Soviet economic assistance policy, aimed at underdeveloped countries, is part of it.'[51] The extent and form of Soviet aid is examined in great detail, also the possible motives and the capacity of the bloc to sustain such aid. The conclusions drawn, however, are somewhat vague. After calling for a more clear-cut separation of aid into the categories of Welfare, Military and Development[52] it is concluded that '. . . should the United States decide to continue such assistance, it should do so in the light of its own national interest. Assistance should go to those countries whose economic growth is considered important to the long-run interest of the United States.'[53] The notion of competing with the Soviets is rejected on the grounds that this would mean involvement in a dangerous game of bluff, objectionable to America on moral grounds. Furthermore the bargaining power of the recipients would be increased and and there was a great danger that in the process she would reduce her diplomatic relations with recipient countries to the same level as the Soviets. However, the United States should not withdraw development aid from a country because it had received aid from the Communist bloc, since this would cause great poverty and leave the way clear for Communism. The third alternative was to develop an independent policy, not based on mere reaction to Soviet initiatives which aimed at a long-term, balanced development programme, taking into account the interests of both donors and recipients. Such a programme should avoid year-to-year operations and aim at long-term planning and flexibility. Tariff barriers, currency restrictions and other hindrances to trade should be removed.[54] In spite of the vagueness of its prescriptions, this analysis indicates the beginnings of coexistence on the aid front between the United States and the Soviet Union, which was later to find a more powerful impetus.

Aid to Promote Democracy?

If fear of Communism is adduced as the chief reason for giving aid to developing countries does such aid in fact 'win friends for democracy'? A decisive negative is asserted by Eugene Black, who states that '. . . The values of freedom and democracy cannot be sold like soap, nor are they the necessary result of economic development.'[55] However, he proceeds to argue that the process of participation in the development of a country's economy can create the habit of democratic cooperation.

An interesting new concept is introduced to the field of international diplomacy—the 'development diplomat'. The function of such a hypothetical personage would not be to give orders, nor yet to provide expertise from a lofty pinnacle, but rather to involve himself deeply in the development problems of his assigned country. His prime purpose would be to 'illuminate choices', to clarify alternatives to economic policy and the consequences of adopting various policies.[56] 'Diplomacy' thus defined would appear to be operating in a vacuum, and in this circumstance the fate of Socrates or even Cassandra could well prove instructive. Nevertheless, this oblique approach to the question of persuading developing countries to adopt democratic methods of development raises important questions, to which some academics have been prepared to give radical answers. The basically oligarchic, socially stratified and undifferentiated nature of transitional developing societies is apparent, irrespective of outward democratic forms. In this context, considerable problems are posed for aid-giving countries, if social transformation is regarded as a prerequisite for economic development.[58] Such views would be widely held, but in the case of India this is not reflected in the political and administrative mechanisms of aid which exist only formally at the highest governmental levels. It has been urged by some that aid be used as a means for reaching to the social and political roots of developing societies, viewing the objective of achieving a more participating, open society as an end in itself, irrespective of economic objectives.[59] This, however, would appear to be a very doubtful proposition, quite apart from the imposition of value-judgments and charges of neo-colonialism necessarily entailed. Though foreign influences may act as a catalyst, social change must primarily be the product of indigeneous forces, and ill-considered outside intervention in this sphere will inevitably prove self-defeating. Official American policy towards India has been confined to developmental aims, in the economic sense, for most of the period under review, but latterly however there have been clear signs that greater political and administrative involvement may be accepted.[60] The scope of possible objectives emanating from aid programmes is thus wide-ranging, from minimum economic objectives to far-reaching political goals, whether in the field of domestic or foreign policy, and thinking on these matters is still very fluid. The conventional division between 'progressive' and 'conservative' opinion is only partially relevant in this context.

Critics of the 'defence against Communism' philosophy of aid are to be found on the 'Right Wing' as well as among 'liberals'. The House of

Representatives Foreign Aid Committee during recent years, under the chairmanship of Representative Passman,[61] has tended to treat all applicants for aid as improvident mendicants, showing a fine impartial disdain for allies and neutralists alike. The view has been taken that foreign aid 'giveaways', by creating resentment arising from suspicion of concealed motives, were more likely to advance the cause of Communism than otherwise. On this assumption, Senator Ellender, in a special report designed to show the extravagance of the foreign aid programme, advocated channelling all aid through the United Nations, with the possible exception of Latin American aid. Such a viewpoint is normally associated with more 'liberal' opinion. The motive here is twofold; first to take away some of the supposed political odium from the United States and secondly, to save money by restricting the American share of total UN aid to one-third.[62]

Non-Alignment

Closely related to the concept of aid as a defence against Communism are the questions of aid to neutral countries and the correct attitude to be adopted towards countries such as India, which adopt socialist or socialistic-type policies. Stated in their extreme form, the two opposing viewpoints can be summarised as follows. On the one hand it is argued that in the fight against Communism, neutralism represents a compromise with evil and is therefore immoral. The form of economic organisation adopted by a a country is an ideological matter, and any form of state ownership or control may be regarded as socialism, which is scarcely distinguishable from Communism. A country therefore reveals its true nature by the form of economic organisation it adopts. Countries such as India, which adopt socialist and neutralist policies, should receive little or no aid, which should be reserved for those who wholeheartedly support the United States in the struggle against International Communism. Against this it is argued that each country has the right to determine its own internal and external policies according to its view of its own self-interest. The United States itself was neutral during the first one hundred and fifty years of her existence. With regard to the question of socialism, each country must adapt its economic policy to its own peculiar circumstances. America's experience is not universally relevant and countries such as India cannot rely entirely on private capital to develop their economy, since the basic public services, such as roads, power and irrigation facilities, education, etc. are inadequate to make large-scale private investment profitable without considerable public expenditure. However, experience has shown, especially in India, that investment in the public sector causes a substantial expansion of investment in the private sector. In spite of her refusal of military alliance with the West, India's internal system of government is democratic and therefore deserves the support of the United States, whose main security interest lies in India's progressive economic development, irrespective of the methods adopted.

The former viewpoint has found several forceful exponents. In moving an amendment to the Mutual Security Act of 1957, which would have reduced aid appropriated to India for that year from $80m to $45m, Senator Bridges enunciated the principle that '. . . those who are not for us are against us'. India was not really neutral but pro-Communist.[63] Senator Knowland has been equally emphatic that the United States should not spend scarce dollars on nations who refuse to accept the principle of collective security, whose leaders preach neutralism, and make no reasonable effort to attract private capital.[64] A more academic statement of basically the same thesis is provided by Milton Friedman, who argues that the inevitable result of economic aid is to strengthen the public sector, to encourage 'monument building' and wasteful state expenditure and control. The tests of efficiency, coordinated planning and so forth applied in granting aid are basically Communist tests, and therefore the whole aid programme is in effect speeding the advance of Communism. America should concentrate instead on such measures as the removal of trade barriers, guarantees for private capital, currency convertibility and other measures of liberalisation.[65] The dogma that public enterprise equals Communism is a common assumption, implicit or explicit, behind all these themes.

If India has been forcefully attacked for her policies, it may well be that these attacks, coupled with her obvious political and strategic importance in the world balance of power equation, have brought her more influential support than other less articulate countries with similar economic problems. So strongly was India's case presented by a certain section of opinion that the Mutual Security Bill of 1959 initially contained a resolution, inserted by Senators Kennedy and Cooper, specifically recognising the importance of India's development plans to America's security and the need to support them with substantial and continuing amounts of aid.[66] The resolution was actually passed through the Senate, in spite of vigorous objections to the effect that India was being given precedence over America's military allies. However, it was deleted after a House-Senate Conference, the House agreeing in principle with the sentiments expressed, but objecting to a specific reference being made in favour of India in a general Act appropriating economic and military aid. India's rights have been vigorously defended by many and some have been prepared to argue openly that Indian neutrality has positive benefits for the United States, in that India can act as an intermediary between the two camps in the 'Cold War'.[67] It has also been pointed out that much depends on how the idea of neutralism is interpreted. Thus Ellsworth Bunker, former American Ambassador to India, declared, in a vigorous defence of that country's position 'India is non-aligned, to be sure, as we were for the first one hundred and fifty years of our national life. But in the great struggle of the present-day–the preservation and broadening of the dignity and rights of men–there is no doubt where India stands. She has chosen the democratic way of life'. After urging the need to fight poverty throughout the world and 'complacency, luxury and smugness at home', he continues ' . . . it means humility to acknowledge that we haven't found all the answers, that nations and people are bound to develop systems suited to their own genius, needs and traditions, that the set of values that they live by may legitimately differ from ours'.[68] Others have urged that a too dogmatic approach to the question of neutralism may incline countries like India towards the Communist camp.[69]

Socialism

Growing acquaintance with India's economic problems has also produced more liberal attitudes towards questions of socialism and planning. Professor J. K. Galbraith, ambassador to India under Kennedy, has insisted that conventional American views on Indian socialism are unsophisiticated, arguing that India's public sector is in fact relatively smaller than that of the United States: 'India has, in fact, imposed a smallish socialised sector atop what, no doubt, is the world's greatest example of functioning anarchy . . . whereas at home the American system is flexible and pragmatic, the export version is somewhat different, i.e. laissez-faire and rugged individulaism . . . Men who wouldn't dream of taking this medicine themselves unhesitatingly prescribe it for foreigners'.[70] After arguing that neither old-fashioned nor modern capitalism are relevant to India's needs, since the latter involves a complex system of administration beyond her capabilities, he concludes that the most irrevelant generalisations come from the higher echelons of power, American officials in India adopting a generally pragmatic view. There is, in fact ' . . . an unquestioned correlation between the majesty of official position with the irrelevance of the generalisations that are solemnly articulated'.[71] President Kennedy, however, did much to invalidate this dictum. He consistently urged the need for foreign investment in both public and private sectors, and further insisted that aid from all sources must be coordinated to ensure the success of the Five Year Plans, to which end the best brains in the West should consult with India. Aid programmes should be put on a long-term basis, instead of voting annual appropriations. Above all, such programmes should not be on a competitive basis, nor designed to achieve prestige, but aimed at balanced long-term development.[72]

The problem of 'strings'

It is clear that the tone of much of this debate is offensive to India, in that the extent of political motivation is revealed, involving extensive and diverse value-judgments concerning her basic policy objectives. The public and often sensational nature of this debate places the United States at a great political disadvantage. Removal or diminution of the more obvious political 'strings' to aid does not alter this fact. Furthermore, apart from ideological considerations, the thesis that the West's main security interest with regard to India lies in the establishment of a prosperous well-balanced economy there involves planning of aid programmes to achieve maximum efficiency. This necessarily entails delicate negotiations as to priorities and also involves an extensive system of end-use reporting. No matter with what finesse such negotiations and procedures are conducted, political sensitivities will inevitably be affected and charges of neo-colonialism, etc. raised in some quarters. Here again the United States is at a disadvantage compared with the Soviet Union, whose aid is concentrated mainly on industrial projects with obvious prestige impact. The Soviets make no apparent attempt to assess the total impact of any project on the economy or to debate with Indian leaders as to the possible alternative use of resources. In the words of B. K. Nehru, Indian ambassador to Washington, '[With Russia] we pay them as we purchase the equipment and then it is our affair whether we sink it into the sea or make good use of it. . . . As far as the United States is concerned there is a very considerable degree of end-use reporting and seeing that things are done as they were promised to be done, and there is quite an army of American officials carrying on this kind of supervision'.[73] An important difference here, of course, is the need for the American government to justify its aid expenditure to the American tax-payer through Congress. However, despite the obvious political acceptability of the Soviet approach, it may well be argued that if American aid strategy is successful in shaping the Indian economy in the direction indicated, this is likely to produce internal political conditions favourable to American interests thus broadly defined.

Bilateralism versus multilateralism

A realisation of the dangers of political involvement implied by bilateralism has led some to argue that more emphasis should be placed on multilateral aid programmes. The advantages of channelling aid through the United Nations have been well stated by Henry Cabot Lodge as follows: 1. The U.N. is less vulnerable to the charge of 'imperialism' than any individual donor; 2. The unpopularity of refusing aid in any particular instance is not borne by one country; 3. There is greater coordination of resources and therefore, presumably, of programming; 4. Recipients are members of the international agency concerned and are therefore involved in questions of allocation; 5. The balance of payments burden is more evenly distributed. According to Mr Lodge an emphasis on the UN would have the additional advantage of exposing Russian insincerity in claiming to give aid without strings, since their contribution to the United Nations aid effort has been negligible, despite Mr Kruschev's declaration to the General Assembly that that organisation should send aid to new states '. . . rising from the ruins of the colonial system to help them speedily to develop their national economies'.[74] From the recipients' viewpoint there is the powerful advantage of being free to purchase from any source.

The opposite viewpoint is well expressed in a Special Report to the Senate in 1957,[75] which argues that although economic aid should be removed as far as possible from the context of East-West competition, aid distributed through a multilateral agency, presumably the UN, might well be inefficiently administered, due to the extensive consultation involved. Furthermore, unless the World Bank system of weighted voting were adopted, recipient countries would outvote donor countries, who having lost control over expenditure, would find their substantial contributions far harder to justify to their voters. If the Communist bloc were included, business confidence in the West would be weakened, but if it were not UN aid programmes would appear as instruments in the Cold War. However, the Report goes on to suggest a number of ways in which bilateralism and multilateralism might be combined. These include a consultative organisation of recipients and donors which would register all aid agreements, dispensing expertise through a high prestige technical and advisory staff. Here there is a difficulty in correlating prestige and expertise with absence of power and responsibility. The most decisive barrier to an increase in multilateralism is that all major donor countries view aid as a means of expanding trade, or at least from a negative viewpoint are concerned that aid should not constitute a drain on their balance of payments. Trade has been a substantial if little publicised factor in persuading Congress to vote large quantities of aid, [76] and caused the abandonment in 1959 of the practice of granting aid untied to purchases in the United States.

Multilateralism does constitute an important element in American policy, however, in that she is the major contributor to the World Bank and pioneered the Consortium concept of aid to India.[78] Although unsuccessful, the efforts initiated under the Kennedy administration to achieve world-wide reduction of trade barriers and a common world policy for the distribution of food surpluses[79] represented some further attempt to relate India's economic problems to their global context. Nevertheless the overall emphasis is heavily bilateralist, despite the pursuit of multilateralist ideas at a theoretical level.

Conclusion

It has only been possible here to outline the main features of a policy debate which has many ramifications, the scope and nature of which has widened vastly since its tentative inception. The period under consideration has witnessed some remarkable developments in basic policy assumptions. Some reasonable understanding of India's attitude towards military alliances and general foreign policy questions has been achieved. In the context of growing Sino-Soviet differences, India's close relationship with Russia has become far more acceptable, while most types of Soviet aid are no longer seen as a direct threat to American interests, though in both respects considerable opposition has continued to be voiced. At the same time the role of the public sector in a developing economy such as India's has gradually been recognised, though the limits to aid in this context are still clearly defined. At a purely economic level, the narrowness of the 'Point Four' approach has long ago been recognised and capital assistance has assumed a dominant role. There has been a general easing of loan terms, placing the United States in most respects ahead of the Soviet Union in this regard, though repayment of loans in dollars represents a heavy burden. A greater proportion of loans are now untied to projects and this trend seems likely to develop.

Future policy trends are hard to predict. It certainly appears, however, that a major review of American objectives and methods is in train.

The far tougher bargaining approach during the past two years indicates that the generally clear guidelines of the Kennedy period are being obscured. Aid is likely to be cut sharply and insistence on tangible results become more vigorous, though pressure could ease if the situation in Vietnam were to improve. Emphasis on modernisation in agriculture and fertiliser production indicates a clear determination to identify and eliminate 'bottlenecks' in the Indian economy. Whilst India seems likely to refuse more obvious demands for quid pro quos, such as a compromise on her Kashmir policy, she may prove less capable of withstanding American pressure for involvement in determining her major economic priorities and strategies.[80] Such an approach may take the United States far beyond the field of economic planning per se. Although many basic assumptions from the Nehru era are now being strongly questioned on the Indian side, and in many cases being quietly set aside, the United States would be wise to proceed with caution, resisting the temptation to take undue advantage of India's present weaknesses. Although short-term successes may be recorded in modification of Indian economic policies, the political price in terms of resentment, consistently strong due to arms aid to Pakistan, could possibly undermine her long-term objectives. Nor, without active Indian cooperation, will economic progress be sufficient to compensate for such political losses. Involvement naturally increases with the magnitude of aid, but as Eugene Black has indicated, the quality of the dialogue between donor and recipient is all-important.[81] The inevitable contradiction between enlarged responsibilities and the achievement of a correct balance in administrative method and diplomatic style will pose progressively more acute problems for American policy-makers in the future.

Chapter 4

Objectives of Soviet aid policy in India

As with all bilateral aid, Soviet aid must be viewed in its overall diplomatic and strategic context. Complex political and economic motives intertwine with questions of power and capability. It is beyond the scope of this study to analyse Soviet aid on a global basis.[1] In the specifically Indian context, whilst important ties of economic interest have been established, it is my main thesis that foreign policy considerations have been dominant. Purely Communist objectives have played a secondary part and to substantiate this proposition relations with the Communist Party of India have been analysed in some detail.

The previous chapter has illustrated some of the confusions in American policy. It has often been thought, by contrast, that Soviet aid is the product of brilliant planning and strategic thinking. It is argued that the Soviet Union does not suffer from the disadvantages of Western democracies. Critical legislatures and public opinion do not have to be satisfied, tedious and often undignified open debates can be avoided and resources mobilised speedily to achieve carefully designed objectives, with economic projects planned as part of an elaborate grand design.[2] While it may be true that the Soviet Union has avoided some of the grosser political and psychological errors committed by the United States, and at times, as in the case of the Bokaro steel mill project, displayed a notable opportunism, detailed consideration of Indo-Soviet relations does not fully substantiate these claims. At a diplomatic level Soviet aid has achieved considerable success, but its objectives have been almost as equally confused and ill-defined as those of the United States. Leopold Labedz comments that '... there is a curious parallel between the processes which led to the loss of political innocence by the Americans, and those by which the Russians, in the course of their policies towards the developing countries are losing some of their doctrinal ignorance'.[3] He continues that while the West has tended to regard economic aid as a 'cure-all' for post-colonialist ills, without linking this to necessary social reform, the Soviet Union offers a panacaea consisting of a generalised revolutionary theory, an emphasis on the evils of colonialism as the explanation for all problems and 'a myth of accelerated industrial development'. The deficiency of this approach is that 'it does not understand the sociological or anthropological elements of the real situation and consequently misjudges the behaviour-pattern of social groups and political elites'.[4] There has of course been no open debate, as in the United States, as to fundamental objectives and there is therefore less information as to what was really expected from aid programmes. However, it is apparent that the economic method adopted was in accordance with Russia's traditional thinking on industrial development and was regarded as a model which would encourage a certain pattern of development, thus bringing about a pattern of politics favourable to Communism. In India, while the economic model has been partially applied within a limited sector, the theoretical political dividends have not accrued, but in view of its diplomatic successes Russia has paid little attention to the effect of its policies on the domestic front. Labedz's analysis holds specially true for India. This is best illustrated by an analysis of Soviet relations with the CPI, which are characterised from the earliest days by dogmatism and indifference, while inter-governmental relations have been given highest priority. The Soviet aid effort emerges with remarkable urgency about 1954, in marked contrast to the whole pattern of relations in the previous Stalinist period. It is necessary to study this earlier period in order to view the policies of the Kruschev era in proper perspective. In this context, internal struggles within the CPI provide valuable clues to subsequent developments.

Moscow's attitude towards India's independence struggle constantly varied according to global considerations of international Communist strategy, and more particularly according the the needs of Russian foreign policy. Indeed, during the second world war the CPI adopted a pro-British line. The period 1945-7 is one of particular confusion, with an uncertain debate being conducted amongst Soviet theoreticians as to the correct view of the Congress movement, Jawaharlal Nehru and the question of partition. One economist, Eugene Varga, went so far as to question whether India could be considered an entirely 'imperialist' economy, but this view was soon condemned as heretical.[5] There was a tendency to distinguish between 'progressive' forces in Congress led by Nehru, and 'reactionary' forces representing 'monopoly capitalism' and the 'big bourgoisie' led by Sardar Patel.[6] Although this view had been discarded by Moscow far earlier, it was not until the replacement of P. C. Joshi by

B. T. Ranadive as general secretary in February 1948, that a policy of outright opposition to the Nehru government was adopted, varying in intensity and tactics until about 1953, since when a more 'constitutional' approach has been adopted. During this period of closest rapprochement Moscow offered only theoretical support, even at the height of the armed insurrection campaigns of 1948-9 in Hyderabad and Andhra (then part of Madras state).[7] By 1951 control of the CPI had returned to the Joshi-Dange-Ghosh 'rightist' faction, with Cominform support. From 1950 (approximately) the Soviet Union appears to have taken little direct interest in CPI affairs, being preoccupied with wider international problems and observing the relative failure of 'revolutionary' strategy in India. The struggles and polemics within the CPI, however, during the last three years of Stalin's life, reflect changes on the international scene and foreshadow subsequent developments in Indo-Soviet relations. Nehru's mediatory role in the Korean war appears to have brought a new Kremlin appraisal of him.[8] Direct contacts between Moscow and the CPI during this period appear to have been minimal, the British Communist Party, through the medium of R. Palme Dutt, acting as interpreter of the official Cominform line. The earlier view of Congress as being divided into 'progressive' and 'reactionary' wings was tentatively resumed, though this time a distinction was drawn between domestic and foreign policy, Nehru's policy in the latter respect being regarded as a 'hesitant and limited opposition to the imperialist war policy'.[9] From this assumption Dutt went on to argue for a 'united front from above' programme with the 'peace' issue paramount. The CPI did not immediately fall into line. Local conditions were favourable to militancy but external pressure was brought to subordinate these to (Soviet) foreign policy requirements. A continuous debate was sustained as to whether British or American imperialism was the chief enemy, which may be interpreted as a question of whether domestic or foreign policy was to take priority. However, it was not until the Madura Congress (27th December1953-4th January 1954) that the CPI hesitantly opted for the latter course, which automatically involved a return to 'constitutionalism'. This, however, was not formally admitted at that time.[10]

The foregoing analysis gives some essential background insight into the triangular relationship between the Soviet and Indian governments and the CPI. What seems to emerge is that although theoretical and doctrinal influence from Moscow on the CPI was strong, there appears to have been no automatic chain of command even in the period of tightest Stalinist orthodoxy. Time lags appear during which the enunciation of a new Moscow line causes intense internal debate before its adoption. It can be argued that Moscow had abandoned its objectives of internal subversion in India—if indeed these were ever serious—as early as 1950, when Nehru's role in international affairs became an important factor in Soviet calculations, whereas the CPI did not formally abandon these objectives until 1956.[11] In the light of this analysis, I shall therefore proceed on the assumption that one must view aid primarily as an instrument of Russian foreign policy rather than an aspect of international Communist strategy. With the emergence of the strategy of 'peaceful coexistence', of which aid was an important instrument, good relations with the Congress government became all-important, while the CPI's political interests were totally ignored.

Changes in Soviet attitudes towards newly independent and potentially non-aligned countries were apparent even before Kruschev's enunciation of the 'peaceful coexistence' philosophy. Nehru's initiative with regard to Korea[12] opened up considerable opportunities for Soviet diplomacy, of which the immediate result was a broadening of the Korean question into the wider issue of recognition of Communist China,[13] thus providing a world platform for the propagation of the 'peace' issue. At the 19th Party Congress in 1952, Malenkov indicated that the economic factor would henceforth play a major role in Soviet calculations.[14] He expounded the view that conflict was growing between the United States and other capitalist countries, owing to the shrinking markets of the whole capitalist world. This was due to the development of the 'socialist' camp, including China, as an independent economic force, and the upsurge of 'national liberation struggles' in 'colonial and dependent countries'. These problems were only partially solved by the arms drive. The economic growth of the 'socialist' camp would create a need for exports rather than imports.[15] Thus the 'third world' was now viewed as the major area for competition with the West. It is not clear whether a trade war was envisaged, as this can be said to have emerged only in a very limited context.[16] However, the economic factor had now been clearly recognised, though the strategy of 'aid and trade' had yet to be formulated.[17]

In view of the almost barren relationship between India and the Soviet Union during the period 1947-54, the speed with which and the extent to which cooperation was subsequently achieved is most remarkable. Apart from the global change in Soviet strategy, foreshadowed under Stalin and implemented by Kruschev, there were substantial factors of common interest to account for such a successful rapprochement.

A radical interpretation of the new Soviet philosophy was necessitated by the coincidence in 1954 of markedly closer Western involvement in the affairs of the subcontinent, in the form of Pakistan's adherence to SEATO and CENTO, and the supply of American F.84 jets to that country. From the Soviet viewpoint it can well be argued that these factors upset the power balance in the area, bringing Western power nearer to her own southern borders. At the same time however this situation presented excellent opportunities to exploit Indian resentment, her search for freedom from American pressures, and Mr Dulles' obsession with pacts.

The high proportion of Soviet aid directed to India and Afghanistan,[18] both of whom had border disputes with Pakistan, indicate her concern to bolster her position in the region. Russian policy may quite plausibly be interpreted as a defensive reaction to these developments, India's neutrality now becoming a minimum requirement for Soviet security, to which end it was necessary to reduce dependence on the United States for assistance. Such a strategy could easily be accommodated within the framework of promoting the independence of ex-colonial developing countries while still maintaining the new philosophy of peaceful coexistence.[19] There is thus a marked parallel between Soviet and American strategy towards India, and indeed, following the Sino-Indian war in 1962 and the growth of the Sino-Soviet ideological split, India has provided perhaps the clearest focal point of Cold War detente between America and Russia. India as one of the leading Asian powers, and as the leading exponent of the doctrine of 'non-alignment' provided the Soviet Union with her best opportunity of emerging from her long period of self-imposed diplomatic isolation.

On the Indian side, deteriorating relations with the United States[20] provided a strong incentive for establishing counter-balancing good relations with the Soviet Union, especially as the latter appeared willing to accept her basic foreign policy assumptions and had declared a doctrine of non-interference in domestic affairs. At the same time, India was preparing to move into a new stage of economic development, with maximum emphasis on heavy industry, especially in the public sector.[21] In view of World Bank and American hostility towards this type of economic strategy, India had a strong incentive to accept Soviet assistance, especially on the attractive terms offered. Above all Soviet aid proved crucial in allowing India's particular chosen pattern of development to evolve. In this respect the amount of Soviet aid was infinitely less important than its orientation.

Soviet aid, whatever the original intention, has clearly failed to influence India towards Communism, private enterprise having been accorded a progressively expanded role,[22] and a generally rightward trend being observable within Congress since about 1962. Nevertheless, the continued increase in quantum indicates that foreign policy objectives remain paramount, indeed even more urgent with the incursion of Chinese interests into the region. One may reasonably question, therefore, whether aid was ever viewed as a means of influencing India's internal policy towards Communism, though certain statements of Kruschev might be interpreted as indicating such an intention. Defining the concept of 'peaceful coexistence' at the 20th Soviet Communist Party Congress in February 1956, he maintained the inevitability in a number of capitalist countries of 'the overthrow of the bourgeois dictatorship by force . . . the fact that we support peaceful coexistence does not mean that one can relax in the struggle against bourgeois ideology'. At the same time it was 'likely that the forms of the transition to socialism will become more variegated'.[23] These words reasonably invite the reaction that 'the Cold War is still on. The present Soviet economic assistance policy aimed at underdeveloped countries is part of it'.[24] It is likely that these sentiments were mainly intended for internal consumption, to protect the newly expounded concept of 'peaceful coexistence' from the charge of 'revisionism'. There seems little doubt, however, that the total effect of Soviet economic and diplomatic policies towards India has been to strengthen the Congress government vis a vis the CPI. Since this trend has been persistsent and Soviet policies have remained largely unaltered, it may be assumed that this effect is accepted, though the possibility of miscalculation in the original formulation of policy cannot be entirely ruled out. However, convincing evidence of Moscow's prime concern for good relations with successive Congress governments and its total lack of concern for the effect of its policies on the CPI was provided during the crucial elections in Andhra state in 1955, when *Pravda* published an editorial praising not only the government of India's foreign policies but its domestic policies also. The Congress Party circulated thousands of reprints of this editorial during the campaign.[25] The CPI was totally excluded from official participation in the Kruschev-Bulganin visit during December 1955, from which the Congress government derived considerable prestige.[26] Opinion polls show that while the visit enhanced

Soviet prestige and was generally thought to have promoted Indo-Russian friendship, it achieved little effect for the Communist cause.[27] In order to retain some semblance of political activity while accommodating itself to the Soviet line the CPI has been forced to resort to 'opportunist' tactics in a variety of situations ranging from labour disputes to linguistic agitations. With the possible exception of West Bengal the Communists have achieved significant success only where they have successfully identified themselves with regional pressures. Their identification with particular caste groups in these regions has equally been demonstrated.[28] Regionalism, linguism and casteism within the CPI could only be aggravated by the loosening of links with Moscow. The Sino-Soviet division has enhanced these trends still further.

There was a widespread tendency in the West, especially in the United States during the initial period to give various interpretations of Soviet aid in vaguely conspiratorial terms. Thus a Special Report to the Senate declared that 'American aid is intended to foster economic growth and higher living standards. . . . This cannot be the long-term purpose of Soviet economic assistance; national independence in the American sense is incompatible with Moscow's long-term design'. However, it is conceded that 'they might believe that economic growth deters communism, yet feel constrained to participate for short-term political advantage'.[29] On this view, Soviet aid will presumably provide industrial 'white elephants' designed to undermine the economy. At a more sophisticated level, it has been argued that, unlike the United States, the Soviet Union is not involved in the complexities of the status quo and need not therefore concern itself with problems of overall economic balance.[30] It is clear that this approach is highly acceptable to India,[31] and alleged economic irresponsibility is therefore at least balanced by political calculation. However, Soviet prestige, though not openly staked on the success of the total planning effort, is involved in the success of particular projects. The full weight of Soviet resources, capital, technical and managerial skills, are concentrated on a small number of carefully selected projects, which in most cases have been accorded the highest priority in India's Five Year Plans.[32] Of particular attraction to India is the importance accorded to training and managerial responsibility for Indians during the establishment of the project, which on completion is turned over to full Indian control. The Bhilai steel mill project and oil exploration ventures in Gujerat have been clear successes. On the other hand the Ranchi (Bihar) heavy machine-constructing plant has suffered from serious administrative difficulties on the Indian side and is experiencing a slackening of demand during the present recession. On balance, however, the successes clearly outweigh the failures.

Early prognostications to the effect that Soviet promises of aid were insincere having proved false, two opposing hypotheses remain, assuming that an evolution of the Indian economy in a Communist direction is intended. First, that industrialisation, which once started becomes an irresistable process, may be regarded as a means for unbalancing the economy, ultimately creating economic chaos and so producing the long predicted 'crisis of capitalism' to be followed by the establishment of 'socialism'. An incidental advantage from this point of view would be the rapid growth of the urban proletariat, thus providing a class basis favourable to the growth of Communism. It is a matter of lively and indeed vital debate whether the Five Year Plans represent a correct economic balance. Criticisms of inbalance and 'giganticism' have long been heard in the West and in recent years with growing force in India itself. However, it must be stressed that the choice of emphasis has been India's, the Soviet Union merely benefiting from the coincidence of views. While the question of intention must remain in the realm of hypothesis, it may be suggested that the pattern recommended for developing countries is that pursued by the Soviet Union itself. Thus the insistence on rapid industrialisation irrespective of other social and economic objectives[33] could perhaps be better interpreted as dogmatism rather than Machiavellianism.[34] This leads to a second and more tenable hypothesis–that the Soviet Union aims, or at least originally aimed, to export its own pattern of industrialisation, with a view to demonstrating that its method represents the true path to rapid development.[35] In this regard, some measure of success has been achieved, even Jawaharlal Nehru acknowledging India's indebtedness to Soviet experience.[36] Of particular importance was the influence of Soviet economic thought on P. C. Mahalanobis, chief architect of the Second Five Year Plan. Yet it is at this point that Soviet doctrinal confusion becomes apparent, for it is neither consistently opportunistic nor ideological. It has been suggested that 'in all the underdeveloped countries, a viable political order depends no less on the present agricultural policy than on the future rate of industrialisation, and the chances of subversion are inversely proportional to the degree to which local political elites are ready to act upon this rather obvious observation'.[37] If this holds good for India, which the mounting agricultural crisis indicates to be the case, then Soviet policy is totally failing to take advantage of the situation, either for subversive purposes or for the purpose of exporting a Soviet agricultural model.[38] Here again, theory and practice may well be in conflict. Official theory still supports the concept of revolution, but even under Stalin it was laid down that 'the export of revolution is nonsense. Every country makes its own revolution if it wants to and if it does not want to there will be no revolution'.[39] Thus revolution, according to traditional Leninist theory inevitable, must in India's case be viewed as the function of the CPI, whose low rating in Soviet priorities has already been indicated. Russian stress on heavy industry coincided with the development of the Second Five Year Plan, which indeed bears some definite resemblance to Soviet Planning concepts.[40] One may speculate whether the Soviet industrial emphasis in India stems from the theoretical desirability of fostering the growth of an industrial proletariat, the desire to export her own economic model or from reasons of economic convenience. All three motives would probably play a part, but so far as the first is concerned, theoretical considerations do not necessarily imply practical policy intent. The CPI has not proved especially strong in major cities, other than Calcutta, and indeed the experiences of Kerala prove that the 'Left' Communist tactic of alliance with the rural masses is the most profitable. No serious charge of clandestine Soviet support for CPI subversive activities has been brought from any responsible quarter, though this is not to deny the possibility. Yet it seems unlikely, for in addition to her demonstrable lack of concern for the fate of Indian Communism, hostile relations with China provide the Soviet Union with a strong incentive for the maintenance of India's stability, demonstrating further that foreign policy considerations have always been paramount.

Some striking attempt to reconcile ideology and diplomacy in favour of the latter was provided by an article publised in Moscow by M. Rubinstein under official auspices, in which the Congress Avadi Conference resolution of January 1955, envisaging a 'socialistic pattern of society' receives approval:

> Steps to develop state industry are not, in themselves, of a socialistic character. . . . However, in India as in other economically backward countries that have recently embarked on the path of independent development, state-capitalist enterprises assume a special character. . . . State capitalist enterprises in India, under present conditions, play a progressive part . . . given close cooperation by all the progressive forces of the country, there is the possibility for India to develop along socialist lines. . . . The economic plans. . . . can be carried out

only with the active participation of their workers and peasants, their young technical intelligentsia, scientists, students, etc.[41]

Apart from the radical reverse in traditional dogma involved in recognising the merits of a mixed economy, the abandonment of class-consciousness apparent in the final statement is still more remarkable. The CPI line had been to regard the Avadi resolution as 'a hoax perpetrated by the big bourgeoisie to deceive the masses'.[42] Rubinstein's article provoked Ajoy Ghosh, general secretary of the CPI from 1951-62 and normally a faithful disciple of Moscow, to reply in scathing terms that socialism, which was based on new property relations, could never be achieved under the leadership of the bourgeoisie, however radical–'power in the hands of the democratic masses led by the proletariat–this is the essential condition for the building of socialism'.[43] This exchange indicates more clearly than ever Moscow's emphasis on pragmatism. Yet the Soviet Union has shown no overall interest in India's economic development, and thus statements approving her economic policies are more in the nature of diplomatic gestures. A similar conflict exists over attitudes to Western aid. Whilst the CPI is violently hostile, Moscow, though often denouncing Western political motives in general terms, rarely does so in a specifically Indian context.[44] Perhaps the most realistic appraisal of the situation is provided by Kruschev's view of the function of Soviet aid in acting as a catalyst to produce still larger quantities of Western aid: 'I will venture to say that if the Americans give India a loan for economic development, this loan to the extent of 60 or 70 per cent may be considered a result of the existence of socialist countries'.[45] While this may well express the sentiments of the Indian government, it does also imply Soviet approval of India's enjoyment of the economic fruits of "non-alignment".

Soviet aid policy in India has generally been diplomatically unexceptionable, in that aid is given without too much haggling, in spheres where it is required. Projects are carefully selected for their impact value, while at the same time interference with Indian planning priorities is scrupulously avoided. Projects are planned in detail, though an advisory role is carefully maintained.[46] Yet precise priorities are hard to identify, for the Indian economy tends increasingly towards private enterprise,[47] despite a significant expansion of the public sector. Diplomacy and doctrine preclude an overall interest in the Indian economy, so neither conspiratorial nor altruistic motives, nor even enlightened self-interest according to the American pattern provide consistent explanations of Soviet objectives. Clearly some economic benefits are derived by Russia from aid and trade policies, in that materials and products not available at home can be purchased in return for export of heavy equipment and manufactured goods in which she enjoys some comparative advantage.[48] The extent of subsidy is hard to determine, though it has certainly been significant, but there is now evidence of far tougher bargaining in the light of lessening Cold War tensions and changing economic relationships with the East European countries of the bloc.[49] It is interesting to note that the validity of the subversion theory of Soviet aid must necessarily be in inverse relationship to the extent of economic advantage that may be expected to be derived from exchange of trade. Lingering doubts on this score may thus be set aside. Yet economic advantage is more a derivative effect than a basic motive of Soviet policy. It does not explain the dichotomy between the absence of apparent ideological purpose, informality of style and ease of relationship on the one hand and the contrasting rigidity of form in the actual content of aid on the other hand.

One is moved to the conclusion that Soviet aid has been the product of nothing more precisely definable than a general desire for good relations with India. Foreign policy considerations have undoubtedly provided the prime motivation, but here again objectives have been no more precise, developing piecemeal according to a changing situation. While limited and sometimes substantial agreement has been reached between the two countries on particular issues, there has never been any question of alignment, though conceivably the Soviet Union may have hoped originally for such an evolution. However, it can be assumed that the primary Soviet foreign policy objective is defensive—to keep India out of the Western camp militarily and in the economic sphere to limit influence from and dependence on the West, to which end economic aid is a most appropriate tool.[50] Thus American and Soviet objectives, though the United States came more reluctantly to accept Indian neutralism, are very similar, and in view of India's basic foreign policy assumptions mutually limiting. On the evidence of limited public opinion surveys, it would appear that the Soviet Union's most notable diplomatic successes have been effected by their support for India's cause in Kashmir and Goa, but economic aid has played a useful role in gaining popular support.[51] Since her aid is directed to no clear economic or political objective within the domestic Indian scene, Soviet policy seems only capable of explanation in these terms. Aid was given in the form it was since this was the most mutually convenient arrangement, but the question of adaptability has not proved very important up to the end of the period under consideration. The pattern established, though subordinate to foreign policy objectives, may initially have been viewed as a panacaea for economic development, which would bring automatic internal political dividends. These failed to materialise, but since the all-important diplomatic advantages did accrue, no attempt at adaptation was made. No doubt the Soviet niche within the developing public sector is secure for a long time ahead, though should a greater American pragmatism develop in this context, along with a continued growth in the European economy, competition could become far keener. At the same time past experience may not necessarily point the pattern for the future, for the growing diversification and sophistication of the Indian economy, together with the probable future emphasis on agriculture and private enterprise, will create challenges to the existing stereotyped pattern of Soviet aid. The growing military emphasis in India's development will create further pressures.

Finally, it should be noted that although the implications of the 1966 Tashkent conference are not yet entirely clear, the Soviet Union is now more involved in balance of power questions on the subcontinent. While she may continue to offer India an alternative focus to the West in terms of economic method, ideology and diplomacy, it becomes increasingly plain that she shares a common interest with America in the preservation of an overall framework of regional stability. India's bargaining power, though still considerable, has thus contracted to fairly well defined limits.

Part 2

The political impact of foreign aid in India

Chapter 5

The politics of aid: the Indian response

Hitherto, economic aid has been largely considered from the donor's viewpoint. It is now time to assess its impact on India. The impression may have been created that initiative comes primarily from the donor countries, but such a passive concept of India's role would be entirely misleading. For this reason it would be unrealistic to attempt, in isolation, an analysis of Indian political reactions to the various aid programmes. On the contrary, I shall argue that it is India itself that has largely determined the pattern of aid negotiations. There are two basic reasons for this; first, the fact that all aided projects have until recently come within the scope of the Five-Year Plans means that initiation and administration has been an Indian responsibility. Foreign experts are always used in an advisory rather than a supervisory capacity. Naturally, donor counries have the power to give or withold aid, subject to scrutiny and modification of programmes but this is an essentially passive function. Requests are formulated in terms of Indian priorities, which in turn largely determine the nature of the various agreements. The more important reason why initiative lies substantially in Indian hands is that she has insisted on formulating her own economic priorities, refused to link aid with question of alliances and ideology and stoutly defended herself against attacks on her domestic sovereignty. In the end her viewpoint has gained reluctant recognition by the donors. The present reassessment of the role of foreign aid must be seen in this light. India has succeeded in obtaining massive help for the purposes stated in her Five Year Plans. The Plans thus provide the basis for the continuing dialogue between India and the donor countries. It follows that the political impact of the various aid programmes will be determined mainly by the relevance of the donors' response to India's economic needs. The donor countries are sometimes accused of exercising influence through aid programmes to 'indoctrinate' recipient countries. In India's case it may fairly be argued that she has successfully educated, to use a more palatable word, the donor countries to an acceptance of her own viewpoint on many important issues, even if the quantity of assistance has fallen short of her own estimated requirements.

India's diplomatic, political and strategic situation gives her a somewhat special relationship to the donor countries, compared with smaller and less influential recipients. An implicit theme in this chapter is that the significance of economic aid to the so-called East-West ideological struggle has been markedly over-rated, at least in its application to India. However, ideology apart, India is important in terms of power politics, both in the direct sense that neither major power bloc could contemplate with equanimity her military or political alignment with the opposite bloc, and in the indirect sense that she wields considerable influence on world opinion through her relations with the 'non-aligned' group of nations and within the so-called 'Afro-Asian bloc' at the United Nations. Though economic aid must be related to other tools of diplomacy, it is nevertheless a factor of considerable importance. However, a realisation of India's potential power and importance, and therefore the establishment of realistic negotiating relationships, has been accomplished rather slowly. In the case of the Communist bloc, once Stalin's rigid policies had been abandoned, relationships with India became rapidly cordial, though for the West the political and psychological stumbling-blocks have been more substantial. Ironically, the reduction of tension between East and West to some extent reduced India's bargaining power, and it is expected that aid from both blocs, especially the Western bloc, will decline from its present level. At the same time it must be recognised that India has won a significant number of her major objectives with regard to aid except as regards quantity. The pattern of 'peaceful coexistence', truce or stalemate, howsoever described in this context, between India, the Soviet bloc and the West, has been substantially influenced by India's tenacious view of her own interests.

Stated briefly, India's basic policy towards aid is that it should assist in the achievement of her own stated economic objectives, filling gaps as they appear. This involves a continuous dialogue with aid-givers. In some cases, particularly in recent years, policies have been substantially altered subject to pressures of various types; however, there is no evidence to show that India has made any changes she considers to be against her interests, simply in order to receive aid. This is even more certain in the sphere of foreign policy, where sovereignty is quite clearly asserted. Within these limits, her aim is simply to obtain the best terms possible.

The very nature of India's international position makes the

whole question of economic aid an especially delicate one. Despite her bargaining power, however, the reverse side to the coin is that she is subject to various pressures not experienced to the same degree by other recipient countries. She is necessarily in the 'limelight' of world politics and the receipt of aid on a massive scale emphasises this fact. An extensive, continuous and public debate is carried on in the West, especially in the United States, through Parliamentary and Congressional debates, through press, radio and television media, at World Bank consortium meetings (though actual sessions here are private) and through periodic statements by heads of state, ambassadors, etc. A veritable army of diplomats is to be found in Delhi itself, in addition to the substantial number of foreign technicians, field workers, officials and journalists spread throughout the country. A continuous stream of advice, official and unofficial, is received by India on the conduct of her economic affairs. Her actions, statements and policies are subject to continuous and not always disinterested scrutiny, and she is obliged to make constant explanations and justifications for her policies and actions. However well-intentioned and numerous her well-wishers, there is no doubt that this continuous and at times somewhat undignified publicity and scrutiny create psychological difficulties which may partly account for the view held in many Western quarters that Indians are highly sensitive as negotiators.[1] In this sense, therefore, the need to seek assistance on a large sacle has produced a situation where India, although in every practical respect sovereign and independent, experiences some sense of inhibition and restraint in the development of a distinctive economic and political philosophy, due to the weight and diversity of foreign influence. This may, to some extent, account for the marked lack of enthusiasm with which vast sums of aid are received and for the dogged persistence with which potentially explosive political issues are neutralised within a narrow technical and administrative framework.

Levels of response

In this chapter it is intended to comment on a few aspects of the 'political impact' of aid in India. It is clear from earlier chapters that donor countries expect some kind of political dividend from their aid. However, if their motives are hard to identify, the task in this chapter is still more complex. There have been no obvious short-term quid pro quos, such as military bases, support on particular issues, overflying rights, etc. that are easily identifiable.[2] The aims of the donor countries are long-term and therefore somewhat hazily defined. However, some political response is clearly expected by them, and its measurement is of prime importance to their legislators and policy-makers. This notion, however, is not very meaningful as it stands. Responses will be obtained at all levels in various forms. Of greatest importance, however, is the fact that a recipient country's response to a donor country on account of aid cannot easily be separated from its general view of that country as determined by a whole host of political, cultural and psychological factors. Statements of politicians, both in India and the donor countries, have a tendency to over-dramatise political issues. A sense of perspective is best achieved by distinguishing various levels of response. The most obvious distinction is between the administrative or 'decision-making' level and the more overtly political attitudes of party politicians. Outside these two circles are the general public, with their varying degrees of influence, knowledge and political awareness. These categories inevitably overlap. Thus, senior ministers are both policy-makers and politicians, while below a certain level of seniority, public servants may reasonably be regarded as part of 'public opinion'.

The factor stressed in the first chapter is of particular relevance in this context, namely that political attitudes to aid are related to far wider questions of foreign policy, internal politics, economic, social and administrative issues. Aid cannot easily be considered in isolation, and will thus always be viewed by any given group, especially 'decision-makers', in terms of their own preoccupations. It must be stressed, however, that the nature of policy-making and debate is necessarily different in India from the donor countries, the most striking contrast being with the United States. In the latter case aid is also tangential to other issues, but yet stands out far more as an issue in its own right, being considered as a major means whereby the United States may achieve certain objectives, whereas in India political issues mainly arise when the form or terms of aid, its diminution, withdrawal or threat of withdrawal conflict with established policy objectives. There is thus not the same regularity or continuity in consideration of aid issues and political opinions are largely reactive. Here one must distinguish between two problems. The first relates to immediate issues of a political nature arising from aid negotiations. The second raises long-term questions as to the extent and direction in which foreign aid ultimately changes the Indian economy, which will in turn naturally affect the shape of internal politics. I am here mainly concerned with the first question. Certain aspects of the second are raised implicitly at various points, but without an exhaustive analysis of the Indian economy, beyond the scope of this work it cannot usefully be considered here as a separate issue. It is sufficient to our purposes to note that India's development was organised up to 1966 within the framework of Five Year Plans. The control structure so created has still been retained even though the Fourth Plan is now in abeyance. The principle of these plans is that all resources for developmental purposes are allocated according to a system of priorities, finance being provided accordingly. This involves a complex system of licensing and controls, especially with regard to foreign exchange. The prime function of foreign aid, therefore, from the Indian viewpoint is to fill the exchange gap entailed by development projects. Although the quantities involved are vast, India would nonetheless view aid as performing only a marginal function. She is continually redefining her priorities and objectives in response to strong and often competing pressures, in which context aid-givers will naturally make their presence felt. Aid should properly be seen, therefore as a major piece to be fitted into a very large jigsaw. Whatever the pressures, in the last analysis it is the Indian government which must decide those projects for which it will seek foreign support and in what form, taking account of availabilities.

Aid 'strings'

Before dealing with specific issues, some preliminary comments are necessary on the political nature of aid administration. It has become almost a truism that India does not accept aid to which she considers there are 'strings attached'. This all too familiar phrase needs some clarification. 'Strings' may be of various kinds ranging from the crude and obvious to the subtle and scarcely perceptible. In the former category are attempts, through hints of withdrawal, reduction or unfavourable modification of aid, to persuade the recipient country to alter its foreign or domestic policies. In the case of India, the most obvious targets have been her policies of 'non-alignment' and socialism. Certain specific issues of foreign policy have at times also caused difficulties, such as the annexation of Goa, the Kashmir issue, and the refusal of transit to American troops en route to Korea. India has stood firm against all these pressures. Equally, the decision to accept substantial arms assistance from the Soviet bloc has caused some disquiet in the West, but his has not prevented India from obtaining substantial military assistance from that quarter also. However, it is clear that since the negotiation and processing of a project requiring external assistance must be formalised in a contract, the recipient must, by the very nature of the process, accept some conditions. What is at issue, therefore, is not some emotionally clouded question of aid, with or without strings, but the more specific question of the nature of the relationship between lender and borrower. It is reasonable to expect a donor country to satisfy itself before allocating funds and resources that a particular project is soundly conceived, will be properly administered and will prove of ultimate benefit to the recipient's economy. If assistance is given on a substantial and continuous basis, regular administrative machinery must be established to vet requests, negotiate agreements, disburse funds, check administration of projects at every stage and submit reports to authorities and legislative bodies at home. This necessarily entails a continuous dialogue between donor and recipient, during the course of which the latter may be persuaded to change direction in her own interests. There is no evidence to suggest that India's recent substantial changes in domestic policy[4] were regarded as against her own interest by the government. Considerable internal pressure has existed both for and against these changes. The extent of American and World Bank pressure is not known, but it would probably be correct to say that by continuous exchange of views these issues were pressed upon the Indian government in sharper and more urgent form than would otherwise have occurred, decisions being taken upon the basis of realities. It should be noted, however, that pressures over Kashmir and defence deployment,[5] where existing policies are considered vital to Indian interests, continue to be resisted. Nor has India changed her basic stand on Vietnam, though in this case she has been less active as a mediator than would have been the case during the 1950s. Again this can mainly be attributed to a change in her own outlook whereby she is less eager to be involved in external disputes between other powers.

In an ideal world an administrative framework would be established according to the principles of Mr Eugene Black,[6] with 'development diplomats' deeply involving themselves in the recipient country's economic problems, but contenting themselves with 'illuminating choices'. Something of this relationship has in fact been achieved in India. However, such a concept involves a sharp distinction between decision-making and advice, which in practice is somewhat blurred. Decisions as to the exact shape of projects requiring external assistance and the terms of such assistance are necessarily reached by a process of hard bargaining and finally of mutual consent. It appears, therefore, that any country which intends to accept foreign assistance must also be prepared to accept a certain irreducible minimum of 'interference' with her internal economic affairs. Such a relationship is unlikely to prove offensive, providing 'unreasonable' pressures are not applied, and can be defined, to the satisfaction of all parties, as 'mutual cooperation'. The significant elements in the relationship between India and donor countries are those pressures over and above the 'irreducible minimum' so defined. These pressures fall fairly naturally into the categories of 'political' and 'economic'. Between the two extremes of the 'irreducible minimum' acceptable to India and the more unreasonable demands of the donor countries there is an area which is negotiable and an area which is not, but technical and administrative matters must be clearly distinguished from major issues of principle. With regard to the latter, there is also far greater scope for negotiation over issues of domestic economic policy than over foreign policy issues.

Administrative framework

Before considering wider issues of economic policy, the following principles with regard to aid negotiation and administration should be noted (see appendix no. 3 for a more detailed account).

1. All foreign assistance is allocated and planned within the framework of the Five Year Plans. Therefore, initiative with regard to the formulation of projects lies with India, though suggestions are made from outside through various media. Presumably in drawing up her Plans and long-term foreign exchange budget, India sounds out foreign opinion as to the quantity and type of aid she may reasonably hope to obtain. Nevertheless, her tight system of planning and control tends to reduce the donor countries to a supplementary and advisory role, notwithstanding their all-important power of accepting or rejecting projects.[7]

2. The fact that all negotiation is centralised in one department, the Department of Economic Affairs, strengthens India's hand *vis à vis* the numerous donor agencies. Admittedly this is slightly less true since the rationalisation of the American agencies in 1959,[8] and the establishment of the World Bank Consortium.[9]

3. Since control is maintained, officially, over all imports and foreign exchange expenditures, control is thus exercised over aid and investment in the private sector. It is not possible for donor countries, either through direct negotiation with Indian businessmen or by private capital investment to bypass the government. Institutional barriers thus make it difficult to channel aid funds in such a way as to alter the balance between public and private sector laid down by the government.

4. The Indian government, through its agencies, maintains control of the administration of projects, despite various forms of surveillance by the donors. However, some qualification is necessary here in that the

point made earlier,[10] that the distinction between decision-making and advice is somewhat undefined, should be kept in mind. Thus, if an American engineer sends in an adverse report to the AID on some aspect of a project, the Indian authorities may choose to disregard such criticism, but they are unlikely to do so in summary fashion, since if this were done frequently, confidence and goodwill would be undermined. The normal procedure would be to work out a solution by mutual consent. As John P. Lewis puts it, 'each bilateral aid relationship, like every marriage, is in a measure unique'.[11] Foreigners and Indians are so interwoven at every level of operation, that it could hardly be otherwise.

5. The multiplicity of donor agencies, each with their several points of view, gives India ample room for manoeuvre in obtaining a balanced pattern of aid. Cold War differences and the policy of non-alignment enhance her bargaining power still further.[12]

In spite of the shelving of the Fourth Plan and some consequent weakening of bargaining power, the basic institutionalisation of aid procedures is retained as a source of considerable strength.

Some modification of the foregoing analysis is necessary in the case of the World Bank. In the first place it need have fewer inhibitions with regard to Indian political sensitivities. Although the Bank may initially have been regarded as a neutral international body, it has later come to be identified with a far more ideological viewpoint. Whilst the Bank has played a vital part in coordinating aid to India and through the medium of the 'Aid India' Consortium encouraged a liberal and wide-ranging view of her problems, its refusal to assist industrial development in the public sector outside 'infrastructure' projects has remained rigidly unaltered. For this reason its advice on more technical matters might receive less than the weight it deserves. The World Bank has often been identified in India as working in close harmony with the United States. The former is in fact jealous of its own independence, but the strong weight of American business opinion in its counsels, the location of its headquarters in New York, and above all the weight of the American contribution to its finances, inevitably lends it a bias in favour of American-style 'free enterprise'. Given the limitations of such an outlook, the Bank has always taken an extremely broad view of India's problems, recognising the extensive role to be played by government in a developing society and the need for large-scale planning. It is over questions of method and the proper balancing of objectives in the Plans that disagreement has arisen. The World Bank is more closely integrated into the planning process than any other donor, having an established consultative status on the Planning Commission. From India's viewpoint it occupies possibly an even more strategic position than the United States, for apart from its contributions being the only source of non 'country-tied' aid available to her, its role in the Consortium is crucial.[13] No individual country is in the same position to evaluate Indian planning and administration, which in any case would involve too great political embarrassment. The World Bank's evaluation of these factors, especially at the beginning of a Plan period, will strongly determine the attitude of donors. Important in influencing American public opinion, it will also have considerable effect on the smaller donors whose facilities for assessing the implications of the Plans are limited. In practice the Bank does not appear to have concerned itself beyond the broadest questions of financial viability, balance of resources and objectives. It gave its approval to the broad concepts of the Third Plan, including the budgeted estimate for external assistance and encouraged maximum participation by the various members. This must have involved an assumption and presumably a tacit assent that the Soviet bloc would finance a substantial part of public sector industrial investment, which formed a key part of the Plan. The conclusions so far offered, therefore, with regard to the limited ability of donor countries to exert influence on policy as a condition for aid, must be modified in view of the World Bank role, although there too India has generally maintained strict limits. American influence with the Bank gives her additional leverage with the Indian government. Amongst Indian officials the connection is fairly well established, though probably in reality the relationship does not extend far beyond the existence of a broad concensus on questions of economic philosophy. In these circumstances the Bank is in a position to take up with India questions which are concerning the donor countries, but which might prove too embarrassing if raised directly, with regard to overall balance, soundness of objectives, and capacity to coordinate large-scale projects. Within this formal technical, administrative and advisory framework the Bank may act as a medium of communication on matters with far more obvious political connotations.

A programme of external assistance, whether operated on a multilateral or bilateral basis, and administered according to the above principles, necessarily involves a continuous process of contact, negotiation and adjustment between Indian 'decision-makers' and foreign representatives. The relationship between India and the donor countries may thus be viewed as a series of dialogues, embracing both 'narrow' economic and technical issues and 'broad' issues of policy. Rigid distinctions cannot be drawn here since the overlap is considerable; for example, the government's general policy of 'Indianisation' of enterprises[14] is a major issue of principle, though in each project the proportion of Indians employed in senior positions is a technical and managerial question, concerned with qualifications, ability, etc. Similarly, the issue of public versus private enterprise can be considered at both the general and particular level. For convenience I shall consider the main continuing issues at stake within these two broad categories, beginning with the more obviously economic issues. It is evident, however, that though much of the discussion will remain at a purely 'economic' or 'technical' level, the various issues are of such a nature as to be capable of taking on sudden and vital political significance.

The external debt problem

One of India's primary economic interests in aid negotiations must be to secure the most advantageous terms possible with regard to interest payments and period of repayment. A vital related factor, when a loan is tied to purchases in a particular country, is the price negotiated for the equipment, machinery, etc., which the loan is intended to finance. It would thus be superficial to conclude that low interest rates necessarily represent generous terms, since loan interest is only a fraction of the total price. Comparison of loan terms offered by various countries to India have already been made elsewhere.[15] This is a vital question in view of the extent of India's external debt. Interest and amortisation on official loans took 19 per cent of gross official assistance during the Third Plan, compared with 8 per cent during the Second Plan.[16] In relation to foreign exchange earnings on current account, debt service on official loans rose from 3 per cent during the Second Plan to 14 per cent in 1965-6 (over 20 per cent when remittances on private capital are included).[17] Before the Fourth Plan was shelved out of a total of Rs 4,000 crores to be requested in foreign aid, Rs 1,350 crores were required for debt service. The corresponding figures for total aid and aid financed debt service during the Third Plan were Rs 3,200 crores and Rs 500 crores respectively.[18]

Despite more generous terms during the Third Plan the increasing proportion of loans relative to grants emphasises the debt problem. This trend is emphasised by the changes in American policy in 1959. One factor in her decision to switch the emphasis of her aid to loans was the belief that this form of aid was more politically acceptable to

Table 10
Breakdown by grants and loans of external assistance utilised (excludes PL 480, 665, etc.).

	first plan		second plan		1961-1964	
	Rs. crores	per cent	Rs. crores	per cent	Rs. crores	per cent
grants	70.2	35.7	160.3	18.1	65.3	4.4
loans	126.4	64.3	724.7	81.9	1420.8	95.6

India. There are various statements by Indian leaders, notably Nehru, to support this view.[19] However Shastri's request for a food gift from Australia in February 1965[20] indicates that this principle may have predominantly reflected the thinking of Nehru, rather than any deep-rooted belief among Indian planners. It appears likely that India will need periodic refinancing and moratoriums in order to meet growing debt obligations, while the need for aid may extend well into the 1970s and beyond. The only long-term solution would be a sustained improvement in the balance of payments. In this respect, the Russian system of trade and aid does provide the means for repayment of loans, whereas the high tariffs on India's main export commodities is a source of constant frustration to her. Commodities particularly affected are jute and textiles, though if India is successful in diversifying her exports, especially expansion of capital goods exports,[21] she will presumably meet similar opposition in this field also. Indian leaders and officials are not much given to making public statements on this issue,[22] though it did figure prominently at the United Nations Conference on Trade and Development at Geneva during March-June, 1964[23] and again at the 1968 UNCTAD Conference in Delhi. It is clearly of vital importance for India, as indeed for all developing countries, to increase her export earnings in order to finance a growing bill for development imports. It would seem supremely illogical to pour huge sums of money into India to assist her industrial development, and then to deny her marketing outlets for the industrial products so created. However, this is obviously a question involving the whole organisation of international trade.

Tied aid

A most important economic issue, with strong political overtones, is the question of tied aid. Aid may be tied in two ways–by country or by project. In the former case the recipient is obliged to use aid funds for the purchase of goods, equipment, etc. in the donor country. In the latter case funds must be spent on a particular project or projects. Many loans and grants are tied both ways. Between these two lies a third category where aid is allocated for the development of a particular industry or sector. Table 11 shows an increase in the proportion of country-tied aid over the whole period of the first two Plans.[24]

Table 11
Percentage breakdown of total aid tied to country of origin

period	tied	untied
first plan	53.3	46.7
second plan	78.9	21.1
first and second plan	75.8	24.2

Table 12 shows the percentage of aid from multilateral and bilateral sources respectively.[25]

Table 12
Percentage breakdown of total aid into bilateral and multilateral by plan periods

period	bilateral	multilateral
first plan	74.5	25.5
second plan and after (up to 31 December 1961)	85.0	15.0
total up to 31 December 1961	83.7	16.3

Multilateral aid is by definition untied to purchases in any particular country. Comparison between tables 11 and 12 shows a correspondence between the increase in both bilateral and tied aid. Rao and Narain noting this connection, and observing that the Second Plan period witnessed a substantial increase in the absolute amount of aid, argued that this indicates a strong desire on the part of the donors to maintain control of their aid programmes while at the same time promoting their own trade. In the economic sense, therefore, 'strings' are a strong feature of aid received by India.[26]

Table 13[27] shows project-tied aid as representing an extremely high proportion of total aid up to 1961.

There has been a marked liberalisation since the start of the Third Plan. Out of a total of Rs 1,865 crores external assistance authorised for the Third Plan up to 31st March 1963, Rs 395 (21.2 per cent) was allocated for non-project purposes.[28] This trend has largely been initiated by Britain and the United States.[29] However, far greater liberalisation is still needed, in India's view. Ironically, although the World Bank consortium has been the medium through which these views have been urged, the

Table 13
Percentage breakdown of total aid into committed, partially committed and uncommitted by plan periods

period	committed to specific project or programmes	committed to specified category of projects or programmes	committed to projects to be agreed upon	uncommitted
first plan	100.0			
second plan and after	84.8	4.7	2.7	7.8
total to 31 December 1961	86.7	4.1	2.4	6.8

World Bank itself has not followed the trend.[30] On the other hand, alone among aid givers it does provide resources of free foreign exchange.

India has several reasons for criticising the practice of 'tied' aid, in each of its main forms.[31] In both cases she argues that tied aid leads to inflexibility, inefficient use of resources and distortion of her development plans. In the case of 'country-tied' aid, she complains of restrictions on her freedom of choice and inability to buy in the cheapest market. A surplus of one currency cannot be used to cover a deficit in another, and thus the task of matching demand for foreign exchange with the available supply is made more complicated. At the technical level a large project may well comprise a wide variety of machinery, plant, etc. purchased from different countries according to availability of various currencies. Optimum use of resources and technical cooperation are thus rendered more complex, increasing the likelihood of 'bottlenecks' (e.g. lack of versatility amongst technical personnel, shortage of spare parts, etc.). Lack of standardisation will generally render the operation of such 'mixed' plants more costly. Aid tied to projects suffers from these defects of inflexibility in even more acute form. The basic purpose of tying loans in this way is to ensure that funds are spent for some definite purpose and not wasted. However, experience suggests that the notion of a 'project' is somewhat vague, and that the donor countries' interpretation is often too rigid. An inclusive interpretation would comprehend every aspect of operations from installation to marketing, but for aid purposes a 'project' is too often defined as the installation of heavy equipment, without sufficient account being taken of the need for import of components, spares, raw materials, etc.; thus a 'project' ceases to be a project after it is ready for production, and so future import requirements, necessary to maintain efficient operation, must depend on the limited quantity of 'untied' foreign exchange available. Inadequate allocation of such currency means that plants must operate well below their economic capacity, thus creating 'bottlenecks' throughout the economy. India argues that if a substantial quantity of 'non-project' currency were available, even if this were 'country-tied', these could be far more quickly eliminated. From the donor's viewpoint there is also the question of availability of supplies, which may not harmonise with the demands of the recipient. This factor may lead to further distortions.

The consequences for the recipient are most severe when aid is tied both to a project and to purchases in the country of origin.[32] Often the equipment or plant required will be produced only by one or two firms in a particular country, who are thus in a commanding position with regard to price, terms of technical assistance, etc. It has been pointed out that Indian antagonism on this issue was most marked in the case of America.[33] American officials were apparently surprised at the strength of Indian reaction to the 1959 reorganisation, whereby AID loans were tied to purchases in the United States. As theirs was the last country to adopt this practice, Americans were impelled to ask why the volume of protest was so much greater in their case than against other donors. John P. Lewis argued that the explanation lay in the generally higher level of American prices.[34] He further argued that prices were exceptionally high for those items which India most requires. Table 14 illustrates that during the first two Plan periods the prices of machinery, metal products and capital goods increased to a greater extent than prices of other items.[35]

Table 14
United States bureau of labour wholesale price index (ave. of 1947-9 = 100)

	1953	1960
all commodities	110.1	119.6
metals and metallurgical products	126.9	153.8
machinery and motive products	123.0	153.3
consumer finished goods	107.1	113.6
producer finished goods	123.1	153.7

Lewis argues that the effect of the 1959 change was to arrest a trend, which had recently appeared, towards price competition and sales aggression.[36] It is clear that both forms of restriction can limit the effective use of aid funds. However, the distinction should not be over-emphasised. Experience shows that an increase in 'non-project' aid weakens the effect of country of origin tying, since non-project funds can be used to purchase imports, outside the scope of existing aid arrangements, which would normally have been purchased in any case. This releases normal exchange funds for purchase of development imports, which can now be freely bought anywhere.

The foregoing analysis is closely related to the question of utilisation. A variety of factors will influence the rate of utilisation, of which the most important are: 1. Relative efficiency, administrative and technical, of both donor and recipient. Here the relative priority accorded to projects by India is a factor influencing comparisons; 2. The form in which aid is made available.

Information as to utilisation of assistance from various sources is shown in table 15, broken down by type of aid.[37]

Table 15
Percentage and utilisation classified by type and source

country or institution	repayable in foreign currency	loans repayable in rupees	grants	PL 480, etc.	all aid
IBRD	88.9	–	–	–	88.9
IDA	47.9	–	–	–	47.9
United States	70.8	89.4	95.8*	81.9	80.1
Canada	48.0	–	85.9	–	76.1
Australia	–	–	94.7	–	94.7
United Kingdom	75.7	–	60.0	–	75.6
New Zealand	–	–	87.8	–	87.8
Poland	–	24.3	–	–	24.3
Yugoslavia	–	22.5	–	–	22.5
Czechoslovakia	–	9.5	–	–	9.5
Austria	41.0	–	–	–	41.0
Belgium	12.5	–	–	–	12.5
Netherlands	17.7	–	–	–	17.7
Norway	–	–	87.0	–	87.0
Sweden	0.0	–	–	–	0.0
Denmark	0.0	40.0	–	–	16.7
West Germany	73.4	–	85.7	–	73.4
Japan	56.6	–	–	–	56.6
Soviet Union	–	68.0†	100.0	–	68.1
Switzerland	13.1	–	–	–	13.1
France	27.3	–	–	–	27.3
Italy	14.0	–	–	–	14.0
total aid	68.1	65.8	91.2	81.9	71.6

*Includes Ford Foundation. †Excludes Bokaro, negotiated January 1965

The countries and institutions with above-average rate of utilisation are thus the IBRD, the United States, Australia, New Zealand, Norway, Canada, Britain and West Germany, the first five exceeding 80 per cent compared with the overall average of 71.6 per cent. Of the below-average countries, the vast majority consist of smaller donors, though included in the list, but still averaging far better than the small donors, are the Soviet Union, the IDA, and Japan. In the Soviet case her utilisation rate is held down partly by her willingness to authorise aid for major projects substantially in advance, thus facilitating India's planning problems. Nevertheless comparison with the larger Western donors is distinctly unfavourable. The IDA and Japan are relative newcomers as donors, Japan entering the field later in the Second Plan period and the IDA commencing operations during the Third Plan only. This is also true of most other minor donors.

The most clearly marked contrast is that between grants and loans. Utilisation of grants was 91.2 per cent compared with an overall average of 71.6 per cent. Four countries give an above-average proportion of their aid in grant form–Canada, Australia, New Zealand and Norway, and all four show an above-average rate of utilisation. Grant aid is generally for small-scale purposes and therefore more easily absorbable. Similarly it comes mostly in the form of specific offers of equipment, expertise and services and thus negotiations are complete in most cases before aid is 'authorised'. Utilisation is below average in the case of loans. In this connection it appears to make little difference, perhaps surprisingly, whether loans are repayable in foreign currency or rupees. The overall percentage of loans to total aid is 65.9 per cent. Seventeen out of twenty-two donors devote a percentage of their total aid to loans in excess of 99 per cent.[38] Of these, fourteen have a below-average rate of utilisation, in most cases very substantially below, only West Germany, the United Kingdom and the IBRD achieving an above-average performance. The United Kingdom and West Germany are two countries which offer a significant proportion of their loans in non-project form,[39] and it is noteworthy that the United States, the prime source of non-project aid, also achieves an above-average rate. Thus a clear correlation is suggested between grant and non-project aid and speed of utilisation. The high rate of utilisation achieved by the World Bank would appear to contradict this conclusion, since this institution's aid is 100 per cent loan and project-oriented.[40] A reasonable conclusion would be that the Bank's methods are most rigidly directed to efficiency, projects being more carefully surveyed and planned in advance than with any other donor. At the same time the Bank takes a more active part in actual administration of projects and in the overall planning of the Indian economy than would be politically possible for any single donor country. Free use of foreign exchange is also a factor. In general, therefore, the official Indian view [41] that utilisation is delayed where aid is tied rigidly to projects seems well substantiated.

PL 480 and 665 loans have achieved a high rate of utilisation, though not as high as grant aid. This type of loan is somewhat hard to classify for the purpose of establishing correlations between utilisation and type of aid, for such aid does not relate to projects in the first instance and therefore the notion of utilisation is somewhat misleading.

Though India clearly finds all forms of tied aid irksome, it does not follow that she wishes to see multilateral substituted for bilateral aid, in the sense that aid would be channelled through an international agency instead of coming direct from the donors. John P. Lewis suggests three reasons why India would probably lose by such a change[42] : 1. The United States and other major donors would probably be less willing to contribute to an international agency on the same scale as at present if they did not have direct control over their funds; if such an arrangement were operated on strictly democratic principles, the donor countries would be massively outvoted by the recipients. 2. Such an arrangement would probably be slow and cumbersome and might well increase rather than decrease tensions. 3. An international arrangement based on the principle of equal voting rights for each member nation would place India on the same level as many other countries at a far lower stage of development and with considerably less sophisticated notions of economic planning. Thus if Andrew Schonfield's principle of 'unfair shares'[43] is a valid criterion of efficiency in the allocation of aid funds, then such a change is neither in India's interests, nor in the interests of developing countries generally. A compromise arrangement would be some form of weighting on the basis of funds contributed (or more improbably on the basis of population), though such proposals are most unlikely to prove politically acceptable. Thus, although the theme of 'multilateralism' is often advocated in the donor countries, especially in the United States, by public figures as diverse as Eugene Black and Senator Ellender,[44] such proposals are rarely advanced in India, and where they are they may be taken to imply a demand for untied funds, rather than any concern for the establishment of theoretically improved international arrangements.[45]

Budgeting and planning

The problem of long-term planning has been a matter of some concern to India in integrating external assistance into development programmes. It is cogently argued that efficient long-term planning involves advance forecasting of foreign exchange requirements and availabilities.[46] Estimation of the latter is, however, quite unpredictable when the majority of donors can only make formal advance commitments for one financial year. Projects, of course, generally take a much longer period of time to complete and the phasing of operations affects other aspects of the economy. Under existing systems of Western democracy this problem is inevitable. The Soviet Union has an advantage in this respect and was able to state advance commitments for the entire Third Plan period. Most donor countries outside the Communist bloc have resolutely refused to request their legislatures to alter traditional arrangements, except that in the United States an unsuccessful effort was made by President Kennedy. A compromise arrangement was reached, however, with the establishment of the World Bank consortium (popularly known as the 'Aid India Club') to cover the Third Plan period.* This forum did encourage encourage several countries, whose number unfortunately did not include the United States, to indicate advance commitments over a two-year period, subject to legislative approval.[47] Uncertainty was introduced by the United States during the first two years of the Third Plan in the form of the 'matching' principle, whereby America would match assistance offered by other consortium countries dollar for dollar, the object being to stimulate them to further efforts. This system was abandoned in 1963 due to its failure to evoke any clear response from other consortium members.

It can be argued that there is a tendency to overstate the case for long-term commitments.[48] From the foregoing discussion on utilisation it is clear that appropriated funds lie idle for some considerable period. J. Lewis[49] argues that in the case of the United States, the AID and other agencies already have sufficient funds and flexibility to give receiving countries adequate security in the preparation of their plans, without long-term appropriations by legislatures, providing proper phasing and programming is undertaken. Given the limited capacity of any recipient to absorb aid, an increase of funds 'in the pipeline', or indeed a lengthening of the 'pipeline' itself, would not improve the rate of utilisation. Indian economists would no doubt counter this reasoning by arguing that if more 'non-project' assistance were offered, these objections would not apply.

*This consortium also covers aid to Pakistan.

Foreign experts: Indianisation

There have been undercurrents of discontent in India as to the quality and remuneration of foreign experts, periodically expressed in the Lok Sabha. One fairly common theme is doubt as to whether foreign 'expert' knowledge is relevant to Indian conditions.[50] A senior minister, T. T. Krishnamachari, then Minister for Commerce and Industry, once went so far as to say that India was chary of accepting technical assistance due to the large number of 'casualties' in the past. He further stated that often, if four men were sent out, one would be good, one moderate and two quite unsuitable. The United Nations was not careful enough in the matter of selection.[51] The criticism of the level of fees paid to German consultants engaged in planning the Rourkela steel project provides a striking illustration of the theme of alleged excessive remuneration of foreign personnel.[52] By contrast, a project where technical assistance appears to have been satisfactorily accepted is the Uttar Pradesh Agricultural University scheme, American specialists being supplied by the United States/AID (TCM).[53] It would appear that a successful relationship was achieved here, due to the adaptability of the Americans concerned to local conditions, and careful definition of their relationship to the Indian authorities. In this case their status was strictly advisory. These factors are perhaps as important in the formation of a favourable image as the salaries and benefits they derive, actually or reputedly, from their employment. The basic problem here is that only the most dedicated are prepared to live at the level of an Indian peasant, worker or even middle-grade administrator. On the other hand, a standard of living notably above average is likely to cause tensions. One suggested solution is to bank a substantial part of the income of aid personnel in their own country,[54] but in view of the health hazards and the cost of safely maintaining a family in India, this would appear to oversimplify the problem. The role and image of aid personnel are clearly questions that deserve further investigation.

Progressive 'Indianisation' of enterprises is a major policy objective of the Indian government, necessarily involving extensive training programmes. Arrangements are incorporated into all projects where foreign aid or investment is supplied, providing for training of Indians at all levels. This question is referred to in more detail subsequently.[55] At this stage it is sufficient to observe that there has been no obvious disagreement in principle between India and the donor countries, and there has been a general progress in the direction desired by India, in spite of some criticisms of the quality of various countries' or companies' training programmes, and some differences of opinion as to the correct and desirable pace of 'Indianisation'.

This completes discussion of the more technical aspects of aid. Issues arising from PL 480 food aid programmes are discussed separately in chapter 6.

Conflicting goals

Turning to broader policy issues, the reaction of foreign donors to the relative allocation of roles between public and private sectors in Indian economic policy (which may be construed as a question of socialism versus free enterprise) is an important factor in shaping official attitudes towards foreign aid. The policy of the various donor countries in this respect should be evident from chapter 2. Opposition has been most vigorous in the case of the United States and the World Bank. Two dominant reactions on the part of Indian policy-makers seem to emerge. First, in spite of some considerable irritation with such hostile attitudes, there seems to be an attitude of philosophic acceptance of such ideological 'bottlenecks', coupled with the outlook that within the wide framework of India's mixed economy, everyone's preferences and prejudices can be accommodated. The sharper edges of this issue are somewhat blunted by the fact that both America and the World Bank are prepared to aid public sector projects in such basic services as power, irrigation, communications, etc. However, as the Indian economy grows, manufacturing industry will presumably constitute an increasing proportion of the gross national product, and thus policy issues here are likely to become more sharply defined. Secondly, there seems to be a wide measure of agreement that 'non-alignment' has paid off in economic terms. The substantial inflow of Russian funds from 1954 acted as a spur to vastly increased Western, and in particular, American aid. Of more importance, probably, is the fact that Russia's willingness to support public sector projects, unacceptable to the United States has made possible a breakthrough to patterns of economic development otherwise unattainable. Not merely have desirable public enterprises been established and India's bargaining position vastly improved, but at the same time many Indians have gained vital managerial experience. Simultaneously, however, American and World Bank attitudes have sharpened the internal conflict over the issue of 'socialism', or more specifically, the respective roles of the public and private sectors. Many Indians would see a connection between American ideological priorities and Western and Indian business interests. This question is discussed further in chapter 9.

Overall, however, it would appear that in so far as the Indian appraisal of American aid policy has been adverse, this has occurred not so much because of an unfavourable view of American aid in general, but because of her opposition to a major aspect of Indian economic policy.

A sensitive and in many respects more basic issue is whether leading Western opinion, especially as it finds expression at the World Bank consortium, supports the fundamental goals of India's Five Year Plans. To some extent this relates to the ideological issue of planning versus competition. Western doubts seem to focus particulary on the scope and direction of the Plans. Criticism was especially vehement during the 1957-8 foreign exchange crisis. Thus, a two man World Bank mission is reported to have argued that India should consolidate existing projects before undertaking new ones, especially as foreign exchange was already heavily mortgaged; that there was a tendency to promote welfare at the expense of efficiency; that the policy of equalising income and wealth, after a point, conflicts with the aim of achieving rapid economic growth; that the administrative machine had become overstrained, and that although the state had a vital part to play in stimulating development programmes, it should avoid assuming new responsibilities, especially in the sphere of mining and industry.[56] Clearly in this analysis the technical judgment that the Plan is too large is linked with a partly ideological judgment that the government is doing too much. A substantial debate developed during this period as to whether India was being over or under ambitious, with forecasts of economic collapse coming from both sides, but with divergent opinions as to the role of economic aid in the solution of India's foreign exchange problems. Perhaps the judgement of Mr A Schonfield that '. . . there is already a tendency among the peoples of the underdeveloped countries, particularly in Asia, to see the West as fixed in a trance like posture with its hand raised saying "Go Slow" while the Russians wave them on, shouting "Faster"',[57] reflects the views of many Indian planners at this time. A closely related factor has been the obviously far greater enthusiasm of the Soviet Union for heavy industrial development as reflected in the overwhelming proportion of their aid devoted to this sector. It is further argued that developing countries are likely to intepret the West's advice to concentrate on agricultural rather than industrial projects as being motivated by a desire to protect its export markets.[58] Furthermore, this emphasis is often seen as being linked with ideological factors already mentioned.[59] Since the Fourth Plan has been shelved and a new emphasis given to agriculture, it is clear that the Indians themselves have changed their views. This is mainly a response to internal pressures and only indirectly to foreign influence. In any case, the potential sources of friction inherent in these opposing developmental philosophies have been substantially reduced as in the private versus public sector issue, by the different emphases or preferences of the main donors.[60]

The relative efficiency of aid programmes

Significant as these issues are, however, it seems reasonable to assume at the 'decision-making' level under consideration, that external aid is judged ultimately on its economic effectiveness. This, however, will be assessed in accordance with Indian economic criteria and will in turn depend on her own economic and administrative efficiency and pattern of priorities. There is an obvious connection between this comparison of economic effectiveness and India's search for the economic model most relevant to her needs.

This last issue, though of vast importance, is too wide to be dealt with in this work, since it would involve a major study of Indian economic policy and thought.[61] The evidence from policies adopted, however, is that India is fairly eclectic in economic philosophy and has produced a blend of ideas adapted to her particular circumstances. In the narrow context of efficiency, in so far as this is within the control of the donor countries, what slight evidence that is available would seem on balance unfavourable to the Soviet bloc. Utilisation of bloc aid has already been shown to be slower than that of the United States.[62] Particular delays seem to have occurred in the case of electrical generating equipment, thus causing serious 'bottlenecks' in power supply projects,[63] and at Gauhati oil refinery.[64] Conflicting reports have also been circulated with regard to the 'model' mechanised farm, established with Soviet aid at Suratgarh (Rajasthan), but it appears to have suffered from serious inadequacies in planning.[65] The Ranchi (Bihar) heavy machine building plant has yet to prove itself. There are no comparable examples of American inefficiency, though in the important 'demonstration' steel sector, the Soviet Union clearly made a supreme effort to ensure full completion of the Bhilai project according to schedule,[66] whereas the German aided Rourkela project suffered continual delays and reorganisations, and even the British assisted Durgapur steel project experienced serious technical difficulties in the early stages.[67] Thus Soviet success at Bhilai, where prestige was most obviously at stake, supplemented by considerable successes in oil exploration and refining projects have largely diverted attention from the inefficiencies mentioned.

Of special importance is the fact that Russia's successes have been concentrated on those projects to which the Indian government attached the highest priority. Claims which the West might advance for superior technical efficiency, however, to whatever extent these may be admitted by Indian officials, are almost certainly offset by objections to the extensive system of controls, especially in the case of the United States and the IBRD, by which these standards are maintained. Furthermore, due to the diffusion of Western efforts over a wide field, any potential efficiency impact is overshadowed by the general complexity of India's economic and administrative problems.

The political debate

It is now appropriate to consider political responses to foreign aid outside the circle of 'decision-makers'. Broadly speaking, the categories to be considered are professional politicians, 'informed opinion' and the general public. As already stated, such distinctions are extremely tenuous. Senior ministers are both 'decision-makers' and politicians and their actions in the former role are not necessarily reflected by their speeches in the latter capacity. 'Politicians' represent a cross-section of opinion, 'informed' and otherwise, both influencing and reacting to the views of the 'general public'. At the same time the notion of 'informed' opinion is an extremely relative one, education level being probably the only concrete defining characteristic. Even here, whether graduation or matriculation is taken as the standard, there are wide variations of political knowledge and awareness within the 'educated' class. A further problem in attempting such an analysis is that all that can be attempted, short of massive public opinion survey evidence on a scale not yet attempted in India, is to present a cross-section of opinion on the question of foreign aid. The most tangible evidence comes from public opinion polls conducted by the Indian Institute of Public Opinion, but these are only used to assess overall Indian attitudes. Useful evidence is to be found from parliamentary debates, periodicals and newspapers. From these latter sources, however, one can only speculate as to how far particular expressions of opinion would receive general support. Two further difficulties should be noted. First, comment from the second category of sources is in many cases critical towards foreign aid. This is partly because adverse comment makes for more dramatic publicity and political posturing; however, it also reflects a tendency not to express strong approval of and gratitude for foreign aid. The rationale for this state of affairs becomes apparent in subsequent paragraphs. Thus, a large number of critical viewpoints are allowed to pass by default. Secondly, related 'opinion-forming' factors must be identified and given their proper weight in evaluating the extent to which a donor country's 'image' is determined by economic aid *per se*.

The general case for receipt of foreign aid has been accepted by the Indian government since the beginning of the Five Year Plans, but especially since the foreign exchange crisis of 1957-8, in spite of some evidence of reluctance on the part of Mr Nehru. Outside the government there has been a minority offering spasmodic opposition. Apart from Communist opposition,[68] the primary considerations seem to be a distaste for receiving 'charity', playing the role of beggar, loss of independence, dignity and above all sense of self-reliance. These ideas are always a factor in Indian thinking, though in actual formulation of policy, economic necessity overrides such fears. Jawaharlal Nehru constantly warned against relying on foreign aid for any longer than necessary. Such speeches would be made with particular emphasis at times of diplomatic tension with the United States. Thus at the time when that country began its policy of giving military aid to Pakistan, Nehru described aid as 'a crutch that should be done without'.[69] The view is quite frequently expressed that a country, like an individual, cannot consistently take without giving in return; aid must therefore lead to dependence, since even if no conditions were attached, the recipient must be involved in a moral obligation to the donor country.[70] This would seem to be a theoretically logical point, but it is hard to see that such considerations have had any practical impact on Indian policy. A common reaction in Parliament in the early years of Indo-American technical cooperation to the announcement of missions by American experts in various fields, ranging from physical education to agriculture, was first to question the relevance of such expertise to Indian conditions, and then to demand whether corresponding Indian experts had been sent to America.[71] Straightforward private charity has received, in general, an even more sensitive reaction. On one occasion the nature, quantity and purpose of a consignment of Christmas toys for Indian children was questioned in Parliament, the member naturally wishing to know whether any Indian toys had been sent to American children.[72] In reply to a question on the proposal of a Mrs Johnson (an American citizen) to collect funds to deliver a hundred thousand small agricultural implements to India, the prime minister replied that although there was no question of conditions, 'we do not fancy any person making nation-wide appeals on behalf of India anywhere'.[73] The case for refusing economic aid has been stated on numerous other grounds, notably to achieve better Indo-American relations,[74] as a rejection of hypocrisy,[75] and more unusually, by C. Rajapopalachari, to prove the sincerity of India's opposition to nuclear bombs, by sacrificing something she really needed.[76] Technical assistance has also been seen as a possible barrier to utilisation of India's educated unemployed.[77] From such fragmentary examples it is impossible to accurately assess the strength of opposition within India to the idea of accepting aid, but they do give an impression of unease and sensitivity, however superficial such arguments may appear to outside observers. Some indication is thus given to donor countries of psychological considerations to be taken into account. Yet lately these vague feelings of unease have crystallised into something far more concrete. While a few years ago the majority of influential opinion would reluctantly have accepted aid as an inescapable necessity, today there is a substantial body of opinion which would regard it as a barrier to realistic thinking in planning circles. Planning is in some considerable disrepute at present as the immensity of India's food problem becomes apparent, foreign aid being associated in the minds of many with the failures of recent years. In this mood, distinctions between donors are blurred, but it is probably true to say that public opinion blames Congress politicians more than foreign aid-givers.

As already indicated, the question of 'interference' by donor countries is one of considerable complexity. The most outstanding direct political issue in this respect is undoubtedly India's policy of 'non-alignment'. It is not my intention to evaluate this policy, since it has been amply stated and analysed elsewhere.[78] The relationship of this question to American aid policy has been considered in chapter 3. Pressure on this issue has been of little avail. This is demonstrated by two simple facts– 'non-alignment' has not been abandoned, though its importance has diminished since the outbreak of the Chinese border dispute, and until recently the quantity of assistance received from all sources has continuously increased since 1951. Perhaps the most concrete demonstration of Indian independence is the fact that a survey of India's voting record in the United Nations from 1958-62 (see appendix no 4) shows that she voted substantially more often with the Soviet Union than with the United States in resolutions where those two countries were opposed, in spite of the fact of receiving approximately six times the amount of assistance from the latter than from the former.

However, 'non-alignment' has been a source of strain in Indo-American relations,[79] and to a lesser extent with other Western countries. Economic aid and the continuous public debate necessary in the West, but not in the Soviet bloc, to obtain the necessary funds has aggravated these tensions. In India there has been nothing to parallel this debate on aid and terms of aid, since attention has been largely centred on her total economic effort, as expressed in the Five Year Plans. This is not to say that foreign opinion is discounted, but rather that it represents one more obstacle to be overcome on the road to economic development and national progress. On the whole, India's leaders have remained fairly imperturbable in the face of attacks on their foreign policy, and have largely contented themselves with periodic justifications of 'non-alignment', as opposed to denunciations of Western 'interference', 'imperialism', etc., though such denunciations have been more frequent in Parliament and the press than at official level.

Another sphere in which attempted influence has until recently been strongly resisted is that of basic principles of economic policy. The question of socialism in the Indian context is a most complex one, embracing wide-ranging semantic, theoretical, sociological and policy issues, outside the scope of this work.[80] The question is considered subsequently in the practical context of foreign aid to public sector enterprise. At this stage it is sufficient to note that many points of criticism, of seemingly minor technical and economic importance, particularly in the case of American aid, can be traced back to this fundamental issue, though naturally much of the criticism is ill-informed and/or propagandist.

Closely allied to the question of 'interference', we can identify a certain type of political approach that inevitably meets with hostility. This may loosely be described as the missionary approach, usually characterised by overtones of extreme and doctrinal anti-Communism. Thus the Indian Parliamentary Communist leader was able to extract considerable propaganda value for an attack on the Indo-American Technical Agreement, on the basis of a book by Sherman Kent (described as a key official of the Office of Strategic Studies) allegedly urging that all agencies of government abroad, all delegates, Congressmen, learned institutions, game hunters, etc. should be used for intelligence purposes.[81] A pertinent observation was made by Dr Neil H. Jacoby on a visit to Delhi as special adviser to the United States government on Indian economic development, to the effect that he found Indians somewhat annoyed that America tended to send 'humanists' rather than engineers: '. . . they feel that they are in the vanguard as humanists; what they need is technical help'.[82] This cannot easily be reconciled with an earlier declaration that 'American capitalism entails a dynamic answer to world need' and a declared intent to preach 'the power of a free competitive economy at every opportunity in India'.[83] Even an enlightened and intelligent idealist such as Lady Barbara Ward Jackson is not immune from criticism. An Indian correspondent to the Christian Science Monitor (Boston)[84] contrasts her approach of applying Christian humanity and Western ideals to poor countries unfavourably with Mr Richard Nixon's declared principle that the battle against poverty must be fought irrespective of Communism.[85] It is improbable that Lady Jackson's sentiments are misunderstood in this way to any significant extent by those that are properly aware of them; however, it does represent a certain type of reaction. That Western 'liberals' however dedicated, are liable to be stigmatised as 'paternalists' is well illustrated in a review (in the highly reputable *Economic Weekly* of Bombay) of a symposium by Max Millikan and Donald L. M. Blackner.[86] The theme of the authors that American aid is an expression of enlightened self-interest, following evolutionary rather than violently radical aims, is cautiously approved; however, their disapproval of recipient countries 'playing politics' is characterised as academic, a charge that is considered finally proven as authors become progressively more 'dedicated' and urge the need to 'imbue the technical expert in each professional field with a realisation that institution building is at least as important a part of his mission as the transfer of special knowledge'. Evidently too much dedication may prove embarrassing.

It is worth noting that India's leaders have themselves periodically used the potential expansion of Communism as a lever towards obtaining increased economic assistance from the United States, though it is also worth noting that such pleas are normally made in America rather than India. Thus B. K. Nehru, commissioner general for Economic Affairs, Washington and subsequently Indian ambassador to the United States, argued that given a choice between bread and liberty, the former would be preferred. The Communist system could provide bread at the price of subservience and through the sacrifice of one generation. India was well placed to achieve stable democracy, due to the democratic tradition of the Congress movement, the influence of British liberal traditions, and her administrative experience. To achieve this a slower rate of economic growth was acceptable than that of Communist countries, but not stagnation. Hence the need for economic assistance.[87] Ambassador C.

Chagla used the same argument more obliquely in a series of talks to Boston audiences in 1959,[88] by talking of the Indian farmer's growing impatience as he hears of the construction of dams and steel mills elsewhere in India and of progress reported in China. However, Shri Chagla attacked the conventional anti-Communist apologists for foreign aid by commenting that in the 'free world' some of the worst type of reactionaries are entrenched and that support for them, because they wear the anti-Communist badge, may suppress the true forces of freedom. Economic aid should be considered more vital to America's fight against Communism than rockets, pacts and bombers.[89]

In general, this type of approach is not reflected in public discussion within India, though as will be seen in chapter 9 a more pro-Western approach is reflected in Indian business circles than elsewhere. In Parliament the prevailing emphasis is on the need for freedom from foreign aid as soon as possible, coupled with a consistent undercurrent of suspicion of donor countries' motives.* Here the attitude of the late prime minister, Jawaharlal Nehru, was crucial. It must be admitted that any conclusions on this matter must necessarily be tentative, due to the charismatic nature of Nehru's personality and style of leadership. However some assessment must be attempted, due to his dominating role in determining this and so many other policy questions. In all his speeches on the question of aid, the theme of self-reliance was paramount. At the height of the 1957 foreign exchange crisis, he stated that although foreign aid was most welcome, if not a rupee came from outside, India would 'fight the present foreign exchange crisis and win it'.[90] This was not to be interpreted as an unfriendly statement, but India was not going down because someone else did not help her. Neighbouring countries had grown politically and psychologically weak in depending on aid.† Only the Soviet Union, he claimed, had achieved economic development without foreign assistance. Finally in the same speech the prime minister stated that he preferred investments to gifts, since the former was less of an affront to national pride. This speech amply illustrates the various tensions experienced by Indians, reflected in the sensitive mind of their late leader. Aid was recognised as a necessity, if the appalling experiences of the Soviet people were to be avoided. Yet, in terms that would be dismissed as bravado by many, both Westerners, and Indians, he proclaims

*There is a tendency, however, for criticism to come mainly from a limited number of individuals, notably from the CPI.

†Presumably the reference is to Pakistan.

India's willingness to make heroic sacrifices for the preservation of national integrity in the process of achieving economic development. Whether bravado or not, this approach was undoubtedly necessary in the context of domestic politics, increasing India's bargaining power abroad if used fairly infrequently. I can find no statements by Jawaharlal Nehru in the same vein as those of B. K. Nehru and C. Chagla, recently quoted.[91] Perhaps the only hint of such an approach was during an official visit to the United States, when in the course of an address to the Senate[92] he emphasised the common democratic ideals of the two countries, the influence of the American founding fathers on the Indian constitution, etc. and then urged the need for economic development in India, for which purpose she would require economic aid without conditions. It has been urged that Nehru was too proud to ask directly for assistance. Two reports in the New York Times in 1957[93] (a year of acute foreign exchange shortage in India and of strained relations between India and the United States) claimed that the authorisation of aid to India was being held up, due to India's sensitivity and reluctance to ask for specific amounts. For fear of rebuff, it seemed that India was waiting to be told how much the Administration was willing to seek from Congress before submitting formal application. However, this theme should not be overstated in view of the fact that Indian finance ministers (e.g. T. T. Krishnamachari in 1957 and M. Desai in 1962) have been prepared to travel abroad extensively in search of funds when necessary.

Except on a few rare occasions[94] it has been noted that Indian leaders have seemed reluctant to make more than conventional expressions of gratitude for foreign aid.[95] This was particularly true of Jawaharlal Nehru. When inaugurating projects, he would often use the occasion to stress the need to be free from outside help.[96] On one occasion, in the process of expressing satisfaction at Indo-American collaboration in the establishment of India's first nuclear power station at Tarapore (Maharashtra), and general gratitude to the World Bank consortium and the Soviet Union, he claimed that 'we are getting all this help because of our non-aligned policy'.[97] If this attitude seems somewhat ungenerous to Western observers, perhaps the real explanation is that Nehru was less concerned with foreign reaction than in building up the morale of the Indian people.[98] Perhaps this idea was best expressed in a speech at Bhopal, when he stated that to build a strong, proud and soundly based nation, it was essential that the masses feel a firm sense of national accomplishment, and be able to look back on what they had achieved.

Aid, however well administered, marred this feeling. The forthcoming Second Plan would therefore place greater stress on self-reliance through the medium of community development projects.[99] In spite of these sentiments, the quantity of external assistance has, of course, progressively increased; but it is important to take seriously the aspirations expressed by the late prime minister. Foreign aid represents only a part, however crucial, of India's total development effort, and the achievement of her major economic objectives would represent more solid political gain for the West than mere repetitious expressions of gratitude.

Opinion surveys

The only significant source for a general consideration of public opinion on this issue are the Monthly Public Opinion Surveys of the Indian Institute of Public Opinion. Two preliminary comments are necessary. First, the same difficulty has been experienced as hitherto of separating the issue of foreign aid from other tangential issues. Some polls deal directly with the subject. Others measure attitudes to donor countries on a variety of issues. From these some tentative correlations and hypotheses are possible, though the number and coverage of the polls is very limited. This raises the second and more serious difficulty of sampling, for clearly these polls would need to be verified by further empirical research, both extensive and intensive. The Indian Institute is affiliated to the International Association of Public Opinion Research and therefore has full access to modern techniques, though within India its work is unique. Sampling difficulties are still considerable in the conduct of opinion polls even in relatively homogeneous Western societies. India, with its endless subdivisions of language, caste and race, its vast differences of wealth, education and social status, and its relatively poor communications in rural areas, presents almost insurmountable difficulties in establishing a fully representative sample on any given issue. In general, there is a clear under-representation of the lowest social, economic and educational categories, but since the breakdown of each sample by age, income group, education, sex, occupation and often religion and state of origin is given, proper qualifications can be made (tables of sampling tolerances are provided by the Institute). The high proportion of 'Don't Know' answers, their incidence being highest among the groups where one would expect apathy and ignorance, namely among the least educated groups and in the rural areas, serves further to validate the polls. On the other hand, given India's state of development, it is the informed, or at least moderately articulate section of the population that is politically significant. The under representation of the categories mentioned is therefore perhaps not unduly important. A large number of the polls cited are backed with questions designed to test knowledge, awareness, etc. Thus, although opinion surveys are a relatively new methodology in India, if used with circumspection they do seem to provide reasonable justification for the limited conclusions and hypotheses set out in this chapter. It must also be stated that the Institute predicted the percentage Congress vote at the last two general elections within 0.5 per cent of the actual vote.

The polls cover the period 1956-66. Two important points stand out over the whole period. The first is the infinitely improved awareness of aid and the effect of such awareness on the Indian public's rating of individual countries that has developed during the course of the period under review. The second is the vastly improved standing of the United States compared with the early years of the Second Plan. Thus table 16 shows the results of a survey conducted in 1958 covering 793 respondents in Delhi, Calcutta, Bombay, Kanpur, Madras and Lucknow, designed to test the knowledge as to which country was providing India with most assistance towards her (Second) Five Year Plan.[100]

Table 16
Public opinion Survey

(per cent)

age	respondents	United States	United Kingdom	Soviet Union	West Germany	others	don't knows	total
20-29	181	33.2	1.6	24.3	0.5	2.7	37.6	100.0
30-49	448	35.3	0.2	17.6	0.2	–	46.5	100.0
50	163	33.8	1.2	15.9	0.6	–	48.5	100.0
unspecified	1	–	–	–	–	–	100.0	100.0
education								
illiterates	239	5.8	–	11.7	0.8	0.4	81.3	100.0
under-matric	289	36.4	1.0	20.2	0.3	0.9	41.2	100.0
matrics	188	53.9	1.5	27.7	–	1.0	15.9	100.0
graduates	77	69.0	–	12.9	–	–	18.1	100.0
total	793	34.4	0.7	18.7	0.3	0.7	44.8	100.0

Thus only one-third correctly named the United States as the country providing most assistance.[101] Slightly more than one-third of those who gave definite answers named the Soviet Union, this response being most marked among the young. It is possible that some may have interpreted the question qualitatively rather than quantitatively,* but in any case the result bears eloquent testimony to Soviet propaganda. Earlier surveys in West Bengal and Travancore-Cochin,[102] asking whether the Soviet Union or the United States provided more of given categories of aid, showed far more correct answers in the case of gifts and loans than with technical or training assistance, though the sample is admittedly small.

Table 17
Public opinion survey

(per cent)

category of aid	United States	Soviet Union	don't know	total
Travancore-Cochin (489 respondents)				
gifts	40.3	15.3	44.4	100.0
loans	55.4	11.0	33.6	100.0
training of personnel	21.9	35.2	42.9	100.0
technical assistance	19.1	42.7	38.2	100.0
West Bengal (908 respondents)				
gifts	37.7	5.8	56.5	100.0
loans	42.1	3.2	54.7	100.0
personnel training	26.3	13.5	60.2	100.0
technical assistance	21.1	18.5	60.4	100.0

The Soviet Union was more favoured in the case of Travancore-Cochin than West Bengal, though the same confusion is apparent in both cases. Travancore-Cochin included the region which subsequently became Kerala state, reputedly possessing one of the highest rates of literacy in India, but also an area of great poverty and of greatest Communist strength. These factors would presumably account for the pro-Russian response there, but a likely factor in both cases[103] would be the impact of the Bhilai steel mill agreement, which placed great emphasis on training and technical assistance.[104] However, it should be noted that in all categories 'Don't Knows' constitute the largest group. When the West Bengal survey is broken down into Calcutta, District Towns and Rural Areas, an ascending scale of ignorance is most marked.[105] In the four categories of aid, 'Don't Knows' range from 26.0 per cent to

*The actual question was 'Kindly name the country assisting India most on the Plan'.

Table 18
Public opinion survey

(per cent)

education	no. of respondents January 1966	no. of respondents May 1966	United States January	United States May	Soviet Union January	Soviet Union May	Japan January	Japan May	United Kingdom January	United Kingdom May	United Arab Republic January	United Arab Republic May	France January	France May	West Germany January	West Germany May	don't know January	don't know May
some secondary	96	363	85	89	74	73	9	13	26	27	3	2	5	5	14	16	8	7
secondary completed or some university	231	834	94	94	84	73	27	16	47	34	8	33	9	—	34	15	3	3
university degree or more	419	627	95	98	87	83	42	29	55	53	6	7	12	16	48	42	2	1
primary or less	254	176	58	60	44	49	3	4	10	12	3	2	2	1	3	—	31	28
total	1000	2000	89	91	79	74	24	13	41	37	6	4	8	9	30	25	7	5

N.B. No check: Provision for multiple answers

35.4 per cent in Calcutta, and from 84.5 per cent to 86.9 per cent in Rural Areas.[106] One observer has concluded that the aid that does arrive seems to many villagers to have come from New Delhi and is likely to be seen as a means employed by the Congress party for gaining votes.[107] Thus accurate knowledge of the source of foreign aid, and even of its existence seemed at that time to be largely confined to the relatively educated classes and to large towns and cities, though even in these groups much confusion existed.

By 1966 a totally different level of awareness seems to have been reached. Two polls achieved the following response to the question 'Do you happen to know whether or not India has been receiving economic aid from any country'?[108] (table 18)
Breakdown by education standard indicates that even the lowest educated showed a marked degree of awareness. It may perhaps be significant that the order in which countries are placed is generally in accordance with the quantum of aid they have provided, though the question as to who gives most is not specifically asked.

Later polls will show that in subsequent years aid has become increasingly important, but polls conducted in 1956 indicated (table 19) that a country's stand on foreign policy issues of vital importance to India were of greater importance than its aid contribution in determining popular attitudes. The overall survey conducted soon after the visit of Bulganin and Kruschev established a very strong pro-Soviet trend. In this context the question asked of 1,372 respondents in Delhi, West Bengal and Travancore-Cochin, 'Could you indicate whether your attitude towards America and Russia has been influenced by

Table 19
Public opinion survey

(per cent)

America	respondents	1st preference	2nd preference	3rd preference	4th preference	don't know
Kashmir	1,372	14.1	28.0	3.4	2.6	51.9
Goa	1,372	25.9	15.5	4.8	2.7	51.1
China	1,372	2.6	4.1	26.0	9.6	57.7
economic aid	1,372	5.5	1.7	8.0	21.9	63.1
Russia						
Kashmir	1,372	41.5	12.8	1.7	2.3	41.8
Goa	1,372	10.3	40.6	5.3	0.8	42.9
China	1,372	4.5	1.7	35.8	7.6	50.4
economic aid	1,372	2.2	1.9	6.8	32.9	56.3

their stands on the following problems?'[109] was of specific relevance. Economic aid thus ranked lowest of the four issues as an influencing factor. This issue was obviously more abstract and remote at that time in its impact on the consciousness of most Indians compared with issues of more dynamic nationalist appeal. On both Kashmir and Goa, the Soviet Union had adopted an unequivocal pro-Indian stand, whereas the United States appeared to many Indians to be leaning towards Pakistan and Portugal. John Foster Dulles had recently made a speech on the Goa issue[110] which received a most unfavourable reception in India. A poll to determine the extent attitudes towards the United States had been affected by Mr Dulles' statements achieved the following results[111]:

Table 20
Public opinion survey

(per cent)

				West Bengal	
	Delhi	Travancore-Cochin	Calcutta	District towns	Rural areas
very much	11.0	18.4	9.0	15.0	1.6
somewhat	13.7	27.4	15.3	13.5	3.2
not much	23.8	7.4	22.0	7.9	1.6
no change	8.8	16.1	13.3	6.0	9.1
don't know, etc.	42.7	30.7	40.4	57.6	84.5
total	100.0	100.0	100.0	100.0	100.0
no. of respondents	227	489	300	356	252

Despite the preponderant trend towards indifference or ignorance, the positive and presumably hostile response shown by these figures is in fact very large, in view of the limited extent of education and political consciousness over the whole population.

Another aspect must be mentioned as contributing to the general 'image' of donor countries prevailing in India at that time. In the matter of alliances the West emerged in a far less favourable position than the Soviet Union. While the prevailing view seemed to be generally hostile to all military alliances, regarding them as inimical to freedom, economic well-being and by nature aggressive,[112] a far greater number were prepared to view Russian alliances as 'defensive in nature'[113] than were prepared to take a similar view of Western sponsored alliances. A poll on the question 'Do you approve or disapprove of the following military alliances?' revealed the following, and from the Western viewpoint, unhappy result;[114]

Table 21
Public opinion survey

	approve	disapprove	don't know, etc.	total
Sino-Soviet military pact	314	174	1,136	1,624
Warsaw pact	262	225	1,137	1,624
NATO	69	457	1,098	1,624
Baghdad pact	38	673	913	1,624
SEATO	34	693	897	1,624

The evident double standard of many respondents was most striking, though indifference and ignorance as usual predominate. It should further be noted that the strongest hostility was reserved for pacts directly involving India's borders. One may reasonably speculate as to whether hostility to NATO would have been nearly as strong in the absence of SEATO and the Baghdad Pact.

Later polls, however, registered a substantial improvement in America's image and opinion rating compared with Russia, as shown in table 22.[115]

Table 22
Public opinion survey

(per cent)

	respondents	very good opinion	good opinion	fair neither good/bad opinion	bad opinion	very bad opinion	don't know	total
United States								
1963	653	17.3	47.6	11.9	1.1	–	22.1	100.0
1965	2,000	16.0	58.0	13.0	4.0	1.0	8.0	100.0
1966 January	1,000	19.0	52.0	18.0	4.0	–	7.0	100.0
1966 May	2,000	21.0	56.0	14.0	3.0	–	6.0	100.0
1967 July	1,000	11.0	44.0	23.0	9.0	1.0	12.0	100.0
Soviet Union								
1963	653	2.9	25.7	26.9	14.9	2.3	27.3	100.0
1965	2,000	16.0	64.0	11.0	1.0	–	8.0	100.0
1966 January	1,000	39.0	51.0	4.0	–	–	6.0	100.0
1966 May	2,000	30.0	56.0	7.0	1.0	–	8.0	100.0
1967 July	1,000	2.0	22.0	44.0	10.0	2.0	20.0	100.0
United Kingdom								
1963	653	7.5	53.5	15.0	1.2	–	22.8	100.0
1965	2,000	8.0	55.0	21.0	3.0	–	13.0	100.0
1966 January	1,000	2.0	23.0	39.0	17.0	7.0	12.0	100.0
1966 May	2,000	1.0	21.0	48.0	15.0	4.0	11.0	100.0

Table 22 continued

(per cent)

	respond-ents	very good opinion	good opinion	fair neither good/bad opinion	bad opinion	very bad opinion	don't know	total
China								
1963	–	–	–	–	–	–	–	–
1965	2,000	–	1.0	5.0	28.0	57.0	9.0	100.0
1966 January	1,000	–	1.0	4.0	24.0	63.0	8.0	100.0
1966 May	–	–	–	–	–	–	–	–
United Arab Republic								
1963	–	–	–	–	–	–	–	–
1965	2,000	10.0	36.0	19.0	1.0	–	34.0	100.0
1966 January	1,000	3.0	43.0	31.0	2.0	–	21.0	100.0
1966 May	–	–	–	–	–	–	–	–
1967 July	1,000	2.0	25.0	39.0	9.0	2.0	23.0	100.0
France								
1963	–	–	–	–	–	–	–	–
1965	2,000	2.0	18.0	29.0	2.0	–	49.0	100.0
1966 January	1,000	1.0	25.0	40.0	4.0	1.0	29.0	100.0
1966 May	2,000	1.0	30.0	39.0	5.0	–	25.0	100.0
1967 July	1,000	2.0	22.0	39.0	3.0	1.0	33.0	100.0
West Germany								
1963	–	–	–	–	–	–	–	–
1965	2,000	4.0	30.0	20.0	1.0	–	45.0	100.0
1966 January	1,000	4.0	39.0	32.0	1.0	–	24.0	100.0
1966 May	2,000	3.0	37.0	33.0	5.0	–	23.0	100.0
1967 July	1,000	5.0	30.0	33.0	2.0	–	30.0	100.0
Japan								
1963	–	–	–	–	–	–	–	–
1965	2,000	7.0	38.0	15.0	1.0	–	39.0	100.0
1966 January	1,000	9.0	49.0	20.0	–	–	22.0	100.0
1966 May	2,000	5.0	50.0	25.0	–	–	20.0	100.0
1967 July	1,000	13.0	38.0	24.0	1.0	–	24.0	100.0

These polls are open to a substantial degree of interpretation. Except in the 1963 poll the United States still trails the Soviet Union (total of Good and Very Good Opinions), but the difference is far narrower than earlier polls and both countries have a clear lead over all others. It may be noted, however, that in the 1967 poll, the ratings of both countries fell markedly, most probably due to their behaviour during the Middle East crisis. Amongst donor countries ideological opposition has been sharpest between the Soviet Union and the United States but nevertheless they are both given the highest popular ratings. Of the various factors producing a common involvement in India that might reasonably be expected to cause a favourable response, economic aid is the most obvious. Other donor countries follow in nearly approximate order according to the amount of aid given. There are, however, significant indicators that foreign policy factors weigh very importantly. In 1966 belief in the United States support for Pakistan was still, no doubt, a factor influencing some respondents. In 1963, by contrast, Russia's rating was well down, and possibly at this time the Indian public were not clear if there was any Soviet involvement in the Chinese border war, a doubt which was later completely dispelled by the time of the war with Pakistan and the Tashkent Conference. Secondly, the United Kingdom was clearly rated third up to the middle of 1965, but unfavourable opinion as to her role in the Pakistan war gave her the worst rating after China by 1966. China consistently achieved the lowest rating and her border activities are clearly responsible. Economic aid is not involved in this instance. The United Arab Republic had by early 1966 achieved the fourth highest popular rating of those countries polled. Since this country provided no aid to India, common foreign policy interpretations must be the main factors here. Finally Japan's relatively high rating* should be noted being, above all Western donors except the United States, despite a lower aid contribution than the United Kingdom and West Germany (whose rating has also climbed steadily). It is possible that her identity as a friendly Asian power is a factor of significance here. The broad overall conclusion would seem to be that aid has become a factor of great importance in determining the Indian public's opinion of a foreign country; however, it is by no means the only or ultimate factor. At the same time, if a foreign country is considered to be in opposition to India's vital interests as in the case of Britain over the 1965 war with Pakistan, the effect on popular opinion may be very drastic, despite the quantum of aid provided.

Various polls make clear that the overall view of a particular country and its people plays an important part in determining Indian public images of that country. This further complicates attempts to isolate the effect of economic aid. Table 23, for instance, provides an example of how an overall view of a country may be subjectivised.

*Probably due to absence of ideological factors.

In 1956, replies to the question 'Which of the following qualities would you apply to the Russians and the Americans?' were as follows[116]:

Table 23
Public opinion survey

	Russians	Americans	both	neither	don't know	total
hardworking	153	41	419	105	379	1,097
intelligent	94	96	519	1	387	1,097
generous	159	101	284	18	535	1,097
good natured	148	47	314	21	567	1,097
spiritual	53	168	117	119	640	1,097
brave	106	35	545	2	409	1,097

It thus appears that while a majority conceded that the United States had given aid more generously than the Soviet Union, Russians were still regarded as more generous and good-natured than Americans. The conclusion seems inescapable that a significant number of respondents saw other motives behind American aid. The only quality where the United States achieved the honour of a clear success over the Soviet Union was in being more 'spiritual'. One may only speculate as to the meaning of this expression. It might have implied a more religious or less materialistic approach, but it could also have implied an image of Americans as very concerned with ideological issues.

The same series of surveys conducted in 1956 established that a generally favourable view of Communism was taken at this time by a significant, though not spectacular section of Indian opinion.[117] In order to establish the popular image of Communism in more detail, the following question was asked of 1,924 respondents: 'Thinking about Russian Communism, what is the most notable feature, if any, that you feel India should adopt'?[118] (table 24)

Full employment has been the objective of most American administrations since the presidency of Franklin Roosevelt, and although an issue of considerable dispute, some measure of state social services are provided in that country. The aim of a classless society, though stated in a quite different socio-economic context, also finds an important place in American political thought. The economic features of Communism most objectionable to the United States, namely nationalised industry, planned economy and collectivised agriculture, found far less support than the three above-mentioned acceptable features of 'socialist'societies.

Table 24
Public opinion survey

	class-less society	nationa-lised indust-ries	social services	collec-tive farming	planned economy	patrio-tism	full employ-ment	don't know	total
Travancore-Cochin	50	26	10	–	–	4	7	392	489
West Bengal									
Calcutta	16	26	76	9	13	–	35	125	300
District Towns	16	20	51	4	6	–	104	155	356
Rural Areas	15	4	13	5	6	–	11	198	252
Delhi	21	10	2	7	–	2	1	184	227
total	118	86	152	25	25	6	158	1,054	1,624

Thus the survey is less ideologically unfavourable to the United States than might at first appear

A further question, 'Thinking about Russian Communism, what is the most notable feature, if any, that you feel India should avoid?' elicited some information as to the type of objection Communism may produce, though the proportion of 'Don't Know' answers is too high for the result to be significant.[119]

Table 25
Public opinion survey

	dictatorship	intolerance of other parties	harassment of the masses	disbelief in god	regimentation of thought	don't know	total
Travancore-Cochin	36	32	2	4	–	415	489
Delhi	11	1	2	5	–	208	227
West Bengal							
Calcutta	27	27	3	5	33	205	300
District							
Towns	40	16	2	13	19	266	356
Rural Areas	6	3	–	2	4	237	252
total	120	79	9	29	50	1,331	1,624

The general conclusion which seems most obvious from these surveys of the earlier period is that while a generally favourable view of Russia was being established during the crucial period of the mid-1950s, for reasons which had little to do with economic aid, the vast majority of Indians were either indifferent or ignorant towards the major ideological issues of Communism and anti-Communism. What opposition was expressed to Communism, however, was in terms generally common in the West. At the same time, favourable aspects of Communism, as seen by the Indian public, were largely those incorporated in one form or another into the mixed-economy, semi-socialist pattern to be found in most Western societies, and indeed in India itself.

Table 26[120] by contrast, shows a sharp improvement in the overall view of American society, its attitudes towards India and its effectiveness in solving its economic problems, to the extent that by 1953 it was leading the Soviet Union and all other countries.

Table 26
Public opinion survey
'In your opinion which of the following statements apply to (relevant country)?'

	United States	Soviet Union	United States-Soviet Union both 1956	United States-Soviet Union neither 1956	United States-Soviet Union don't know 1956	China	United Kingdom	West Germany	France	Japan
1. no. of respondents										
1956	1,097	1,097	1,097	1,097	1,097	–	–	–	–	–
1961	1,080	1,080	–	–	–	1,080	1,080	1,080	1,080	1,080
1963	653	653	–	–	–	653	653	653	653	653
2. friendly to Asian countries										
1956	7.9	22.9	9.1	4.2	55.9	–	–	–	–	–
1961	43.8	33.6	–	–	–	2.5	28.0	14.6	8.7	17.5
1963	67.5	36.3	–	–	–	0.5	50.5	23.4	11.6	20.1
3. generous aid to India										
1956	22.2	3.1	16.0	2.4	56.3	–	–	–	–	–
1961	51.7	41.3	–	–	–	0.5	27.8	20.9	4.0	13.3
1963	84.4	62.6	–	–	–	–	50.5	37.8	8.1	29.6
4. has solved unemployment problem										
1956	4.1	24.3	15.9	4.7	51.0	–	–	–	–	–
1961	17.1	23.4	–	–	–	4.4	7.4	6.9	1.3	6.9
1963	42.1	29.2	–	–	–	0.9	26.0	15.5	4.6	13.3
5. economic system leads to exploitation										
1956	21.1	0.1	7.8	3.2	66.5	–	–	–	–	–
1961	7.9	7.9	–	–	–	7.9	4.6	2.1	2.4	1.7
1963	15.5	11.8	–	–	–	8.1	13.2	5.7	4.6	4.7

6. economic system leads to rise in standard of living of all in country										
1956	9.3	15.9	20.3	1.2	53.3	–	–	–	–	–
1961	26.3	18.0	–	–	–	3.0	11.1	9.9	4.7	8.6
1963	44.4	22.4	–	–	–	1.7	23.0	10.6	5.7	11.0
7. war loving										
1956	–	–	–	–	–	–	–	–	–	–
1961	12.4	14.1	–	–	–	27.4	4.5	7.2	7.9	1.6
1963	4.6	7.2	–	–	–	68.1	2.6	3.1	2.1	0.8
8. peace loving										
1956	22.3	17.4	–	–	–	2.3	21.4	10.4	6.7	15.4
1961	23.9	16.4	–	–	–	1.4	19.8	15.5	12.4	18.7
1963*	0.9	1.7	–	–	–	0.3	0.6	0.8	0.8	0.8
9. none										
10. never read or heard about the country										
1961	15.6	16.6	–	–	–	18.0	16.7	17.1	17.9	17.7
1963	16.1	20.5	–	–	–	29.6	19.9	45.6	72.9	49.2
11. unable to specify										
1961	26.5	28.2	–	–	–	49.4	35.2	44.4	59.2	48.6
1963	0.9	1.7	–	–	–	0.3	0.6	0.8	0.8	0.8

*Response too small to be significant.

Whilst Russia led on all counts in 1956, other than providing generous aid to India, by 1963, of the two major countries, she was ahead only in one respect—that more people thought that the American system led to economic exploitation. The change from 1956 is thus very dramatic. It should be noted that the rating of all countries (except China) has risen steadily as they have become more familiar, but it is reasonable to attribute a large part of this trend to economic aid. In 1956, although the majority of respondents had favoured aid from both countries, of those who favoured aid from only one of them a definite majority favoured the Soviet Union.[121] By contrast, table 27 shows the response to two polls in 1966.[122]

Table 27
Public opinion survey
'Would you say that (relevant country) helps a lot or just a little in the economic development of our country?'

(per cent)

	United States		Soviet Union		United Kingdom		West Germany	
	January 1966	May 1966	January 1966	May 1966	January 1966	May 1966	January 1966	May 1966
number of respondents	1,000	2,000	1,000	2,000	1,000	2,000	1,000	2,000
a lot	70	65	65	51	12	8	7	6
just a little	11	21	13	21	23	25	20	17
not applicable*	19	–	22	–	65	–	73	–
neither helps nor hinders	–	14	–	21	–	67	–	77
total	100	100	100	100	100	100	100	100

*January 1966—Question only asked of those who had earlier shown awareness of country's aid.

The pattern of response generally follows the order of aid quantum provided, though Britain still shows ahead of West Germany, and the Soviet rating is quite disproportionately high by this test.

The same group of respondents were asked (table 28) the question, 'Why do you think (relevant country) is giving economic aid to India?'[123] (The question was asked only of those who knew the country concerned was giving aid).

Again the response is hard to evaluate. It would seem that nos 3 and 5 provide the most disinterested motives, in which case the Soviet Union

Table 28
Public opinion survey

(per cent)

	United States 1966		Soviet Union 1966		United Kingdom 1966		West Germany 1966	
	January	May	January	May	January	May	January	May
1. no. respondents	1,000	2,000	1,000	2,000	1,000	2,000	1,000	2,000
2 win over India to Western camp. Keep India under obligation. Counter influence of Russian aid	21	24	–	–	–	–	–	–
3.help development of India's economy	13	15	17	12	1	2	5	5
4. strengthen democracy in India	10	10	–	–	–	–	–	–
5. friendly relations win goodwill	15	8	22	16	4	5	4	6
6. to fight Communism in India	11	8	–	–	1	1	–	–
7. own interest. Prevent India joining Western bloc. Counter American influence	–	–	17	15	–	–	–	–
8. political reasons: gain influence/domination in Indian politics	–	–	4	5	3	3	–	– 1
9. isolate Chinese; counter Chinese influence; build India as a counterpoise against China	–	–	2	1	–	–	–	–
10. India being a member of the Commonwealth	–	–	–	–	10	8	–	–
11. commercial reasons: gain/hold markets	–	–	–	–	8	4	7	4
12. to promote socialistic pattern of society	–	–	3	3	–	–	–	–
13. prestige reasons	–	–	–	–	2	2	2	1
14. other favourable comments	–	–	–	1	–	–	1	1
15. other unfavourable comments	–	2	–	–	–	–	–	–
16. don't know	23	25	18	21	12	12	11	8
17. not applicable	11	9	20	26	60	63	70	75

N.B. No check: provision for multiple answers.

is more highly rated on both polls. Most questions are, however, open to a wide degree of interpretation.

In one respect, that of strength, especially space development, the Soviet Union has clearly stayed ahead.[124] Thus table 29 shows the response to a question in 1961, 'Which country is further ahead in the field of long-range missiles and rockets, the United States or Russia?'[125]

Table 29
Public opinion survey

no. of respondents 1961		United States 1961		Soviet Union 1961		don't know 1961		total 1961	
urban	rural	urban	rural	urban	rural	urban	rural	urban	rural
895	2,165	6.0	2.6	59.9	28.7	34.1	68.7	100.0	100.0

(per cent)

In the same poll a further question was asked which appears to show a related trend, though the positive response in favour of the Soviet Union was far weaker 'Who is winning the Cold War, Russia or the West?'[126]

Table 30
Public opinion survey

(per cent)

no. of respondents 1961		Russia 1961		The West 1961		neither 1961		don't know 1961		total 1961	
urban	rural	urban	rural	urban	rural	urban	rural	urban	rural	urban	rural
895	2,165	23.5	9.9	5.4	2.2	23.6	5.7	47.5	82.2	100.0	100.0

These results were confirmed by further polls in 1965 and 1966 on the question, 'All things considered, which country do you think is ahead at the present time in space development, the United States or the Soviet Union?'[127] (table 31)

The percentage who believed that the Soviet Union was ahead increased sharply among the better educated groups. By contrast only a very slight majority believed the Soviet Union to be ahead in general scientific development.[128] (table 32)

It should be noted that the two highest educated groups show a slight lead in favour of the United States in this respect. The overall conclusion of this group of polls, however, is that the impression of Soviet strength has remained, despite America having succeeded in reversing earlier

Table 31
Public opinion survey

(per cent)

education	no. of respondents 1965	1966	United States ahead 1965	1966	Soviet Union ahead 1965	1966	about equal 1965	1966	don't know 1965	1966	total 1965	1966
primary or less	576	176	5	9	18	38	41	18	36	35	100	100
some secondary	430	363	6	12	31	50	44	18	19	20	100	100
secondary completed	487	834	7	11	45	61	43	22	5	6	100	100
univeristy or more*	507	627	6	8	61	71	31	17	2	4	100	100
total	2,000	2,000	6	10	38	60	40	19	16	11	100	100

*1966 poll specified degree.

Table 32
Public opinion survey
'All things considered, which country do you think is ahead at the present time in scientific development–the United States or the Soviet Union?'

(per cent)

education	no. of respondents	United States ahead	Soviet Union ahead	about equal	don't know	total total
primary or less	176	12	31	23	34	100
some secondary	363	21	30	28	21	100
secondary completed or some university	834	34	33	26	7	100
university degree or more	627	39	34	23	4	100
total	2,000	31	33	25	11	100

unfavourable impressions in other respects. It would be a reasonable assumption that this impression of strength would be a factor in Russia's continued favourable rating and in particular would affect the view of many Indians favourably towards the utility of Soviet economic aid.

From such limited evidence it is only possible to postulate a few hypotheses and conclusions with regard to general public opinion. These may be summarised as follows:

1. From being a factor of very little significance in earlier years, aid appears to have become a factor of substantial importance in determining popular attitudes towards particular countries. Other considerations are foreign policy, especially as regards issues of immediate importance to India, belief as to motivation and overall image of the country itself.

2. It would appear that the public are little aware of the extent of dependence on foreign aid, or if they are they are not unduly concerned. At the same time they show little concern for questions of gratitude and obligation which have concerned the more politically sensitive. Indeed, national pride would not appear to be nearly so involved at the popular level as earlier analysis would suggest, unless the affront is very direct indeed.

3. The complex political battles mentioned earlier fought out at government and political levels appear also not unduly to concern the general public, e.g. such questions as socialism, public versus private sector, the direction and magnitude of the Plans, etc. Thus critical consciousness of the implications of aid seems very low. Indeed the

relative equality between the United States and Russia would seem to indicate a considerable degree of political unsophistication, when taken in conjunction with the general gradation of other countries approximately in order according to their aid contribution.

4. Dogmatic anti-Americanism displayed by some politicians and in some quarters of the government seems to have found only limited popular expresssion after the early years of the Second Plan, which were indeed the worst period in Indo-American relations.

5. 'Non-alignment' still appears to be an important factor with the general public, as evidenced by the high rating for both Russia and America, the majority being willing to take aid from both countries.

The range of potential political conflict should be apparent from this chapter and points of conflict are continually shifting. The extent of awareness and opinion is equally diffuse. Even at the highest levels judgments tend to be clouded by immediate objectives and preoccupations. India's response to foreign aid *per se*, though a matter of great concern to the donors, does not easily admit of measurement, but an indication of the range of political issues involved does substantially clarify the situation. These may be more adequately understood from the case studies which follow.

Chapter 6

Food aid

The system of surplus commodity food assistance to developing countries was established by the United States Congress in 1954, under Public Law 480.[1] In outline the programme provides for the United States government to dispose of surplus food, mainly wheat, by agreement with recipient countries. Terms are negotiable for each consignment, but the greatest part of supplies to India come under title 1 which provides for a complex local currency loan procedure. Normally the Indian government would pay at least half the shipping costs. Initially supplies are received as a gift and sold on the market through government agencies. The rupee proceeds are then paid to a special account, the funds so created being known as counterpart funds. 10-15 per cent of these funds (precise details are not published) are used for American local aid administration costs. The remainder are disbursed on a long-term loan basis for mutually agreed development projects. Under the Cooley Amendment procedure a minimum of 5 per cent of counterpart funds must be devoted to the development of the private sector.

India's dependence on food imports has increased markedly, as shown in table 33.[2]

Table 33
Production and imports of foodgrains (million tons)

	average annual production	average annual imports	imports as per cent of total supply
first plan period	65.8	1.8	2.6
second plan period	75.2	3.8	4.9
third plan period	80.5	6.5	7.5

Since a large proportion, possibly two-thirds, of the crop is consumed by the producers, the proportion of imports relative to domestic marketable surplus is far higher. Over 90 per cent of food imports in 1966 consisted of wheat, flour, sorghum and maize. In the same year, approximately 80 per cent of purchased imports of these products came from the United States.[3] PL 480 constituted an increasing proportion of total grain imports as shown in table 34.[4]

Table 34
Level of food imports through PL 480 (crores of rupees)

year	total imports of foodgrains–value	PL 480 imports of foodgrains–value	per cent foodgrains imports through PL 480
1956-7	108	33	55.6
1957-8	165	96	58.2
1958-9	151	88	58.3
1959-60	150	91	60.7
1960-1	213	150	70.4
1961-2	117	64	64.7
1962-3	166	107	64.5
1963-4	197	162	82.2
1964-5	282	240	85.1

Viewed from the American side, PL 480 exports constituted 26 per cent of total value of agricultural exports to all countries from 1954-5 to 1965-6. In the case of India they constituted 93.5 per cent of total agricultural export value to that country.[5] By 1966 India was receiving over half the total PL 480 food aid supplied by the United States. She has thus provided a very important outlet for America's surplus agricultural produce, a factor that should be borne in mind when making political judgments. PL 480 aid represented 55.9 per cent of total aid supplied to India up to 31st March 1965,[6] and in the fiscal year 1966 represented almost two-thirds.[7] These figures indicate the extent to which food aid determines the overall image of American aid. The agonies and complexities of India's food distribution policy add further to the political burden such aid entails.

While PL 480 has undoubtedly kept India afloat through times of crisis and while it has been a vital prop to the Second and Third Plans by stabilising food prices in the major urban centres, it has also caused a great many political tensions. These have contributed to India's determination to achieve minimum self-sufficiency in foodgrains by 1971 and equally to America's determination to spur her to this end. At several points Indians regard the whole system as an infringement of their sovereignty. The accumulation of rupees by the United States is a particular point of tension. No details are available, but the amount is said to be very high and is a source of embarrassment to both governments. Several fierce exchanges have occurred in the Lok Sabha over American use of their retained share of counterpart funds. Though the government has firmly asserted America's right to spend these funds as she wishes, some members have demanded tighter controls.[8] These demands are naturally related to fears of foreign exchange losses on invisible account.[9] Minor sources of irritation include the provision that a small minimum of purchases of American agricultural products must be made through normal trade, loss of dollars on freight carried in American Flag vessels and the provision which allows the American authorities to use 1 per cent of their rupee holdings for sale to their citizens, resident or tourist, in India.[10] At a more serious level, suspicions that the United States is using food imports to give herself political leverage over Kashmir and other defence and foreign policy issues are heightened by the frequency of PL 480 negotiations. If American pressure does exist here it would seem to be mainly motivated by a desire to avoid aid funds being wasted for non-economic purposes. As already indicated, the main weight of American influence has been directed towards persuading India to tackle her problems of population and food production.

Both India and America have set clear time limits to the continuance of PL 480 imports, which are to end by 1971. The real question therefore is the extent to which this programme has assisted or retarded the solution of India's food problems. On the one hand the price stabilisation effect has reduced political and economic tensions. At the same time some breathing space has been given for the solution of long-term problems. Against this it is argued that large quantities of food imports both destroy the political urgency to tackle problems and have disincentive effects for producers by depressing prices. During recent crisis years these arguments would seem rather academic and in any case the Indian government has been torn between the need to set support prices sufficiently high to give incentives to producers and sufficiently low to provide for the needs of the poorest consumers. Without massive internal subsidies, the only alternative was large-scale imports. While the shift in priorities towards agriculture has largely been the result of changes and tensions within India itself,[11] the Americans have long been pressing for such a new approach. The beginnings of a real American effort in this direction can be traced to a formidable and devastating Report in 1959 by the Ford Foundation, under the auspices of the government of India.[12] The problems were stated in terms of crisis, on the basis of an estimated population of 480 million by 1966 and a foodgrains demand of 110m.[13] During the Third Plan production was virtually stagnant and during the drought year of 1966 reached only 72m tons, though this rose to an estimated 95m tons in

1967–a record crop. Population in 1967 was estimated at 510m.[14] The Report recommended extensive changes over the whole field of agricultural policy, including production, marketing, land-reform, finance, administration and a whole host of other technical matters. In many ways the Report was an impressive achievement and its influence has been profound. Particular stress was placed on incentives and price support schemes. It is therefore most surprising to find that the Report assumed not only the continuance of large supplies of imports as buffer stocks, but also that support prices should be 10-15 per cent below average import prices.[15] The question of depressing prices was not discussed at all. In 1960 a four year agreement was signed with the United States for 16m tons of PL 480 imports.[16] While one would not blame the massive failure of the Third Plan agricultural effort on PL 480 alone, but on a whole range of causes, it is hard to refute the widely held Indian view that these imports have caused many producers to divert acreage to cash crops other than cereals, and at the same time provided the central government with a cushion for administrative and policy-making complacency.

Table 35 shows that total United States stocks of grains have been reduced drastically in recent years.[17]

Table 35
United States wheat stocks (thousand metric tons)

beginning of crop year	
1961-2	38,406
1962-3	35,975
1963-4	32,520
1964-5	24,527
1965-6	22,254

This change has been the result of deliberate policy measures, related both to domestic considerations and a clear reversal of earlier views as to the contribution Western food surpluses should make towards the under-developed world. The prevailing expert view in the United States would appear to be that food aid should only be available for temporary crises, disasters, etc., and must be geared to local production programmes, which should receive the main weight of assistance.[18] This undoubtedly makes very good sense, but in the light of the above figures the Indians can scarcely be blamed for cynicism both towards the original programme and the efforts to abandon it.

India's response to this changing situation at last shows signs of becoming positive. Vigorous efforts are being made to reach the target of 120m tons of foodgrains by 1971, the estimated requirement for achievement of minimum self-sufficiency. Internal pressures to reach this goal are compulsive, quite apart from American pressures. Population is expected to reach 560m by 1971,[19] while projections for 1986 have been put as high as 854m, though this must depend on the failure or success of birth-control programmes. Efforts are being concentrated on one or two selected areas in each state, bringing together all available inputs of fertiliser, seed, credit, expertise, etc. This approach follows closely the 'package programme' foreshadowed in the 1959 Ford Foundation Report. Special efforts are being directed towards the introduction of high-yielding varieties of rice and wheat, which have already shown spectacular potential under Indian conditions in the last two years. Many would argue that these will provide India with the vital breakthrough, and the growth and anticipated decline of PL 480 must properly be seen in this light. Efforts are also being concentrated on raising fertiliser production. The target capacity for 1970-1 is 2.4m tons compared with 681,000 tons in 1967.[20] To this end foreign capital has been offered an open door with no controls on price and marketing other than an undertaking to sell 30 per cent of output to the government at an agreed price. The Third Plan target was little more than 50 per cent fulfilled[21] and the urgency of the problem necessitated the abandonment of the 1956 Industrial Policy Resolution provisions in respect of this industry. In case of failure to achieve the new target, the highest foreign exchange priority is to be given to fertiliser imports. It would appear that the basic decisions with regard to investment priorities have been taken and apart from favourable weather conditions, success will depend on implementation. Despite great political uncertainty and justified scepticism towards Indian bureaucracy, many observers would give India a fair chance of at least coming near the 1971 target. Even if this is achieved, however, output must continue on a steeply rising curve for the foreseeable future to match rising population. In view of all these problems and in view of the deeply rooted institutionalisation of the PL 480 programme it is too early to predict with confidence that food imports can be phased out as quickly as everyone hopes. Nevertheless, the political embarrassments are clearly great enough to give both parties the maximum incentive to achieve this objective at the earliest possible date. All aid involves dependence, but this particular form of aid is deeply wounding to

India's national pride, and gives the United States immense leverage. At the same time the United States is laid open to every possible charge of political manoeuvring, the justice of which can never be properly established, while Indian politicians and bureaucrats are provided with a blanket defence to cover all manner of indecision, maladministration and incompetence.

Chapter 7

Foreign aid and investment in the Indian oil industry

A study of the oil industry in India is of considerable significance in relation to the major themes discussed. The increasing determination of the government to assert its control over the economy has come into direct conflict with the interests of the private oil companies. By a process of ruthlessly hard bargaining, some degree of cooperation has been achieved. An initially monopolistic postion held by three foreign companies, Burmah-Shell, Standard Vacuum Oil Co. (Esso) and Caltex, has been progressively undermined by deliberate policy measures. Five public sector refineries are at present in operation or under construction, and the Oil and Natural Gas Commission is engaged in several exploration ventures either alone or in partnership. The Soviet bloc has rendered substantial assistance in exploration, crude oil extraction, refining and the construction of pipelines. At the same time, however, the government has shown willingness to undertake partnership with private enterprise in all aspects of the industry, where it can negotiate suitable terms. The industry is thus, perhaps, one of the best examples of the Indian concept of mixed economy,[1] admirably reflecting the tensions and conflicts that such a policy produces; but primarily it casts light on the relevance of India's 'non-alignment' policy in the sphere of economics.

The refinery agreements

Prior to 1951, the only oil production and refining in India was conducted by the Assam Oil Co.[2] at Digboi (Assam). The overwhelming bulk of India's demand for refined petroleum products was imported. During the course of the First Five Year Plan three major refineries were established in the private sector. Agreements were signed with Esso in November 1951, with Burmah-Shell[3] in December 1951, and with Caltex Ltd in March 1953.[4] Finally agreed refinery capacities for the initial constructions were 1.21 million tons, two million tons and 675,000 tons per annum respectively.[5] The estimated initial costs, including working capital, were \$35m, £16.5m and \$15m respectively.[6] In the context of India's subsequently defined industrial policy the agreements were extemely favourable to the companies. The Esso and Burmah-Shell Agreements were signed within fifteen days of each other and their marked similarity in all but minor matters suggests that those companies presented a solid front in their negotiations with the government.[7] The Caltex agreement[8] was also similar in all essential details, with a possibly even longer list of requirements from the government. This company, negotiating an agreement some fifteen months after the previous two, no doubt benefited from the precedents already established. The agreements gave the companies security in every possible way, and the government was later to come under fire for having been too generous. Increasing pressure was subsequently placed upon the companies to renegotiate these agreements. The main provisions are summarised in appendix no. 5.

In view of the subsequent discontent at the immensely powerful position of the oil companies as a result of these agreements and the continued efforts of the Indian government to undermine their dominance, one may ask why these agreements were ever signed. It would appear obvious that the Indian government was negotiating from a position of weakness. Foreign companies entirely dominated supply and distribution of refined products at that time.[9] India's main concern was to save foreign exchange by refining crude oil within India. At the same time it should be noted that the First Five Year Plan did not place great emphasis on industrial projects, nor was the general ethos at this time so strongly in favour of the public sector as during the Second Plan period and subsequently. Whatever the reason, the refinery agreements left three foreign companies in a position of overwhelming dominance over the Indian oil industry at all levels.

Public Sector Development

The appointment of Shri K. D. Malaviya as Minister of Natural Resources and Scientific Research in 1955 was to open the way for a decisive policy of 'economic nationalism' in the oil industry. Development of national resources was regarded as an obvious way of saving scarce foreign exchange. It became progressively clearer that future developments in exploration, drilling, refining and, to a lesser extent, marketing were to be dominated by the public sector, though more recently it has become evident that private enterprise will be allowed some participation, albeit on considerably less easy terms. Shri Malaviya's philosophy was well expressed in a statement announcing the forthcoming arrival of a Soviet exploration mission in October 1955, as a first step towards state-owned oil companies: 'We are determined to acquire the "know-how" of oil, and we will get it from whatever sources we can, and in the shortest possible time.'[10] The variety of partnership agreements entered into by India subsequently bears witness to the zeal with which this policy has been pursued. At no time was any official statement made suggesting that India might break the refinery agreements.[11] However, it became increasingly apparent that a policy of isolation was being adopted. By establishing crude oil production, refining capacity and distribution networks in the public sector, and at the same time restricting private sector expansion, the government could in the long run reduce India's dependence on the companies and dominate the market itself. The power of government to licence expansion was an important weapon in achieving this objective. Competitive pressures were thus used to extract concessions, the ultimate objective being a renegotiation of the refinery agreements.

To more fully understand the government's strategy it is necessary to study in detail the various sections of the industry.

Oil search

The period under review witnessed a substantial growth of oil exploration and production. However, as shown in Table 36[12] the gap between India's demand for crude oil and her capacity to produce widened and is expected to widen even further.

Table 36
Indian production of crude oil in relation to demand (million tons)

	production	demand
1960-1	0.5	6.0
1965	3.0	9.5-10.0
1966	5.0	12.0-12.5
1970-1 (estimated)	10.0	24.5

The 1970-1 production figure is based on known reserves but it is hoped that existing areas of exploration may yield a further 2 million tons. It is clear, however, that India's crude oil imports will grow in volume.

At the beginning of this period the negligible supply from Digboi (Assam) oilfield represented the only indigenous production of crude and refined oil. The depletion of the Digboi oilfield encouraged further exploration by the Assam Oil Co., a subsidiary of Burmah Oil Co., which led to the development of the Naharkatiya oilfield to an extent where its annual capacity was 2.75m tons at the commencement of the Third Plan.[13]

The proven and indicated reserves of the Naharkatiya and neighbouring oilfields have been estimated at 44m tons.[14] The Indian government has progressively acquired a stake in exploration and drilling in this area. In January 1958, agreement was finally reached on the formation of a new rupee company, to be known as Oil India Ltd, in which the government was to have a third share.[15] Considerable acrimony seems to have surrounded the negotiations, which were evidently protracted throughout most of 1956 and 1957. An important feature of the agreement was a £10m loan by Burmah Oil Co. Ltd for the construction of a pipeline from the Naharkatiya oilfield to the proposed Gauhati (Assam) refinery, subsequently built with Rumanian assistance. This loan was later supplemented by a £3m loan from the British government. The Times (London), 7 December 1957, suggested five reasons for the delay in reaching agreement: 1. India's insistence on the establishment of a rupee company; 2. The governments' desire to participate to a far greater extent in the industry, which was related to a fear of a nationalisation on the part of the companies; 3. The government's attempt to acquire 50 per cent shares in the new company; 4. The late request for a loan towards the construction of the Gauhati pipeline; 5. The companies regarded the second refinery at Barauni (Bihar), which was to be connected by a further pipeline from Gauhati, eventually financed by Soviet Union, as uneconomic. The companies came subsequently to regard the Gauhati refinery in the same way,[16] and from the Burmah Oil Co's point of view, the arrangement must have appeared, at the very least, as highly unorthodox. One may also speculate on the extent to which the government endeavoured to obtain a loan for the second-stage pipeline from Burmah Oil Co.[17] Negotiations were obviously conducted in secret, but several press reports suggest the various additional tensions and complexities accompanying them. At one stage it appears that there may have been some question of three rupee companies to deal with exploration, drilling, refining and transport.[18] Such an organisational structure would presumably have involved government ownership of shares in Digboi refinery. An agreement was apparently reached on the structure of the new company in April 1957, but the terms were kept secret.[19] Just prior to this, rumours that the Assam Oil Co. was trying to retreat from its earlier intention to form a rupee company were officially denied.[20] It would appear that the question of the Gauhati refinery came more into prominence during the summer of 1957. The Assam government was reported to be negotiating with both French and Soviet agencies[21] and on 25 July the Union government, evidently under strong pressure from Assam, agreed to prepare a project report. Clearly this threw negotiations back into the melting pot. However, despite strong indications that the whole scheme was in great jeopardy,[22] the agreement was finally signed in January 1958. Three years later Oil India Ltd was further reorganised to give the Indian government and Burmah-Oil Co. Ltd 50-50 shareholdings.[23] In return Oil India Ltd was granted an exploration licence to cover an additional area in Assam of approximately eighteen hundred square miles. The Burmah Oil Co. evidently had little option but to make this bargain, due to the depletion of the Digboi oilfield.[24] In January 1962 the new arrangement was threatened by the Assamese government's refusal to issue exploration licences, on the grounds that the reorganisation had lost the state a substantial amount of revenue from royalties.[25] This led to a protracted series of talks and the issue was not finally settled until 11 November 1962.[26]

The only other region where oil has so far been successfully exploited is Gujarat, the main production areas being Ankleshwar and Cambay. Reserves in this region are estimated at 45 million tons and by 1963 production had reached 1,800 tons per day.[27] The development of these oilfields was substantially assisted by Russian capital and technical assistance.[28] In September-October 1955, K. D. Malaviya led an Indian mission overseas to explore the question of technical assistance towards exploration in India.[29] Events moved rapidly and a team of Soviet experts arrived in India in November 1955.[30] As a result of a preliminary survey, the Soviet team announced that substantial oil reserves existed within India.[31] On the strength of this, the government announced the establishment of a separate department within the Ministry of Natural Resources and Scientific Research, viz. the Oil and Natural Gas Commission, for the purpose of exploration and development.[32]

This organisation has so far achieved only limited success, although it has acquired valuable 'know-how' and must be credited with considerable versatility in its approach to problems. The operations of Oil India Ltd are outside its sphere of responsibility and therefore the only crude oil which it has so far brought into production has been from Gujarat.[33] Apart from these proven areas, efforts have been made to find oil in West Bengal, the Jaisalmer region of Rajasthan and in the Brahmaputra valley of Assam.[34] In West Bengal a joint venture was undertaken with Esso, but with total lack of success.[35] Agreement was reached with the French Institute of Petroleum, a consortium of private companies partly under government auspices, on 12 September 1961, for joint exploration of the Jaisalmer region.[36] Under this agreement the Institute was to provide technical assistance, but India would bear the risk. The French government agreed to provide Rs 3 million credit to cover foreign exchange costs. Evidently negotiations had taken place with Esso who were reported to have considered the government's terms too tough. In the government's view Esso were holding out for too high prices and tax reliefs, while refusing India's request for a 'buffer zone' near the Pakistan border.[37] Other countries approached for assistance included Italy[38] and Japan.[39]

In view of the fact that the gap between India's demand for and potential production of crude oil is widening,[40] and early hopes that vast unexploited resources might be found have been disappointed, India has attempted to reduce her dependence on foreign suppliers by investing in a joint exploration venture in Iran. An agreement was signed in 1965 allocating 50 per cent of capital investment to the National Iranian Oil Company, the remaining 50 per cent being divided equally between ENI (Italy), Phillips (United States) and the government of India.[41] Success in this venture would considerably strengthen the position of the public sector refineries.

Refining

India has so far established, or is in the process of establishing five refineries in the public sector. These are at Gauhati (Assam), Barauni (Bihar), Koyali (Gujarat), Cochin (Kerala), and Madras. The estimated capacity of these refineries when they are fully operational will be 11.75m tons.[42] The Soviet Union provided Rs11.9 crores of foreign exchange credit for the Barauni refinery, for which the agreement was signed in September 1959,[43] and Rs7.75m credit[44] for the Koyali refinery, for which J. Nehru laid the foundation stone on 10 May 1963.[45] The Gauhati refinery has been constructed with Rumanian assistance. Under an agreement signed in October 1958, Rumania provided credit worth Rs5.23 crores at 25 per cent interest over seven years.[46] In all these cases the refineries, although built with foreign assistance, were to be 100 per cent owned by the Indian government. However, in the case of the Cochin refinery, a quite novel structure was devised, which was further developed in the case of the Madras refinery. Under this first agreement, signed on 27 April 1963,[47] the government own 51 per cent of the shares, the American company Phillips Ltd own 25 per cent, the Calcutta firm of Duncan Bros hold 2 per cent and the remaining 22 per cent is to be issued to the Indian public or other persons determined by the Indian government. Phillips provide the initial foreign exchange and in return are guaranteed the right of nominating the managing director for ten years or until the foreign exchange debt is repaid.* A Board of nine is established, consisting of five government nominees, two Phillips nominees and two others, Duncan Bros being guaranteed one nominee for the first two years. Phillips are to act as import agents and to provide technical assistance, being paid for their services. This agreement provided the Indian government with a most important breakthrough in their dealings with the private companies. In subsequent months a spate of offers were received to build the proposed Madras refinery, conceding majority ownership to the government. Offers were reported to have been received from Esso, Shell International, Burmah Oil Co., Caltex, Gulf, Phillips, Mobil, ENI (Italy), Amoco, National Iranian Oil Co., and a consortium of Japanese companies. The Soviet Union also expressed interest.[48] In November 1965 an agreement[49] was eventually signed between the Indian government, the National Iranian Oil Company and the American International Oil Co. (Amoco). The most significant points of this agreement were: 1. Division of equity capital in the proportions–government of India–74 per cent, NIOC– 13 per cent, Amoco–13 per cent; 2. The majority of finance required for construction to be provided in loan form: the Indian government to provide the rupee equivalent of $4.68m with the other two partners each providing $11.16m. Thus the Indian government acquired 74 per cent control while providing only 17.3 per cent of the initial investment. At the same time all foreign exchange was provided by the two foreign partners; 3. During the period of the loan the foreign partners will have automatic right to nominate two directors each on the board of thirteen. Thereafter all thirteen directors are to be elected at large by the shareholders, giving the government theoretical power to fill all the vacancies; 4. The government of India has power to appoint the chairman of the board and the managing director; 5. Dollar loans are at 5.5 per cent over fifteen years; 6. Darius Crude oil (Persian Gulf) is to be supplied according to an agreed price formula. Substitute crude oil may be used only insofar as the refinery suffers no net economic disadvantage thereby. Indigenous crude must be supplied on terms as favourable as those offered to other Indian refineries; 7. Refinery products must be sold on terms as favourable as those obtainable by other refineries; 8. The foreign partners will have first option to participate in any future expansion programme; 9. Provision is made for arbitration, but in the final analysis the Indian government retains control through the provision that the chief justice

*Initially, this nomination is made for only five years.

of India shall appoint an umpire in the event of a deadlock between the respective arbitrators.

The contrast with the three original refinery agreements could hardly be more complete. India's tough bargaining policy, coupled with the substantial growth in world oil supplies had created a situation where the major world consortiums were competing keenly for outlets for their crude oil, and were now prepared to concede India's demand for public sector control. The nearest unsuccessful offers came from Shell and Burmah Oil Co., who offered to build an ancillary fertiliser plant. The NIOC offer was successful, apparently, because they offered the best terms with regard to supply of crude oil and acceptance of Indian supplies and further offered a more extensive fertiliser plant with 51 per cent Indian ownership.[50]

Negotiations are in progress for the construction of a refinery at Haldia near Calcutta. Only two offers have so far been forthcoming, from a French consortium and a joint American-German offer from Mobil Oil Co. and Phoenix Rheindorf. A number of oil companies are evidently reluctant to bid, having found the government's terms too tough during the Madras negotiations. However, this situation may only be temporary.[51]

A further refinery is envisaged somewhere in north-west India for the Fourth Plan period, but as yet the site has not been selected and must presumably await the outcome of negotiations over Haldia. The shelving of the Fourth Plan may well postpone this project for some considerable time.

Distribution

The government has established its own distribution network with a view to at least partially offsetting the companies' dominance in this field. The Indian Oil Co. (IOC), a government agency, was established in 1959.[52] The main sources of supply envisaged were: 1. Imports from the Soviet Union and eastern Europe; 2. Output from public sector refineries. Initially the new agency was entirely dependent on the former source, but the latter source will become increasingly important. Vigorous efforts were made to persuade distributors, especially state and local authorities, to switch from their original sources of supply. However, many difficulties had to be overcome, notably lack of storage facilities, exclusive dealing discounts offered by private companies, and price competition (in itself a considerable success for the government's policy).[53] The government proposed to spend Rs10 crores during the Third Plan on the distribution programme,[54] which will depend for its success on the IOC's ability to guarantee regular supplies on more favourable terms than the companies. This in turn depends on 1. the terms on which refined products can be imported from sources other than those of the major oil companies. already established, the primary alternative source being the Soviet bloc; 2. The successful implementation of the public sector refining programme; 3. The proportion of refinery capacity controlled by the Indian government in the long period. With regard to the first factor, in the early stages it would appear that India was striking a very good bargain, though official figures are not available.[55] One report stated that Russia was offering prices 15-18 per cent lower than Persian Gulf posted prices.[56] Another report claimed that she was charging her eastern European 'satellites' nearly double the price for which she was offering oil products to the outside world.[57] It may also be reasonable to infer that the Soviet Union was accepting rupee payment.[58] Assuming these various suppositions to be correct, one must thoroughly doubt the long-term willingness of the Soviet Union to continue offering oil on such favourable terms, on three grounds. First, her continued economic capacity to sacrifice substantial foreign exchange earnings is doubtful in the context of the rapid expansion of her external trade, though this will naturally be affected by total world supply and demand for oil. Secondly, there would appear to be a trend towards greater assertion of independence in the eastern European Communist countries, which will make it no longer possible for the Soviet Union to subsidise oil or other exports to developing countries in this way.[59] Thirdly, if the 'thaw' in the Cold War between America and Russia continues, it is likely that the latter will become less sharply competitive in her interpretation of the concept of 'peaceful coexistence'. On the other hand the growing glut on the world oil market is a factor working in India's favour. To date at least, IOC's share of the market has shown rapid growth, increasing from 8.2 per cent in 1963 to 25 per cent in 1965. A target of 50 per cent is envisaged for 1971.[60]

Related to the distribution programme is the establishment of several product pipelines in the public sector, the most notable being two from Barauni refinery to Calcutta (330 miles) and Kanpur (430 miles). Agreement was reached with ENI (Italy) for a credit of Rs2 crores (total cost estimated at Rs11.3 crores) foreign exchange to cover imports of equipment, technical assistance, etc.[61]

Private Sector expansion?

The new efforts of the Indian government in the various directions

indicated have raised the fundamental question of the future of the oil companies in India. Tensions have arisen over a whole range of issues connected with the government's policy of expanded participation in the industry which has led to progressively tougher bargaining. The expansion of the public sector is related to the future expansion of the private sector. In spite of rapidly expanding demand for oil products which at present exceeds India's productive capacity, expansion of the private sector has been curtailed as a matter of policy. No very clear explanations have been offered for this policy, but two likely reasons may be suggested:
1. The intention is to ensure that the public sector gains the dominant share of refining capacity within a few years. The original Fourth Plan target envisaged a total refinery capacity of 24.5m tons by 1971. The private sector is to be pegged at its 1965 capacity of 7.75m tons, while the public sector is to expand from its 1964 capacity of 4.75m tons to 16.75m tons as shown in table 37.[62]

Table 37
Target refinery capacities in 1970-1 (1964 capacities in brackets)

				millions of tons	
	private sector			public sector	
Burmah-Shell	3.75	(3.75)	Gauhati	0.85	(0.75)
Esso	2.50	(2.50)	Barauni	3.00	(2.00)
Caltex	1.05	(1.05)	Koyali	3.00	(2.00)
Digboi	0.45	(0.45)	Cochin	2.40	
			Madras	2.50	
			Haldia	2.50	
			N.W. India	2.50	
total	7.75			16.75	

2. The government may be using expansion as a bait to the companies to make concessions and radically revise the refinery agreements. The companies, on the other hand, maintain that on pure economic grounds there are excellent arguments for their being allowed to expand capacity, placing special emphasis on the growing import gap, in the context of chronic foreign exchange shortage. Burmah-Shell are reported to have claimed that a 1 million ton expansion would cost £2.1m compared with an estimated cost of £18.75m for building the Gauhati refinery, whose initial capacity was only 0.75m tons.[63] Annual foreign exchange costs to meet the deficit in oil products by the end of the Third Plan would be £45m equivalent, a cost which the companies could save India by

expansion. Furthermore they claimed to be partly financing the development of the public sector, in that price reductions were not passed on to the consumer but retained by the government in the form of tax. The concessions over the years were estimated at approximately Rs115 crores, roughly equivalent to the public sector outlay proposed for the industry during the Third Plan.[64] A third possible consideration is that the government might be prepared to allow expansion in return for a willingness by the companies to process Russian crude oil. However, there have been no signs of any such concession by the latter. At present only Gauhati, Barauni and Koyali of the public sector refineries are in commission, but only Gauhati was fully productive at the end of 1965.[65] The private refineries thus still supply the vast bulk of refined products at present. There has been a rise in imports during the Third Plan from 1.0m tons in 1960 to 2.9m tons in 1963. Demand estimates for 1970 are 22.34m tons, and thus in theory adequate Indian productive capacity will be available.[66] In view of the slow performance of the public sector to date and the fact that two public sector refineries included in the original Fourth Plan target have yet to be negotiated, one may reasonably speculate that without private sector expansion, import demand may in fact increase. The companies would therefore seem to be in a position to take the long view.

B. K. Nehru, the Indian ambassador to the United States, expressed fears as to the effect of India's oil policy on the 1961 meeting of the 'Aid India Club', to which the World Bank is stated to have submitted a report describing this policy as 'ideological'. India for her part denies that her policy is ideological. The official explanation for restriction on private sector expansion is in terms of location. It is argued that such expansion would accentuate the already heavy concentration of capacity in the Bombay region, whereas the government's strategy is to establish a balanced pattern of regional location.[68] While conceding that initial costs are higher, it is argued that in the long period the government's policy will produce a more economic pattern of production and distribution. Research into oil transport economics, beyond the scope of this work, would be necessary to establish whether the dispute was in fact being conducted on economic or political grounds, but one suspects the latter.

Challenge to the refinery agreements

Since the later years of the Second Plan there has been continuous dispute between the government and the three Indian companies over prices. This has been related to other issues, of which the most important are the processing of indigenous and Russian crude oil, import of refined products, and capacity expansion. In the background is always the question of the status of the Refinery Agreements. These have so far been scrupulously maintained, though differences of interpretation have arisen. Revision may always be offered by the companies in exchange for other concessions.

The original three Refinery Agreements had established the 'import parity' principle for the pricing of refined products, i.e. prices should not exceed the landed cost, including wharfage, landing charges and import duty available to the companies for comparable products.[69] By about 1960 a radical change had come over the world oil market, compared with the time when the agreements were signed.[70] In spite of rapidly rising world demand, new sources of supply proved still more abundant. The Indian government has been most anxious to take advantage of discounts available on Persian Gulf posted prices, but due to the integrated nature of the Indian companies' operations this has proved difficult. The companies made a series of price concessions, as well as giving up the duty concession on motor gasoline laid down in the agreements; Burmah-Shell also agreed to terminate the complex Valued Stock Account procedure whereby costs were based on f.o.b. Ras Tanura (U.S. Gulf), whereas crude oil was in fact supplied from the Persian Gulf.[71] Dissatisfied with the companies' concessions, the government set up an Oil Price Enquiry Committee (OEPC) under the chairmanship of Shri K. R. Damle, which reported in July 1961.[72] A primary purpose of the Damle committee was to consider the availability of discounts of Persian Gulf posted prices. The companies adopted the position that their prices were competitive, that long-term discounts on a sound commercial basis were not available to their suppliers.[73] A large part of the Damle Report is therefore devoted to establishing that the Indian companies and their suppliers were in fact part of an integrated organisation. The companies' evasions on this score were grossly impolitic. Intermediate companies were named but it was claimed by the refining companies that the original suppliers of crude oil were unknown to them. The main findings and recommendations of the committee may be summarised as follows:[74]

1. The Indian companies were making little or no effort to obtain widely available discounts, and should make every effort to do so, if necessary at the expense of their own sources of supply.

2. A formula was laid down for calculating the discounts available on various categories of refined products, based on f.o.b. Abadan.[75] This

formula was to be reflected in future prices of refined products and to be enforced through foreign exchange control. Technically this is not a breach of the Refinery Agreements though it does involve a unilateral interpretation of the 'import parity' principle by the Indian government.

3. The 'import parity' principle should take account of import sources for refined products other than those of the three major companies.

4. Although the companies' rights under the agreements are recognised, the new factor of cheap Russian crude oil should be recognised and the companies should either show willingness to process Russian crude oil, or if this is impossible obtain equivalent discounts from their suppliers.

The degree to which the Damle Report achieved a further reduction in prices is not clear. The OPEC formula was immediately adopted against vehement protests from the companies,[76] and was officially in operation from 1 October 1961 until 30 September 1965. A new Working Group on Oil Prices (the Talukdar Committee) reported in August 1965.[77] The government had earlier found that the OPEC formula could not easily be applied to a multiplicity of grades and specifications and in order to impose block control over prices and profits and to counter loose control by the companies in certain categories, charged an additional non-recoverable duty of Rs30 per ton in May 1965.[78] The Talukdar Report was intended to establish a more stable formula, while also reviewing the complaints of the companies concerning the OPEC formula.[79]

The Talukdar Report rejected the companies' major complaints and, arguing that higher discounts were available than at the time of the Damle Report, recommended yet higher discounts as a basis for pricing and foreign exchange allocation.[80] Numerous examples of discounts being offered, often by the three companies to other parties, not merely as temporary bargains, but as regular and continuing features of the world oil market, were quoted.[81] The claim that Russian oil sales to India and elsewhere were temporary political arrangements rather than serious commercial transactions was also denied.[82] There is, however, one important inconsistency in the Report. The companies had contested the OPEC formula of 12 per cent on capital employed as being an appropriate profit margin, claiming that after various other factors including taxation had been taken into account, the net return to the marketing companies was in the region of 3-4 per cent. The committee argued that in view of vertical integration of the industry and the profits earned on crude oil for which the Indian companies provided an outlet, it would not be 'appropriate to compare their operations with the other industries operating in this country, unless their overall profitability right from production to marketing of refined products is known.[83] At another point, however, in the process of arguing with most convincing logic that the companies are integrated organisations whose prices are necessarily managed and that, therefore, far from bargaining for discounts, they will actively seek to avoid them, the Report stated that:

One of the companies has stated frankly that it has made sizable investment in India in its integrated refining and marketing operations for the purpose of distributing its own products and cannot be expected to distribute the products of another party having no comparable investment in India. We are here considering the imported products which this country is entitled to get at the most economical price. The marketing companies will get their return for distributing such products, irrespective of the source of supply.[84]

The government of India is hardly entitled to argue the case both ways. A further point on which there is likely to be dispute is the terms on which the Indian companies will be expected to accept indigenous crude. Deliveries from Ankleshwar to the Bombay refineries are growing continually and even after Koyali is fully operational the private refineries must expect to receive one million tons of crude annually from this source.[85] The ONGC argued to the Talukdar Committee that a price based upon the 'import parity' principle was unlikely to cover costs, even when optimum production had been achieved. The committee urged an enquiry to examine what overheads other than those connected directly with Ankleshwar were being included in the ONGC's cost estimates.[86] However, it is always open to the Indian government, if ONGC's costs cannot be brought down sufficiently, to extract a higher price from the companies, either directly or through import duties on their external crude oil supplies. For this reason the companies have put forward a request, as part of a deal to amend the Refinery Agreements, that an agreement should be reached as to the share of indigenous crude oil each company should be obliged to accept.[87] So far the companies have held firm in refusing to process imported crude oil, other than through their own suppliers, but in the event of their being obliged to change their position, they would presumably wish for a similar arrangement. The government has not acceded to this request, preferring to maintain flexibility.

Future prospects

The question as to the ultimate intentions of the government with regard to the future of the private sector in this industry is still open. On record are fairly recent statements by K. D. Malaviya to the effect that ultimately all branches of the industry 'from search to sale' must come under the public sector,[88] and by J. Nehru who, when laying the foundation stone for the Koyali refinery, stressed the future dominance of the public sector, Indo-Russian friendship and the fact that oil search had only been successful in the past six or seven years when conducted in the public sector.[89] Shri Malaviya was ousted from the government in 1963, but his successors have generally continued his policies, even if the tone of the debate has become rather less acrimonious.

The private sector is at present hemmed in at all points. Refinery expansion is curtailed at least until 1971. The government is making every effort to hold prices of refined products on the basis of a bare net profit to the marketing companies while seeking the maximum discounts on crude oil, the remaining source of profit to the companies. At the same time IOC is steadily undermining their marketing position. There appears to be an application of dual standards emerging. While the highest standards of competitiveness, bargaining and efficiency are expected from the private sector, the public sector will probably continue to be supported by numerous concealed subsidies and market distortions. All the political and many of the market advantages seem now to lie with India, but the desperation of her foreign exchange situation must lead her to strike the hardest possible bargain with the companies. From India's point of view it can well be argued that the companies took undue advantage of their monopolistic position at an earler period, and failed to make reasonable concessions in good time. At an earlier stage a revision of the Refinery Agreements to incorporate Indian capital might well have proved a most acceptable gesture. The Indian government would now appear to be little interested in this issue and the public sector philosophy seems more firmly rooted. In the changed circumstances prevailing in recent years most conditions of the agreements, other than nationalisation, have proved amenable to pressure without involving breach of contract.

The industry is still listed under Schedule A of the Industrial Policy Resolution, but as has been proved in the case of other industries, such as fertiliser, its future will be determined by economic rather than political considerations. The foreign companies' existing investments must be regarded as 'captive' and their powers of bargaining are thus strictly limited, but as a short-term measure the threat of witholding supplies could still be a potent weapon, though self-defeating in the long term. The companies foresee little hope of change in their favour before 1971, but hope the situation may thereafter improve. If demand should prove to have been underestimated or public sector plans are seriously delayed, the postion of the private sector would be far stronger. On past evidence, both of these possibilities seem quite likely. Continued upward estimates of demand have been made by government agencies, while the growth of the public sector has been conspicously slow and the market is still dominated at present by the three major companies. The expansion of the public sector will continue to depend greatly on Soviet support, which at present is only showing expansion in the supply of products.

The balance of power situation at present obtaining in the industry may be summarised as follows. India has made definite though slow progress in establishing public enterprise in all aspects of the oil industry. This may have involved an uneconomic use of resources, but perhaps the gain in bargaining power will bring her greater economic return in the long term. It must be admitted that India has shown extraordinary versatility in seeking methods to break the Western companies' monopoly, whatever the judgment may be on her actual administrative efficiency. However, it is clear that no breakthrough to public sector operation could have been achieved without help from the Soviet bloc and the oil industry amply demonstrates the point stressed repeatedly by senior Indian officials that India's 'non-alignment' policy has made possible, both through Soviet bloc aid and the Western response to it, patterns of economic development that would not otherwise have been possible.

The significance of foreign aid in the oil industry is generally clear, and the contrast between the roles played by the Soviet bloc and Western countries equally clear. Apart from some Italian assistance in the construction of product pipelines[90] and some French participation in the as yet unsuccessful exploration venture in Rajasthan,[91] Western governments have given no assistance to the public sector, leaving the initiative to private firms. By contrast, the Soviet Union had authorised Rs57 crores by the end of 1964 (24.9 per cent of total Soviet aid up to then) towards public sector projects in the oil industry.[92] This industry is perhaps the most politically sensitive of all Indian industries in that the question of foreign domination of crucial supplies arises in its most dramatic form. At the same time it represents an important test case in the perennial domestic struggle as to the correct respective roles of public and private sectors. In this context the political significance of Russia's contribution to India's public sector development, by contrast with Western aloofness, can scarcely be overestimated.

Chapter 8

Foreign aid in the steel industry

The political issues in the Indian steel industry relevant to this work are rather different to those in the oil industry. The main feature of the latter is the conflict between the Indian government and the foreign oil companies. In the steel industry, by contrast, foreign investment is a less significant factor, but relations with foreign governments are of vital importance, since foreign aid has played a crucial role in steel development.

The government's general policy has been to establish public sector dominance over the whole industry and complete public ownership of all new enterprises connected with pig iron and basic steel production, though the private sector dominates in respect of steel products. However, the two large private corporations in existence before the First Plan was commenced, Tata Iron and Steel Co. Ltd (TISCO) and Indian Iron and Steel Co. Ltd (IISCO) have not been nationalised, and have in fact been allowed to expand substantially. Table 38 shows that the public sector by no means dominates the industry in terms of production, though on the basis of existing policies this may be expected to happen over a period of years.

Table 38
Production and rated capacity of Indian steel mills (million tons)

during 1964-5	steel ingots		finished steel	
name of project	rated capacity	production	rated capacity	production
public sector				
Bhilai	1.00	1.26	0.88	0.91
Durgapur	1.00	1.01	0.81	0.72
Rourkela	1.016	0.98	0.72	0.70
Mysore iron and steel works	0.047	0.047	0.04	0.04
total	3.063	3.297	2.45	2.37
private sector				
TISCO	2.00	1.95	1.54	1.56
IISCO	1.00	0.96	0.80	0.76
total	6.063	6.207	4.79	4.69

On this basis the public sector produced 53.1 per cent of steel ingots and 50.5 per cent of finished steel, against 6.9 per cent and 49.5 per cent respectively for the private sector.[2] According to the targets for the end of the Fourth Plan, however, it is intended that the private sector's share will diminish considerably. Production in 1970-1 is estimated as follows:[3]

Table 39
Estimated steel production and capacity in 1970-1 (million tons)

public sector	production	capacity
Bhilai	3.0	3.6
Rourkela	2.0	2.5
Durgapur	3.0	3.4
Bokaro	1.5	1.7
total	9.5	11.2
private sector		
TISCO	2.2	2.2
IISCO	1.3	1.3
total	3.5	3.5
grand total	13.0	14.7

The public sector will thus account for 73.1 per cent of production and 76.0 per cent of capacity.

Aid: distribution and terms

Foreign aid towards the development of India's steel industry is shown in table 40[4].

Two main points emerge from these figures. Firstly, a very high proportion (84.15%) of foreign assistance authorised to his industry has been channelled to the public sector, indicating India's success in gaining acceptance of her economic policies among the majority of donor countries. However, it should be noted that both the U.S.A. and the World Bank have contributed only to the private sector. This reflects the policy of those two parties that public enterprise should only occur in the 'infra-structure' sector of the economy.[5]

The steel industry provides a particularly useful opportunity to compare techniques and approaches to aid projects. The three public sector steel mills at Bhilai (Madya Pradesh), Durgapur (West Bengal) and Rourkela (Orissa) have been assisted by Russia, Britain and West Germany respectively. The more or less simultaneous development of these three

Table 40
Foreign aid allocations to steel projects (to 31st December 1964) (crores of rupees)

donor	project	date	amount authorised	amount utlised
Soviet Union	Bhilai	2 Feb. 1955	64.74	64.74
Soviet Union	Bhilai expansion	12 Sep. 1959	56.47	56.47
Soviet Union	Bokaro	25 Jan. 1965	100.50	100.50
United Kingdom*	Durgapur	20 June 1958	20.00	20.00
United Kingdom	Durgapur expansion	23 May 1962	29.33	10.34
United Kingdom	Durgapur expansion	17 Mar. 1964	6.67	0.25
West Germany	Rourkela	26 Feb. 1958	78.57	77.64
West Germany	Rourkela refinance	30 Jan. 1961	11.71	11.71
West Germany	Rourkela refinance	4 May 1962	10.12	10.12
West Germany	Rourkela refinance	25 Apr. 1963	7.31	7.31
West Germany	Rourkela expansion	25 Apr. 1963	47.62	19.66
West Germany	Rourkela expansion	26 Nov. 1963	1.66	–
West Germany	Rourkela expansion	15 Sep. 1964	10.71	10.71
IBRD	IISCO	18 Dec. 1952	13.90	13.90
IBRD	IISCO expansion	19 Dec. 1956	9.50	9.50
IBRD	IISCO expansion	22 Dec. 1961	9.30	1.20
IBRD	TISCO	26 June 1956	35.70	35.70
IBRD	TISCO expansion	20 Nov. 1957	15.50	15.50
total			529.31	465.25

*Excludes Rs 15.33 crores loan from Lazard Bros syndicate on 5th January 1957.
N.B. The Rourkela and Durgapur extensions have subsequently been postponed.

mills, their initially identical capacity targets and the fact that they have all been built for ultimate Indian management and ownership in the public sector have inevitably led to drawing of sharp comparisons and to a high priority being placed on these projects by donor countries. However, great care is necessary in this context, as conditions vary. For example, Rourkela and Durgapur have been far more affected by labour troubles than Bhilai and one might thus superficially conclude that the Russians have handled labour more competently than the British or Germans. This may in fact be the case, but it ignores the fact that from the inception of all these projects Indian management has held an important and progressively more dominant place: Furthermore, local factors have worked more in favour of Bhilai. Rourkela and Durgapur have attracted refugee labour from East Pakistan, which has stimulated communal troubles, especially at Rourkela. West Bengal has been a very unstable state due to the strong Communist influence there[6] and the dynamic and turbulent nature of Calcutta politics. Madya Pradesh is, in these respects, a far quieter state politically; furthermore, one may assume that Communists with influence in labour unions would be concerned not to embarrass a Soviet financed project. Thirdly, it must be remembered that India has been responsible for providing a wide range of services. All three projects have been accorded the highest priority by the Planning Commission, but effective comparisions can only be made in conjunction with intensive analysis (beyond the scope of this study) of the performance of the various Indian authorities.

Loan terms for the three projects are summarised in table 41[7]

Table 41
Interest rates on foreign assisted steel projects

project	interest rate	repayment period	grace period
Durgapur	consolidated fund rate (5½-6 per cent) plus ¼ per cent management fee	11 years	8 years
Durgapur extension	consolidated fund rate (5½-6 per cent))plus ¼ per cent management fee	25 years	7 years
Bhilai	2½ per cent	12 years	1 year
Bhilai extension	2½ per cent	12 years	1 year
Rourkela	6.3 per cent	3 years	3 years
Rourkela services and maintenance	3 per cent	20 years	7 years
Rourkela extension	5¾ per cent	20 years	5 years
Rourkela refinance	5¼-5½ per cent	12-16 years (except 1960-1 4 years)	(variable)

Rourkela clearly offers India the worst bargain. Table 40 has shown the Rourkela price to be the highest, with Durgapur lowest. With regard to extension projects, the Bhilai price per ton capacity works out lowest, with Rourkela again highest.[8] A comparison of initial loan terms shows Rourkela charging the highest interest rates, its initial repayment period–three years–being the shortest. Only in respect of the small loan, negotiated in 1962, for services and maintenance are the German terms at all generous. Constant refinancing of loans has added to India's debt burden, and up to the end of 1963 no repayments had been made on the original Rourkela loan, compared with Bhilai repayments totalling Rs32.92 crores out of Rs64.74 crores due (plus interest).[9] Consultancy fees at

Rourkela have come under sharp criticism, and to a lesser extent at Durgapur,[10] though probably the cumbersome contract arrangements are mainly responsible for the high cost.

Rourkela–Bhilai–Durgapur: Negotiations

Negotiations for the three contracts were very complex and conducted against the background of tension in India's external relations prevailing at the time. However, simultaneous negotiation for the three mills improved her bargaining position. Unfortunately, evidence is somewhat fragmentary, and a full account of this fascinating sequence of negotiations must await publication of official documents. The following account is based on Press reports and government of India publications:

It appears that Rourkela was the earliest project to take definite shape, having been mooted early in the First Plan.[11] The official Review of the First Five Year Plan comments on the 'relatively slow progress' in executing the project, due to the time taken in negotiation and the large volume of preparation involved.[12] No doubt Indian inexperience contributed to this delay, whatever the faults on the German side. There were initial doubts over the capacity, which was finally fixed at 1 million tons in July 1955,[13] though the project itself was not finalised until November 1956.[14] The question of management and ownership was also a source of friction, Krupp-Demag initially acting as consultants and theoretically as coordinators, but in practice the Indian government was negotiating with a multiplicity of sub-contractors either directly or indirectly.[15] Thus each stage involved separate negotiations, and until well into the Third Plan, when Hindustan Steel Ltd had taken firm control, the project appears to have been operating in a managerial vacuum. With regard to ownership, Krupp-Demag initially held a 20 per cent shareholding. Originally this was to last nine years, after which Krupp-Demag had the option to sell at 20 per cent premium on the face value of the shares, thus guaranteeing a dividend, in addition to consultancy fees.[16] However, in November 1956, when the agreement was finalised, the German firm agreed to surrender both its shareholding and its directorships.[17]

The first indication of the Russian offer to build Bhilai came in August 1954, with an indirect approach through a private concern by the Russian Trade Commissioner.[18] On 10 September 1954 India accepted the offer 'without prejudice', subject to a satisfactory project report.[19] India found the terms attractive from the beginning, and only five months later, on 3 February 1955, an agreement was signed, on which occasion Shri K.

Reddy, Minister of Production, compared the speed of negotiation and preparation of the project reports favourable with Rourkela, where, after fifteen months, major issues were still unresolved.[20] However, public opinion and government were not without misgivings. There were some doubts as to whether the Russian offer was genuine or for propaganda purposes.[21] Political exploitation was feared in some quarters, and there is evidence that Dr B. C. Roy, chief minister of West Bengal, refused to allow Russian assistance for the Durgapur project.[22] There were further doubts as to Soviet Union's technical ability and standards of quality.[23] More seriously, India was apprehensive of Western reaction. G. D. Birla, a leading steel industrialist, left for Europe and the United States almost immediately following the initial Russian offer, evidently with the government's sympathy, in order to arouse interest in investment in the steel industry.[24] In view of the timing of this visit, a reasonable interpretation is that it was intended to reassure Western opinion, already alarmed by possible trends towards nationalisation and 'economic nationalism', while at the same time using the Russian offer to apply gentle pressure for more favourable offers from the West. The mission was eminently successful in its impact on British government and financial opinion, resulting first in an offer for investment in the Birla-dominated Indian Iron and Steel Co.[25] and, after this had been refused by India, in an offer to build a mill in the public sector.[26] Although the Russian offer clearly had a catalytic effect on Britain, and indeed stimulated negotiations, albeit unsuccessful, with France[27] and Japan,[28] neither the Russian offer nor the Birla mission affected American attitudes. Although IISCO and TISCO received substantial American investment through the World Bank for their own expansion projects,[29] opinion in that country remained firmly opposed to assisting public sector steel projects.[30] In fact, there was a strong tendency to see American investment in these private steel companies as an excellent opportunity to demonstrate both the technical and ideological superiority of private enterprise.[31] Thus, India's attempts to use the Bhilai offer as a bargaining counter with the United States failed. It is therefore hypothetical to speculate as to the degree of enthusiasm with which she signed the Bhilai agreement. A number of negative reasons have been suggested, in addition to lack of response from the United States. Internal politics may have played a part, in that there was a current of opinion in favour of economic neutrality as a logical extension of political neutrality;[32] secondly, there were frequent reports of inter-departmental rivalries, the main protagonists being K. Reddy, Minister of Production and T. T. Krishnamachari,

Minister of Commerce and Industry and Minister of Iron and Steel after the creation of that Ministry in May 1955. The former is said to have favoured a more vigorous public sector policy than the latter.[33] If this is so, then Krishnamachari's appointment as Minister of Iron and Steel may be regarded as a victory for the 'gradualist' viewpoint and as an effort to reassure Western opinion. However, by that time the Soviet offer had been accepted. It must be remembered that though Soviet aid is now firmly established and welcome, at that time its implications were as yet unexplored, the era of hard Stalinist orthodoxy towards 'bourgeois nationalism'[34] in Asia having only recently passed. Thus, one may argue that as in the oil industry, Russian aid was seen as offering a 'breakthrough' towards the pattern of industrial development required by India, though parallel efforts were made to gain the West's cooperation in achieving such development. One Indian press comment to the effect that the Soviet offer was being accepted 'out of curiosity and as a relief from the feeling of oppression surrounding Indo-American relations'[35] seems to sum up well the uncertain, faintly disenchanted but doggedly empirical approach of the Indian government at that time.

Comparative impact of the Rourkela, Bhilai and Durgapur projects

Initial pointers towards evaluating relative performance of the three mills can be provided, although the complexities are very great. Comparative figures for gross and net profits from 1962-4 are shown in tables 42[36] and 43.[37]

Table 42
Gross profits* of public sector projects (Rs million)

	Bhilai	Durgapur	Rourkela
1962-3	54.68	4.73	5.43
1963-4	114.11	91.08	60.00

*After interest payments but before depreciation.

Table 43
Net profits of public sector steel projects (Rs million)

	Bhilai	Durgapur	Rourkela
1962-3*	-44.89	-84.46	-107.20
1963-4	14.65	-1.89	-63.17

*Allows for adjustment of steel retention prices.

Bhilai's performance is the most impressive, with Rourkela again lagging. The high loss figures for the latter project reflects, amongst other things, the heavy burden of repayments.[38]

Table 44[39] compares performance as a percentage of rated capacity—a pertinent test of the degree to which targets are being achieved.

Table 44
Percentage achievement on rated capacity of public sector steel projects

	Bhilai		Durgapur		Rourkela	
	1963	1964	1963	1964	1963	1964
coke	92	98	107	101	92	83
hot metal	103	114	101	104	97	90
ingot steel	108	113	91	98	95	94
saleable steel	99	103	86	88	74	92

Bhilai leads in all fields except coke production, while Rourkela's performance is the weakest in most instances.[40]

It might plausibly be argued that the speed with which foreign personnel are replaced by Indians is an indication of the degree to which the projects have reached normal operating efficiency. Table 45[41] gives the numbers of foreign technicians working on the respective projects.

Table 45
Foreign technicians employed in public sector steel projects (as of 1st January)

	Bhilai	Durgapur*	Rourkela
1963			
operation and maintenance	42	71	218
expansion	15	–	–
1964			
operation and maintenance	37	57	256
expansion	179	–	–
1965			
operation and maintenance	21	43	95
expansion	298	–	–

*Expansion projects subsequently deferred

Thus until the major expansion project of 2.5m tons capacity took serious shape, Bhilai had been by far the quickest to dispense with foreign personnel, with Rourkela slowest.[42]

Indian administrators have generally rated Bhilai the most efficient of the three plants and Rourkela the least efficient. The above figures, limited though they are, give support to this judgment, which is reinforced by numerous reports of technical and labour difficulties at the Rourkela plant,[43] and to a lesser extent at Durgapur.[44] There do not appear to be any special factors with regard to quality, technical conditions or location[45] which would alter this balance of judgment as to relative efficiency, nor can any clear case be made out that Rourkela's troubles were due to Indian mismanagement, as the Germans have vehemently insisted.[46] Such mismanagement no doubt occurs to some extent in all three mills, but there seems to be no evidence why this should be a special factor at Rourkela. One would suggest that Rourkela's troubles stem primarily from its deficiencies of organisational structure, where there has been no clear relationship between German and Indian authorities, nor any coordination between the German contractors themselves.

While earlier caveats should be observed, it should be noted that Rourkela is officially regarded as the least efficient of the three projects.[47] What is politically significant, however, is that these results provide sufficient evidence for the politically-minded section of the Indian public to make comparisons in the order of merit suggested by the foregoing analysis. To this extent Russian aid has been thoroughly vindicated in the public and official mind and Bhilai has provided the maximum 'demonstration impact' possible of Russian industrial power and efficiency. Against this, serious efforts have been made since about 1961 to correct the major faults at Rourkela,[48] and the tables cited show a marked improvement in performance towards the end of the period under consideration. As all three mills become more obviously Indian enterprises the political significance of the factors mentioned may be expected to diminish.

Intangible factors must influence the drawing of political comparisons. A pertinent though subjective factor in this context is the 'atmosphere' surrounding these three projects. The dilemma here is that there are no objective standards of measurement, but equally one cannot objectively ignore factors that affect political attitudes. The best course, therefore, is to offer a selection of viewpoints.

Several commentators note an atmosphere of austerity and seriousness of purpose at Bhilai[49] compared with Durgapur and Rourkela. One commentator claimed that because of this Bhilai excites young Indians in a way that other foreign aid projects fail to do.[50] There are varying accounts of Russian relations with Indians at Bhilai. They have been described as 'extravagantly friendly'[51] on the one hand and 'friendly but separate' on the other.[52] There seems general agreement that the simplicity of Russian living is well accepted.[53] One interesting and unusual explanation to account for good Indo-Russian relations is the claim that Indians feel more at ease with Russians than with West Europeans or Americans, since they can feel that cultural superiority compensates for technical weakness.[54] If such cultural attitudes exist, however, there seem no valid grounds for applying them exclusively to Indo-Russian relations, and the fact that differences of wealth are less apparent would seem a far more potent factor. There have been widespread accusations of German exclusiveness, based on separate swimming baths, hospitals, social facilities, etc.[55] and defences based on natural language and social barriers carry little weight in this case.[56] In this respect Durgapur seems to occupy a middle position. Apart from Communist sources,[57] there have been no serious charges of British exclusiveness. British facilities are open to Indians earning over £56 monthly, but here financial and social barriers inevitably play a part.[58]

Russian and German training and managerial approaches have been compared, to the detriment of the latter, though evidence is somewhat fragmentary. At a crude level it has been charged that Germans at Rourkela tend to shout and are intolerant and contemptuous of inefficiency, whereas Russians at Bhilai are more patient and stick to an advisory role more carefully.[59] One might argue that sheer weight of numbers of foreign personnel would add to frictions in this context; thus in 1959 there were sixteen hundred German personnel compared with approximately seven hundred Russians.[60] At a more sophisticated level a comparison has been drawn between German technical instruction and the efforts of a Professor of Mathematics endeavouring to communicate his most advanced findings to a raw graduate student. Russians, by contrast, are given credit for endeavouring to communicate with Indians at their own level of technical knowledge.[61] To meet these problems it was suggested that future contracts should lay down that information be provided in the form that India requires it.[62]

Bokaro

The Bokaro (Bihar) project was programmed in the official Third Five Year Plan and was scheduled to commence production before the end of the Plan period.[63] However, it was not until January 1965 that satisfactory arrangements were made for foreign assistance and an agreement concluded with the Soviet Union.[64] During the Second Plan period India was preoccupied with establishment of the first three public sector mills, though tentative negotiations over Bokaro were carried on in various quarters. Although at different times the United Kingdom,[65] the Soviet Union,[66] Japan[67] and West Germany[68] were in the picture, it seemed likely from about 1960 onwards, until withdrawal of the Indian request in September 1963, that an agreement would be signed with the United States. The Bokaro negotiations were an unhappy experience for both countries. A variety of factors played a part in the failure of these negotiations, though undoubtedly the major sources of dispute were concerned with management and ownership. On the first issue American opinion adhered generally to the 'turnkey' concept, whereby Americans would build the plant, manage it for a period and then hand it over to India in perfect working order.[69] Ten years was regarded as a suitable period in this context.[70] American opinion may well have accepted the German view of Rourkela as a perfect technical enterprise marred by Indian mismanagement.[71] Fearing what appeared to be the unjust political odium falling on West Germany, the United States government wanted Bokaro to be a 'show-piece' of American technical skill and enterprise.[72] India, however, was not prepared to accept this degree of American control, believing that Indian managers and technologists should take a substantial part from the scheme's inception.[73] American opinion did not oppose this view in principle,[74] though even within India no agreement was reached during this period as to the degree of Indian managerial involvement desirable.[75] It is held in some quarters that relations with the United States were somewhat complicated by the operations of Dastur and Co., who held a vague status as consultants but whose functions were not satisfactorily defined from the American viewpoint.[76]

A source of considerable irritation to India was the prolonged survey of technical and economic factors carried out by a series of American teams. After some two years of negotiation, the United States insisted, in April 1962, on a full scale investigation by the United States Steel Corporation, to be financed by the Agency for International Development, not merely into resources but into steel demand, economic feasibility and desirability of the project.[77] It was argued that this would set India back one year without committing the United States to anything, that India already had adequate information and that aid was needed in steel and engineering technology rather than economic evaluation.[78] A compromise was shortly afterwards reached whereby Indian statistics would be accepted where they were 'reliable and exhaustive'.[79] One year later, in April 1963, this report appeared,[80] almost simultaneously with the Clay Committee Report,[81] and probably with more devastating effect. The position with regard to raw materials, water supply and Indian managerial 'know-how' were considered generally unsatisfactory. Further reports were called for to solve these problems, which process was estimated to take a further two years.[82] On this basis, had negotiations proceeded, at least five years would have elapsed before even an outline project report appeared.

It is clear that the Kennedy Administration was firmly committed to the view that the fact of the steel mill being built in the public sector should prove no bar to American assistance. Ambassador Galbraith's commitment to this view was consistent and pronounced.[83] Only one week before the House of Representatives rejected the scheme he argued passionately before the House Appropriations subcommittee that public ownership of productive facilities of part of the economy was a matter of deep conviction to the people of India and refusal to aid Bokaro on the grounds of public ownership could jeopardise Indo-American relations and the future of the Indian private sector.[84] However, neither the pleas of the president, Ambassador Galbraith nor even of Indian businessmen who argued that the plant was essential to the development of the private sector which could not provide sufficient capital itself,[85] were sufficient to save the negotiations. The Clay Report which dogmatically stated that 'the United States should not aid a foreign government in projects establishing government-owned industrial and commercial enterprises which compete with existing private endeavour',[86] seemed especially aimed at Bokaro. Together with the United States Steel Corporation's report, this provided weighty ammunition for the project's opponents. Finally, the House of Representatives specifically barred Bokaro from the Foreign Aid Appropriations, in 22 August 1963.[87] The Administration was evidently prepared to fight for the reversal of this decision, but Mr Nehru, to save further embarrassment, officially withdrew India's request.[88]

Reactions to this final breakdown of negotiations were generally 'stoical' on both sides. The United States Administration made little effort to persuade India that it was eager to continue the fight, though Galbraith commented that 'the question arises of whether we must leave the impressive and dramatic projects to other countries'.[89] The official announcement of withdrawal of the aid request by C. Subramaniam, Minister of Steel, Mines and Heavy Engineering, in Parliament, on 11 September 1963, was studiously moderate—the request was being withdrawn to save time and to preserve long-term friendship. At the same time the United States Administration's helpful attitude was stressed.[90] Clearly the government had been seeking alternatives for some time. Initially some optimism was expressed in the press that India might be able to substantially undertake the project herself, with a certain amount of sub-contracting.[91] Reports by Dastur and Co. lent weight to the belief that the United States Steel Corporation had underestimated India's potential contribution, and had in consequence overestimated the total cost.[92] A Report tabled in Parliament on 11 December 1963 was extremely optimistic in this regard.[93] The government-owned firm, Bokaro Steel Ltd, was registered on 29 January 1964.[94] However, prospects of near self-sufficiency being achieved were seriously impaired by a major fire at the Indian Heavy Engineering Co's plant at Ranchi (Bihar), which was intended to play a major part in the Bokaro project.[95] Furthermore, in February 1964, negotiations with Dastur and Co. over fees broke down.[96] In May 1964, the Soviet Union offered assistance on the same basis as Bhilai,[97] this offer being accepted on 4 June 1964.[98]

The author would not concur in the judgment that the success of the Russian bid for the Bokaro contract 'represents a major defeat for the United States in a crucial area of the cold war',[99] on the grounds that such over-dramatisation does not provide any very meaningful insight into Indian reaction. However, it has proved Ambassador Galbraith wrong in a major prediction to the effect that 'a few people have predicted with something almost approaching pleasure that Americans would never give support to publicly owned enterprise. I am not at all sorry to disappoint them.'[100] The error of this prediction, while not causing any serious rift in Indo-American relations, has unfortunately reinforced the stereotype image of the United States in India implicit in this statement, from which the Kennedy Administration had made moderately successful efforts to be liberated. At the same time the Soviet Union has gained prestige by its willingness to assist a maximum priority project, enabling India to pursue her chosen pattern in the development of heavy industry. Final judgments must of course await the completion of the Bokaro project. Priorities have shifted and the whole heavy industry sector is undergoing a period of uncertainty.

Chapter 9

Foreign private capital: some political aspects

This chapter, while not dealing directly with the main theme of foreign aid, provides important related evidence. The distribution of foreign aid has played an important part in establishing the pattern of economic development, while questions of socialism and the proper role of the private sector have been key issues in India's internal politics. The emphasis of the World Bank and successive American governments on the private sector, and in particular the need to attract foreign private capital, has therefore been a factor in determining Indian political attitudes. A quadrangular configuration of interests is in evidence, involving the major Western donors, Indian private capital, foreign capital and the government of India. The complexity of the situation is, of course, multiplied by the numerous contending interests within each group, to which may be added the interests of the Soviet bloc. Therefore, the broader perspective provided by this chapter is necessary to a proper understanding of the main themes of the whole work.

As in the case of overseas governmental capital, India's reaction to foreign private capital has been uncertain and mixed. In defining the aims of this chapter it is immediately necessary to state that it is not intended to examine the role of foreign capital in the development of India's economy, nor is it proposed to argue the relative merits of governmental capital assistance versus foreign capital or the related issue of public versus private enterprise. It is intended rather to examine certain issues of political significance. Of these the most important are 1. India's policy with regard to acceptance of foreign capital; 2. Measures taken to encourage foreign capital; 3. Disincentive factors; 4. Pressures operating from foreign sources to promote (a) existing foreign interests in India and (b) changes conductive to the creation of a more favourable 'climate' for the attraction of foreign capital. To a great extent it is impossible to separate economic and political issues in this context, but economic analysis is only undertaken with a view to evaluating political factors.

Analysis of foreign private investment up to 1960 shows that Britain's dominance proved persistent, but with a declining share of total external

Table 46
Gross foreign investment by source (Rs million)

(outstanding as per June 30th) (per cent in italics)

	1948		1956		1957		1958		1959		1960	
United Kingdom	2,060	*80.5*	3,925	*79.6*	3,988	*73.4*	3,988	*69.7*	4,003	*65.6*	4,464	*64.6*
United States	112	*4.4*	470	*9.5*	575	*10.6*	600	*10.5*	842	*13.8*	1,127	*16.3*
West Germany	1	*0.04*	28	*0.6*	35	*0.6*	38	*0.7*	54	*0.9*	68	*1.0*
Japan	2	*0.08*	2	*0.04*	6	*0.1*	6	*0.1*	14	*0.2*	34	*0.5*
Switzerland	54	*2.1*	82	*1.7*	67	*1.3*	67	*1.2*	76	*1.3*	89	*1.3*
Pakistan	84	*3.3*	42	*0.09*	42	*0.8*	42	*0.7*	42	*0.7*	42	*0.6*
others	245	*9.6*	233	*4.7*	248	*4.6*	262	*4.6*	270	*4.4*	300	*4.3*
IBRD	–	–	148	*3.0*	469	*8.6*	722	*12.6*	804	*13.2*	781	*11.3*
total	2,558	*100.0*	4,930	*100.0*	5,430	*100.0*	5,725	*100.0*	6,105	*100.0*	6,905	*100.0*

investment. Table 46[1] shows the extent of foreign investment according to source of origin.

British supremacy has been based on her overwhelming stake in India prior to Independence. The pattern of diversity in foreign investment has been accelerated, as is shown in table 47.[2]

Table 47
Percentage distribution of foreign stake in new capital issues sanctioned between April 1956-December 1964 by national origin of foreign participants

	(per cent)
United Kingdom	47.1
United States	28.9
West Germany	7.6
France	2.4
Japan	1.8
Switzerland	4.3
Italy	3.3
others	4.5
total	100.0

Besides showing an increasing participation by European countries, it is clear that the gap between the United States and Britain is narrowing rapidly, a trend which may obviously be expected to accelerate.

The pattern of foreign investment is generally towards the industrial and petroleum sectors and away from plantations, trade, utilities and finance.[3] This is in general accord with government policy. Analysis reveals a strong concentration in spheres where the latest modern scientific and technological methods are most applicable[4] – a factor of considerable importance in view of India's official socialistic and nationalistic objective of indigenous control of national development.

The most common and acceptable form of foreign investment is through the medium of collaboration agreements between foreign and domestic capital, which have shown steady though erratic growth during the period under consideration. In addition to rapid inflow of foreign capital through this medium there has also been a notable increase in association of Indian capital with foreign controlled companies. Apart from government policy, there are many reasons why foreign investors should favour the collaboration agreement.[5] Above all the political need exists to obtain national status and treatment. With the growth and complexity of government control, local associates with individual knowledge of the machinery and personnel of key government agencies are essential to efficient operation. Collaboration provides a convenient method of disguised exporting, with often only small investment commitment consisting of limited supply of equipment, semi-finished products or technical services. This is an obvious result of India's high tariff policies.

In spite of the complexities of internal political reaction to foreign capital, the intricacies of the Indian economy and the tortuous nature of planning controls over the private sector, the Indian government's basic policy towards private foreign capital is fairly clear. In certain sectors it is required and in certain others it is not. Generally speaking, it is only welcomed in physically productive enterprise, as opposed to commercial or financial enterprise.[6] Requirements for foreign investment are strictly related to Plan priorities. A number of important conditions have to be satisfied, but once permission is given to invest, a generally cooperative, if not always expeditious attitude is adopted by the government, which has so far ensured, in spite of many frustrations, a general level of stability and security for foreign investors. All proposals for establishing new industrial enterprises or for expansion of capacity where the total capital investment of the enterprise is more than Rs25 lakhs must be awarded an Industrial Licence under the Industries (Development and Regulation) Act 1961. The main factors considered in awarding licences to foreign entre preneurs are:[7] 1. An enterprise's status with regard to the Industrial Policy Resolution of 1956;[8] 2. The priority accorded to the establishment of capacity in the relevant field; 3. Export-earning and import-saving potential of the proposed enterprise;* 4. The extent to which foreign entrepreneurs can supply foreign exchange; 5. The extent to which foreign collaboration will provide technical 'know-how' not available in India; foreign firms are expected to arrange training programmes for Indians and to progressively absorb them into senior management positions.

The government has sought to encourage foreign collaboration with Indian capital, rather than foreign-owned subsidiaries. In general, foreign collaboration is only allowed on a minority basis.[9] Up to March 1962, out of 402 collaboration agreements sanctioned, only fourteen cases of foreign majority control were allowed, these exceptions being necessitated by deficiencies of Indian technical knowledge.[10] With regard to the 1956

*In both 2 and 3, availability of resources within India is highly relevant. The need to save foreign exchange encourages establishment of indigenous industrial capacity, even where this may be uneconomic on other grounds.

Industrial Policy Resolution, exceptions from Schedule A restrictions have so far been made in the case of oil exploration and steel forgings.[11] In the latter case extensive efforts have been made to attract private capital in response to defence requirements and shortfalls in Third Plan industrial projects. There is thus no reason to suppose that Schedule A will remain inviolate for all time.

The 49 per cent rule is in practice not very meaningful.[12] Control may be exercised through various means by a nominally minority foreign partner. A majority of voting shares may be held, or through diffusion of Indian ownership a small number of Indian shareholders made acquiescent to foreign control. The foreign partner may retain control over key managerial posts and exert influence through licences, patents, provision of technical 'know-how', etc. It must also be remembered that the provision of foreign exchange is a crucial factor for any enterprise in India, giving the foreign partner an outstanding advantage, whatever his nominal stake.

Available evidence shows that foreign firms have responded well to the government's call for 'Indianisation', and the latter seem generally satisfied on this score.[13] Since December 1956 all foreign firms have been obliged to publish information on the proportion of Indians in salary categories over Rs1000 per month, as tabulated in table 48.[14]

Table 48
Percentage of Indians in given salary categories

			(as per 1st January)	
Rs per month	1954	1955	1956	1963
1,000-1,500	54.9	61.5	67.0*	–
1,000-2,000	–	–	–	93.6
1,500-3,000	23.0	27.4	33.3	'over 60.0'
over 3,000	6.5	7.9	10.0	31.4

*Source actually says 'Just over two-thirds'.

This would seem to represent a definite trend in the direction desired by India, though there is considerable scope for argument as to the exact pace of 'Indianisation' desirable in relation to efficiency. However, there is good evidence that most foreign firms view this trend with some reluctance.[15]

The main factors influencing foreign capital's willingness to invest, apart from normal market considerations, are 1. Specific incentives offered by government and 2. The general 'climate' for investment. This latter is a somewhat intangible factor, but in general terms it is a question of public sentiment towards foreign capital in particular and private enterprise in general, especially as expressed through the policies of political parties and the relative strength of such parties or groups. The government's attitude is crucial and foreign investors will make their own assessment of likely future government policy, official pronouncements not necessarily being accepted at their face value.

India has, over the course of years, offered an increasing number of specific incentives to foreign investors, through a wide variety of tax concessions, while assurances have been given with regard to nationalisation and repatriation of capital and dividends (see appendix No. 6).

In spite of these various concessions, foreign capital has had, and continues to have reservations as to the long-term 'climate' for investment. The private sector is subject to numerous restrictions, particularly with regard to licencing and imports. Probably, fears of nationalisation are less acute than in the previous decade, when the Life Insurance companies were nationalised in 1956[16] and great fears were aroused by an amendment to the Constitution, whereby terms of compensation in the event of nationalisation became non-justiciable, now coming entirely within the discretion of the Union and State governments.[17] In fact India's policy has been to set up new enterprises in the public sector, rather than to acquire existing enterprises.[18] Regular complaints are made at home and abroad about heavy taxation,[19] and excessive administrative controls and delays, particularly with regard to the issue of licences.[20] In the mid-1950s there was some feeling that India was only accepting foreign capital as a short-term necessity, and that in the long run there was no future for foreign investors there.[21] It must also be noted that there has always been a steady undercurrent of hostility in the Indian Parliament and press to foreign capital, particularly American capital. Apart from sheer doctrinal Anti-Americanism,[22] the main fear has been of foreign domination of the economy.[23] It is also argued that political trouble is inevitable if the interests of foreign companies are in any way opposed.[24] The example of Ceylon was quoted where the United States suspended aid when, following nationalisation of the oil companies, the companies and the Compensation Tribunal failed to agree on terms. It appeared to many Indians that the companies were seeking special treatment and setting themselves up above the law of the land.[25] In view of India's dependence on massive American help, intransigeance on either side in some similar situation in the future could produce considerable confusion. More specifically, economic objections arising from potential foreign control relate to long-term indebtedness with its contingent drain on foreign resources, importing of unsuitable technology to suit the interests of foreign investors, hindrances to growth of Indian exporting capacity, and general monopoly control over price-fixing.[26]

One further factor, the long-term effect of which it is not yet possible to gauge, is the border dispute with China. The initial effect of the Chinese attack in autumn 1962 on private capital, both Indian and foreign, was very bad.[27] Stringent financial measures, notably the imposition of a super profits tax, coupled with general uncertainty as to the effects of the war on the economy, produced a persistent stock market depression.[28] The super profits tax was replaced by a milder surtax, but considerable uncertainty remained, and this mood was intensified by the fighting with Pakistan in 1965.

Against this background of doubt, however, India has stage by stage improved the prospects for foreign capital and by the end of the period under consideration had established a 'climate', if not of burgeoning optimism, at least of relative stability and confidence. An important factor has been the various institutions established by the Indian government to assist the development of the private sector.[29] The two major institutions are the Industrial Finance Corporation of India, established in 1948, which provides medium- and long-term loans to public companies and co-operative societies engaged in manufacturing, processing, generation and distribution of power, mining, shipping and hotels, and the Industrial Credit and Investment Corporation of India (ICICI), a privately owned institution (though with substantial government and foreign financial backing) with the following functions: To assist in the promotion of private industrial investment by means of 1. Provision of loans or equity participation; 2. Encouragement of private investment from other sources; 3. Sponsoring and underwriting of new share issues; 4. Guaranteeing loans; 5. Providing re-finance where appropriate and 6. Furnishing managerial, technical and administrative advice. Other institutions are the various State Financial Corporations, the Refinance Corporation for Industries, which assists banking institutions in providing medium-term loans to suitable enterprises, the National Industrial Development Corporation, whose main object is to pioneer new basic and heavy industries with a high planning priority, by means of 1. Preparation of project reports and 2. The establishment of companies or associations for the execution of such schemes; and finally the National Small Industries Corporation, which in addition to financial assistance to industries with capital assets below the value of Rs5 lakhs, endeavours to exercise quality control and organise markets by means of coordination with larger enterprises.

Since about 1960 India's efforts to attract foreign capital have become more serious and positive. Of particular significance, at least as an earnest of her intentions, was the establishment of the Indian Investment Centre, at first in New Delhi and later in New York and Dusseldorf. The main function of this centre[30] is to act as an information link for both foreign and Indian businessmen: 1. To bring together suitable Indian and foreign firms and investors, with a view to establishing joint enterprises or expanding existing enterprises and 2. To help potential suppliers of capital, both Indian and foreign, in preparation and presentation of their applications for joint ventures for sanctioning by government. This last point is very important, since through its knowledge of the administrative machine, much confusion and time can be saved. It should be stressed, however, that the Investment Centre is an unofficial and advisory body, whose functions are more in the nature of a 'marriage bureau' than of conducting direct negotiations with the parties or with the government. Its style is generally informal which no doubt assists its objectives. Although the new centre plays a valuable part in the provision of information, in initiating contacts and to some extent in smoothing the wheels of administration, its value must basically depend on the status accorded to it by government, particularly by the crucial Departments of Technical Development (Ministry of Industry) and Economic Affairs (Ministry of Finance), and the Planning Commission. One notes an absence of official pronouncements on the work of the centre,* in contrast to the enthusiasm displayed by its chairman, G. L. Mehta.[31] Evidently, it is intended to establish a technical wing as part of the centre's functions, which would help foreign and Indian entrepreneurs frame their projects, provide feasibility studies and maintain constant contacts with the newer generation of Indian industrialists, with a view to anticipating developments.[32] All this would seem to require a very considerable degree of cooperation and coordination with the relevant government departments, which might regard an expanded role for the centre with some jealousy.

Definite efforts have been made to remove one major barrier to foreign investment, namely the time-consuming nature of the licencing procedure.[33] In 1961 processing of applications for foreign investment was concentrated in one department within the Ministry of Commerce and Industry. In 1964, extensive reforms (summarised in appendix no. 7)

*Nor was any positive attitude towards the centre conveyed by officials of the departments concerned whom I interviewed.

recommended by the Swaminathan Committee on Industries Development Procedure were largely approved by the government. However, in spite of some improvement in the processing of applications, many investors argue that it is the extent of the licencing system itself that provides the real barrier to private business, administrative procedures being only a marginal factor.

From the foregoing account it would appear that India is serious in her declared policy of attracting foreign capital, subject to the limitations stated. It is also clear that in recent years efforts to attract foreign capital have been intensified by a great variety of means. Over a period of time, as India has honoured assurances which earlier may have appeared somewhat perfunctory, an atmosphere of political if not market confidence has been established. Nevertheless, the government has been under continuous pressure to offer still more favourable conditions from businessmen both Indian and foreign, from various foreign governments, notably the United States and also from the World Bank. At a strictly practical level the United States and the IBRD, with some assistance from West Germany, have made substantial loans to the various institutions, specified earlier, assisting the private sector. Up to March 1965 authorised aid to these various institutions was as follows:[34]

Table 49
Foreign assistance to Indian credit institutions

(crores of rupees)

institution	USAID	USPL 480 counterpart funds	IBRD	West Germany	total
1. industrial finance corporation	14.3	20.0	–	2.97	37.27
2. ICICI*	2.4	20.0	42.8	3.57	68.77
3. refinance corporation	–	36.2	–	–	36.20
4. national small industries corporation	10.0	–	–	1.18	11.18
total	26.70	76.2	42.8	7.72	153.42

*Also raises additional funds by private loans overseas.

This investment represents a very substantial concern by the American government and the World Bank, for the expansion of the Indian private sector. The donors seem to be mainly motivated by a belief in the necessity of establishing private enterprise as a condition of economic growth, and also in the political benefits they believe will flow therefrom. Probably a widely held belief was expressed by Vance Brand, managing director of the Development Loan Fund, in testimony before an appropriations subcommittee of the House of Representatives, who stated, 'I think it is wrong to make our loans just for big fertiliser plants, steel plants and so forth. Those are needed, and those are good, but you cannot teach people about freedom unless they have property. One of the great freedoms we have is the right to own property. I think we have an obligation to the middle class.'[35]

Steady but quiet efforts have been made by the United States in this general direction, in addition to the substantial financial assistance already mentioned. It is not clear where exactly the idea for establishing the Investment Centre originated, but in May-June 1959, Morarji Desai, then Minister of Finance, made a tour abroad in search of increased aid. M. R. Ruia, president of the Federation of Indian Chambers of Commerce and Industry, leader of a goodwill and trade mission returning after two months in America, told a press conference at Bombay on 27 May 1959[36] that the climate for foreign investment was now much more favourable and that Desai's visit was much appreciated; he further announced his intention to propose at the next Federation meeting the establishment of an Investment Centre in New York. This was the first public suggestion for such a centre, and therefore it seems reasonable to assume that the idea took definite shape during these two Indian visits to the United States. At the same press conference,[37] Shri Ruia announced that a representative of the Export-Import Bank would in future be attached to the American embassy to strengthen liaison between Indian and American capital. The USAID authorised assistance for the establishment of the Investment Centre, consisting of a $704,146 grant towards foreign exchange costs and a grant of Rs3,771,446 towards local costs, to be drawn from PL480 counterpart funds. A substantial part of this assistance took the form of provision of financial, technical and public relations experts and training of Indians in such expertise.[38] Earlier, in September 1957, the American government had established a scheme for insurance against currency inconvertibility, where schemes had the prior approval of the Indian government, and in December 1959 this was extended to cover loss by expropriation. This arrangement is incorporated into procedural agreements for negotiation between the two governments.[39] This latter issue has caused some dispute in India, since earlier American proposals appeared to give Americans greater rights than Indian citizens.[40] Exchanges of trade delegations, missions, etc. between the two countries have been frequent, of which the visit to India in April 1964 of a delegation of over fifty American businessmen provided a spectacular example.[41] Official American statements in recent years have often been favourable and optimistic.[42] Where criticism has been voiced publicly it has, with one or two exceptions,[43] been very moderate and confined to specific issues.[44] Within the specific field of investment 'climate' and incentives, it is most interesting to note the absence of doctrinal pronouncements. In the United States Congress this particular issue hardly ever seems to be debated, though as has been shown in chapter 3, aid to India in general and India's policy of 'socialism' in particular merit considerable attention.[45]

Other countries, especially Britain, make definite efforts to encourage the flow of private investment to India. Although Britain's share of total overseas investment in India is declining, her stake is still substantial. It is clear that leading British businessmen with a stake in India have grasped the essential facts of the situation. These are well expressed in a Report for the Federation of British Industries in 1963 by Sir Norman Kipping.[46] First, in spite of various disadvantages, such as allegedly high taxes, it is recognised that the Indian market has enormous growth potential,[47] but a very substantial capital inflow from all sources is necessary to set the process of growth in motion. Britain's realisation of the connection between governmental assistance and the development of trade and investment has already been noted.[48] The Kipping Report, however, further stresses that the Indian market can only be held by investment rather than exports. Balance of payments problems are likely to make India a high tariff country for a long while and capital investment is the only effective means for overseas firms to get under the tariff barrier.[49] It is also grasped by British financial commentators that investment projects must be worthwhile enterprises, must fit in with India's Plans and must not be regarded as 'export outposts'.[50]

By contrast, West Germany appears to have adopted a less flexible approach. In particular, the idea of minority participation has not proved attractive to German businessmen. Dr Erhard, then Minister for Economic Affairs, visiting Delhi in October 1958, stated that 'given a 51 per cent share in capital and management, capitalists would be prepared to come to India in preference to other countries, particularly in medium-sized industries'.[51] He explained that this did not stem from any desire to dominate, but rather to see that German technology was properly implemented.* Analysis of Indo-German collaboration projects[52]

*No doubt this approach was influenced strongly by the experience of Rourkela.

reveals a strong emphasis on German technical and managerial services, training of Indians on formally agreed lines, and licence and royalty agreements in connection with German processes, technical knowledge, etc. These characteristics are to be found, to a greater or lesser extent, in connection with foreign investment from all sources, but it is particularly noticeable in the case of West Germany. There are probably three main factors to account for this emphasis: 1. Realisation that control of technical and managerial aspects will give effective control of an enterprise, at least for an initial period, even where only minority capital is held. This fact is no doubt appreciated and exploited to some extent by investors from all countries, but since West Germany is the only country to have publicly opposed India's stated policy on this matter, it must be assumed that it has special importance in her eyes; 2. Sale of technical services, licences, etc. is an excellent means of ensuring good income from an enterprise, whatever its overall profit. Again, this factor will play an important part in the calculations of all foreign investors, but the German viewpoint seems to display a special cynicism towards ventures which cannot be controlled by Germans, and therefore this emphasis can presumably be regarded in the form of an insurance policy on their part; 3. The emphasis on acquisition of skills and technology noted in official aid appears to be reflected in West German private collaboration ventures in India.

To many Indians, no doubt, foreign and Indian businessmen seem, in pressing their various claims, to blend in harmonious chorus. Indian businessmen have been active, especially in the United States in urging the need for foreign capital, while using this theme as a basis for attacking the government's general policies towards the private sector. The fears and discontents of the Indian business community in the early years after Independence were no doubt well expressed by J. R. D. Tata, leading industrialist in the field of steel and heavy engineering, who on one occasion stated

> . . . more important, perhaps, than anything else is the need to shed certain preconceptions which have long coloured official and political thinking in our country . . . . For instance that the profit motive is dishonourable; that profit is synonomous with profiteering; that industrialists as a class are inefficient or dishonest or both; that about three per cent net is a fair return on risk capital; that mechanisation means unemployment; that it is more important to impoverish the rich than to enrich the poor; that a welfare state can be built without first creating the means to pay for it;

that nationalisation creates additional wealth; that centralised state enterprise and management is socialism.[53]

In recent years, however, a more mixed and subtle approach can be noted, the main themes being that basically the long-term prospects are good; that government policy has changed for the better, though there is still plenty of room for improvement; that the growth of public and private sectors are largely interdependent, and therefore the old bogey of nationalisation should no longer deter foreign investors; that India is to a great extent misunderstood in the West and 'socialism' is not what it appears to be.[54] Cooperation between Indian businessmen and the government was particularly noticeable during the negotiations over the Bokaro steel project.[55] J. D. Tata made a strong statement in favour of American aid for a state-owned project, since in this instance there was insufficient private capital.[56] Shri Bharat Ram, president of the Federation of Indian Chambers of Commerce and Industry, urged that the project was vital to the expansion of the private sector. A publicly owned steel mill would not compete with private enterprise in this field, since there was a general shortage of steel.[57] No doubt this willingness to cooperate reflects the progressively more favourable policy adopted towards the private sector in recent years.

However, a counter trend may be noted. Certain sections of Indian business appear to have definitely nationalistic views, accepting foreign capital only where absolutely necessary and endeavouring to reduce participation to a strictly non-managerial form. Others, of course, welcome collaboration as a source of foreign exchange and as a means of exercising political leverage. It is often the case, nevertheless, that the government insists on foreign collaboration, particularly technical collaboration, against the wishes of Indian capitalists, displaying in the eyes of the latter a lack of confidence in Indian technological capacity. We thus have a paradox whereby stereotype public attitudes of both government and private sector are often at variance. The government, despite its complex procedures for control of the flow of foreign capital and its official encouragement of Indianisation is nevertheless frequently accused by Indian industry of over-licencing and an insistence on foreign capital against the wishes of local entrepreneurs. The government view in these cases would presumably be based on the need to eliminate Indian monopolies and enforce modernisation, though the initial inflow of foreign exchange will also be a consideration. On the other hand, the private sector uses the official government policy of encouraging foreign investment, within the limits described, as a means of extracting concessions for the private sector generally. At the same time, many Indian businessmen have considerable reservations about associating foreign capital with their own ventures, both from the viewpoint of their own commercial interest and on general nationalistic grounds.

In spite of initial doubts, India has clearly indicated that private capital, both Indian and foreign, has been allotted a part in development planning. Definite incentives have been provided, whatever opinions may be held as to their adequacy, or, from the viewpoint of the private sector's opponents, their desirability. At the same time, India has an excellent record in honouring guarantees offered to investors. However, the real question lies in the precise scope likely to be offered to private entrepreneurs in the future. In some respects it seems that India has been preparing to mount a massive campaign to attract foreign capital. Periodic vigorous speeches to American businessmen by Indian ambassadors on the need to invest in India have for a long while been part of India's diplomatic stock in trade,[58] but the vigorous efforts of the former Finance Minister, M. Desai[59] and of his successor, T. T. Krishnamachari,[60] together with the efforts of the Investment Centre and the overhaul of licencing procedure, suggest that the government is now in earnest. However, a counter-trend may be noticed in official pronouncements. Thus, B. R. Bhagat, then Minister for Planning and Minister of State in the Ministry of Finance, said in the Rajya Sabha on 7 May 1964,[61] that a dominant role for the public sector was envisaged, especially in the fields of power, steel, machine-building and fertilisers; by 1976 over 50 per cent of industries would be in the public sector. Of course, even if this target is fulfilled, it would still be possible for the private sector to have a substantial stake, on the lines of the Cochin refinery agreement.[62] Speaking in the Rajya Sabha on 27 April 1964,[63] T. T. Krishnamachari warned the stock market and the private sector generally that if it did not help the government to reach the goal of socialism, other methods would be found. The private sector must respond, or the public sector would have to find the necessary capital formation through forced savings and vertical expansion.* However, the government did not want to destroy the private sector and would 'give it a place to live'. More recently, the Minister of Planning, Shri Asoka Mehta, has indicated the government's firm intention to move towards greater socialist control over the economy, including greater control over the banking system. He expressed a personal view that the constitutional

*Presumably this must be construed as a euphemistic term for nationalisation.

guarantee about the right to property made it difficult for 'the forces of socialism to operate on the level of a change in the structure of private property', but added that already the government was 'moving towards an enlargement of the social ownership of new forms of property'.[64]

The contradictory nature of these various statements reflects the ideological and power struggle within the ruling Congress party and indeed within the Administration itself. At the same time there is some tension between the need to attract foreign capital and the concessions this may involve towards the indigenous private sector, hostility towards the Marwari business empire being especially bitter. Business interests within the Congress Party appear to have become progressively more influential despite continuing offical assertions of socialist intent.

The clash over fundamental objectives has clearly sharpened since the death of Nehru, and the cabinet composition under both Shastri and Mrs Gandhi has reflected these divisions. The decision to allow foreign capital on a majority basis in the fertiliser industry* clearly represented a major concession to the private sector, and specifically to American opinion. This decision was a major factor in precipitating the resignation of former Finance Minister, T. T. Krishnamachari.[65]

It would appear that a trend generally favourable to the private sector will continue, due to several factors. These are the growing magnitude of India's economic problems, seriously aggravated by threats to her borders, which necessitates rapid industrialisation by any means possible. In the context of the Sino-Soviet split, the competitive aspect of Soviet and American aid has become less important and unless the Soviet Union indicates willingness to increase aid on a massive scale, dependence on the United States will increase. In view of the uncertainty of future aid from this source, growth of the economy will increasingly depend on large injections of foreign capital. If exports were to rise dramatically, the foreign exchange factor here would be less urgent, but this appears problematical. Furthermore, as the Indian economy becomes more sophisticated, medium-sized industry becomes a more important factor, a trend which further favours the private sector. Thus while the public sector may be expected to grow within its existingly defined limits, the private sector, with the aid of foreign capital, may be expected to grow still more rapidly. This trend will certainly produce acute political tensions and resistance from important sections of government and national

*In addition, foreign firms will be allowed a free hand in marketing and distribution, except for an obligation to sell 30 per cent of their annual output to the government at an agreed price.

political opinion. There will no doubt be frequent official reassertions of basic socialist objectives, at variance with the prevailing trend. However, the general conditions for entry of foreign capital stated earlier seem well established and, apart from a few special cases negotiated under political pressure, seem likely to be maintained at least for the immediate future.

Chapter 10

Military aid

This chapter is of incidental interest to the main themes and provides only an outline survey of military aid. However, this issue should be noted for two reasons, first, because it illustrates the interaction of non-alignment and foreign aid in a more dramatic form, and secondly because military expenditure is now becoming a more vital related issue in the perspective of the whole foreign aid programme. In a wider context, some preliminary insight is given into broader power considerations on the subcontinent, against which aid policy must be viewed.

During recent years India has started to import military equipment on a large scale. This is related to a substantial increase in defence expenditure. Table 50[1] shows only a gentle increase during the period of the first two Plans, but a dramatic increase during the Third Plan period, due to pressures in various Chinese border areas, particularly Ladakh and the North-East Frontier, during autumn 1962. Tensions with Pakistan, erupting in widespread fighting in August-September 1965, have also been a key factor in this build-up.

The defence budget will continue to rise sharply in the future, the Planning Commission having estimated a required outlay of Rs5,500 crores for the

Table 50
Indian outlay on defence expenditure

	(crores of rupees)
1951-2	196
1955-6	190
1956-7	212
1957-8	280
1958-9	279
1959-60	266
1960-1	282.
1961-2	317
1962-3	504
1963-4	808
1964-5	835
1965-6	879
1966-7	943

Fourth Plan period[2] wherein the defence outlay will rise from Rs920 crores in 1966-7 to Rs1,110 crores in 1971-2.[3] The foreign exchange component of the five year defence plan, commenced in 1964, is variously estimated in the region of one to one-and-a-half billion dollars.[4] Clearly such a massive build-up could not be initiated or sustained without substantial external assistance.

It is difficult to define the term 'aid' in this context, since the precise terms are not disclosed. Although Mr Nehru stated as late as 1961 that it was contrary to India's dignity to receive military aid, he was prepared to purchase arms from any source and even to negotiate for the building of armaments factories.[5] Taking the definition of 'aid' adopted in chapter I[6] as any purchase or credit negotiated through governmental or voluntary agencies on terms more favourable than 'normal' commercial terms, it is clear that India has been receiving some assistance towards purchasing planes, tanks and other military equipment from the United States since at least 1954.[7] These purchases were made within the framework of the United States Mutual Security Act, for which purpose it was necessary for the United States to recognise India as a friendly country, in spite of her 'non-alignment' policy.[8] Without detailed information it is impossible to know whether such purchases should be classified as military aid. However, at a press conference in New Delhi on 20 February 1957, the director of the International Cooperation Administration, John B. Hollister, expressed the view that development assistance should take the form of loans, whereas military assistance should take the form of 'aid', presumable meaning grants.[9] It seems hard to understand why this statement should have been made in India, if there was no question at that time of India's accepting such assistance. Since about 1960, India has increased its military purchases substantially. A general perspective can be given as follows, though as stated, many details are not available.

Up to 1964 the total value of military assistance negotiated with the Soviet Union was said to be worth the equivalent of $130m.[10] Of this, the main items were $40m worth of ground-to-air missiles, radar equipment, etc., thirty AN12 transport planes,[11] an unknown number of MI4 helicopters,[12] of which twenty had so far been delivered, plus a variety of mortars, machine guns, pontoon bridge equipment, etc. Six MIG fighters had been delivered.[13] Of greatest long-term significance, however, was the agreement for Soviet technical and capital assistance in the establishment of three MIG factories in India, at Koraput (Orissa), Nasik (Maharashtra) and Hyderabad (Andhra Pradesh). Further deliveries of MIGs were also expected. It would seem that Russia has also indirectly assisted in developing India's capability in the sphere of nuclear weapons construction. An 'Atoms for Peace' agreement, signed in Vienna on 6 February 1961[14] provides for:

(Article 1). Cooperation in research over the uses of plutonium, uranium, etc. Exchange of scientists.
(Article 2). Exact projects to be worked out by subsequent protocol.
(Article 3). The Soviet Union to supply uranium materials.
(Article 4). The Soviet Union to supply technical assistance where required and equipment for mining and exploration.

Though this agreement is intended to stimulate peaceful uses of nuclear power in India, such a programme, albeit vaguely defined, could doubtless be converted to nuclear weapons production.

Reports indicate[15] that at the Nassau talks in December 1962 between Macmillan and Kennedy, the United States agreed to grant $60m worth of military aid to India, to be matched by a similar amount from Commonwealth countries.[16] On 21 September 1964 Y. B. Chavan, India's Defence Minister, announced to the Lok Sabha[17] that the United States would provide during the Fiscal Year 1965 1. $60m credit for miscellaneous items such as replacement and modernisation of plant and equipment in ordnance factories and a new artillery shell plant at Ambajhar and 2. Grant assistance for such items as support for Indian mountain divisions, air defence equipment, transport aircraft, and road-building equipment for the Border Roads Organisation.[18] Information concerning British military assistance does not appear to be very extensive,[19] but a full statement of assistance received from other Commonwealth countries was given in a statement Y. B. Chavan in the Rajya Sabha on 17 August 1963.[20] Canada had offered Rs27m worth of military equipment, etc. of which Rs11.4m had been supplied up to that time.[21] In addition, a loan had been offered for the purchase of sixteen Caribou aircraft. Australia had offered arms, notable rifles and mortars, ammunition and woollen garments to the value of Rs23.5m, of which Rs14.15m had already been supplied. In addition, Sir Garfield Barwick, then Australian Minister for External Affairs, announced in Canberra on 20 April 1963 that an exchange of military experts had been arranged on a continuing basis.[22] The Indian Finance Minister, T. T. Krishnamachari, is reported to have stated that he was most impressed with the Australian military complex, which he had not appreciated before.[23] New Zealand provided butter fat. Outside the Commonwealth France supplied Rs20m worth of aircraft spares as a free gift, to be selected by IAF officers, while West Germany supplied Rs40 lakhs worth of winter clothing.[24] India's nuclear capacity, initiated by the Trombay reactor project, undertaken in 1953 with Canadian assistance,[25] was substantially boosted by an $80m loan from America, announced on 1 July 1963, for an atomic reactor plant at Tarapur, sixty-two miles north of Bombay.[26] Under this agreement the United States Atomic Energy Commission would provide the initial uranium charge for two giant reactors. The plant would be ready in 1967 and would have a generating capacity of 380 m.w., second only to Hinkley Point (Britain), which has a capacity of 510 m.w. The loan bears interest at 0.75 per cent over forty years, with no principal payments due in the first ten years.[27] Although at present India is eschewing nuclear weapons production for a variety of reasons,[28] the assistance she has received from various quarters in nuclear research and technology must give her definite nuclear potential in the military sphere.

The decision to accept formal military aid seems to have been taken with extreme reluctance and only under the compelling pressure of Chinese aggression. Nehru expressed profound fears, even at this stage, that such aid would weaken the 'moral fibre' of the nation, by inducing the idea of dependence on outsiders.[29] Hence the present emphasis on large-scale independent defence efforts, with special emphasis on building up the economic, industrial and scientific base for achieving military self-sufficiency,[30] though this may in fact be slower of achievement than India hopes. Acceptance of military aid has also created some tensions and re-definitions with regard to the non-alignment policy.[31] It should be noted, however, that although acceptance of economic aid may have brought a few marginal concessions to external pressure, it has clearly not influenced the formulation of India's foreign policy to any basic degree. Thus, it should not easily be assumed that military aid will have any different effect.

The relative absence of ideological debate in the West over military aid to India is in striking contrast to the passions aroused over the generation of economic aid programmes a few years earlier. Most significant is the generally calm reception given by the American government to Soviet military aid. This reflects the quite different approach to Soviet aid generally, adopted by the United States in recent years, compared with its initial reaction.[32] It also reflects the changing pattern of relationships between the West, the Soviet bloc, India and China. However, some tensions have arisen which to a certain extent have been concealed by issues of a technical and commercial nature. Thus, the decision to purchase Soviet jet aircraft was very much influenced by the favourable terms offered compared with the West,[33] as well as by rumoured disagreements with the Bristol Co. (Britain) over the incorporation of Orpheus engines into HF 24 fighters.[34] However, India's arguments on this score did not prevent Western criticism. The American ambassador to India, Professor J. K. Galbraith, pointed out that buying from the Soviet Union had unfavourable political repercussions in the United States Congress, causing embarrassment to the Administration. It would help if India were to negotiate first with the United States, and if prices proved to be higher, this would at least strengthen her case before the American Legislature.[35] The United States has refused to supply HF 24 supersonic fighters on the grounds, apparently, that the development of two separate Indian fighter programmes would place too heavy a strain on her resources.[36] One may reasonably speculate, however, on the extent to which the unsuccessful negotiations with the Bristol Co. aroused hostility in American business circles. Closely related to the American refusal to supply supersonic planes, is her insistence that there should be no intermingling of American and Soviet military assistance.[37] This is obviously understandable from the security aspect, but poses profound technical problems, both for India and all supplying countries and will probably influence donor countries to limit their assistance to relatively obsolete equipment, at least with regard to aircraft, missiles and communications systems. American fears of 'intermingling' were largely prompted by reports, which later proved correct, that India was negotiating with the Soviet Union for supply of ground to air missiles and radar equipment, much of which was currently being supplied by the United States.[38] However, this same logic would obviously apply to military aircraft. Perhaps the United States government also shared fears expressed in some Indian quarters concerning Soviet pilots training Indians and possibly flying over strategic border areas.[39] On balance, it would seem that the United States has not gone so far in its acceptance of Soviet military aid as with economic aid.[40] On the other hand, there have been no strong expressions of opposition at official level. It is thus an open question whether the United States is applying quiet diplomatic pressure in favour of a more Western bias in arms procurement, or whether the views of Vice-President Humphrey (then Senator) will predominate—that some measure of Soviet arms to India should be encouraged in order to widen the Sino-Soviet split.[41]

Military aid to India involves the donor countries in the cross fire of Indo-Pakistan hostilities. Aid to India has enraged the Pakistanis, just as military aid to Pakistan under SEATO and the Baghdad Pact has caused the United States to incur vehement denunciations in India. Assurances in both cases that the American government would not allow its armaments to be used by the two countries against each other failed to make any impression. In practice it would be very difficult for the United States to enforce this guarantee, since any form of aid, military or economic, allows additional resources to be diverted to military uses. Of course, an aggrieved donor could cut off future aid, and this did indeed occur during and after the Indo-Pakistan war in 1965. The question of Kashmir has been raised several times in relation to military aid. Several suggestions have been made in the United States Congress that aid to India and/or Pakistan should be reduced or suspended, pending a settlement of the Kashmir dispute,[42] but nothing specific has emerged. However, reports appearing in the Indian press[43] that American military aid was dependent on some substantial diplomatic initiative on Kashmir by Prime Minister Nehru in his forthcoming talks with Pakistan leaders were officially denied in Parliament by the Defence Minister Y. B. Chavan.[44] The same pressures have latterly been alleged with regard to PL 480 aid, but India's stand has remained firm. In such a situation it is extremely hard for a donor country to appear impartial, and probably the Soviet Union has derived most benefit from the situation by giving aid to India only, and consistently supporting her over Kashmir and all other disputes.[45] To date, this has remained true, despite the modifications in approach implied in the Tashkent initiative. Though this policy has brought uncompromising hostility from Pakistan, it has earned high praise and goodwill in India, by far the more populous and powerful country. The West, by contrast, has tried to strike a balance and has thus incurred the suspicion of both sides. The various alternatives open to the West, in particular the United States, are fraught with political difficulties. As an extreme measure no aid could be given to either country, pending a solution of major differences. In the current extremist climate of opinion in both countries, neutrality will be interpreted as hostility, and such brutally equal treatment is likely to be viewed in this light. At the same time, such a policy would have economically disastrous results, besides leaving the sub-continent much more open to pressures from Moscow and Peking. A policy of equal aid to both countries, assuming that objective criteria could be established to define 'equality' in this context,* would again be open to the same

*Presumably this would have to be calculated on a per capita basis. Even this formula is not entirely devoid of ambiguity.

dangers of 'neutralism' so defined, besides ignoring economic criteria of efficiency, viability, etc. Alternatively, aid may be biased to one side or the other. However, the West has adopted no clearcut policy and relative allocations have been determined on a variety of vaguely defined economic, political and military criteria, reflected in a correspondingly confused public debate. Pakistan has received a larger per capita total of assistance from the United States,[46] though the substantial inflow of military aid to India since October 1962 has narrowed the difference to some extent. The latter trend represents changing Western priorities in the light of the Chinese border threat. At the same time growing cordiality between China and Pakistan[47] has caused considerable misgivings in the West. It is clear, however, that the foreign policy of both countries is substantially influenced, and probably in the case of Pakistan dominated, by their relations with each other. In this context Pakistan's growing detente with China, as indeed her adherence to SEATO, has almost certainly been motivated by anti-Indian opportunism.

Large scale receipt of military aid is intimately related to the question of 'non-alignment'. It is clearly important to India's 'image' abroad, especially in Asia and Africa, to preserve a balance between Soviet and Western assistance. This, of course, is only possible in the context of intensifying Sino-Soviet antagonism and the growing detente between the Soviet bloc and the non-Communist world. Any factor which might reverse this trend, such as an 'escalation' of the conflict in Vietnam, represents a threat to this uneasy balance. Another factor affecting the balance is the relative priority given by both major powers to the defence of India, which in turn depends on relative estimates of the strength of the Chinese threat. Although the element of competition between the Soviet Union and the West in economic aid has significantly diminished, this factor cannot be discounted. The mere fact of Russia giving direct military assistance against another Communist power is sufficient indication of the gravity with which she views the Chinese challenge to her interests. In the case of the United States, military assistance to a country threatened by aggression from a Communist power is a natural response within the context of her post second world war foreign policy. With regard to India, however, the relative absence of official and Congressional comment on the potential threat from Peking is most noteworthy, compared with the frequency of comment on potential aggression, subversion, etc. in south-east Asia. Resentment was expressed in the Indian Parliament concerning a statement by General Maxwell Taylor, in testimony before the House of Representatives'

Appropriations Committee, to the effect that he did not know who crossed into who's land first or who shot first; also that the NEFA boundaries were not properly marked.[48] Mr Nehru intervened to say that considerable publicity had been given to these remarks at the beginning of a long statement, and that these should therefore be viewed in their proper context.[49] Apparently American coolness may stem from lingering disapproval of India's non-alignment policy, or alternatively from a desire not to embarrass her in her efforts to maintain this policy, in spite of the Chinese threat.

It is questionably how long India can maintain the present precarious balance of military aid and 'non-alignment', although in the latter case both major powers have a substantial negative incentive to prevent a too heavy bias towards the other side. In particular, the economic factor in defence calculations poses a problem for the maintenance of 'non-alignment'. The cost to India of establishing a fully independent and self-sufficient defence capability will be enormous and must inevitably place heavy strain on her resources. In terms of cost it would be far more economical for India to integrate her military resources with the defence systems of external allies. In the absence of positive military integration between the West, the Soviet Union and eastern Europe, which seems a long-term possibility but beyond the pale of practical politics at present, India would be involved, under pressure, in a choice between the Soviet Union and the West. In no sphere is economic logic more inexorable than that of nuclear weapons. For a variety of political reasons India is at present abstaining from nuclear weapons production. No doubt she already has a limited nuclear production capability, but the cost of establishing a comprehensive, up-to-date nuclear arsenal in a sphere where rapid obsolescence is the dominant characteristic, would be truly prohibitive. India's present policy is to seek some form of international nuclear guarantee from the United States, the United Kingdom and the Soviet Union. This concept has as yet been only tentatively defined, while no definite response has been received from Russia, and therefore its success would appear highly improbable. In the long run, if a Chinese nuclear threat appeared an immediate reality, such an arrangement would only be militarily effective if spelled out in far more precise terms. In this case the multilateral nature of such a guarantee, and therefore 'non-alignment' itself, would be placed under considerable strain unless the East-West detente had developed very rapidly in the meanwhile.

One other feature of Indian defence policy should be noted—the emphasis on public enterprise which a policy of independent defence production and economic nationalism necessarily entails, both in direct defence production and in the establishment of the necessary heavy industrial base.[50] This is essential to ensure that the government's economic and military priorities are fulfilled and that the massive diversion of resources implicit in such a pollcy is effected. On this basis Indian and foreign businessmen would appear to have a substantial interest in establishing a closer military interdependence with the West.[51] This factor aggravates the political tensions over and above those created in the normal way by the internal conflict over economic policy.

In the case of the West at least, large-scale military aid was primarily a response to an emergency appeal by India.[52] With the immediate threat lifted and the future pattern of Chinese intentions towards India uncertain, the donor countries, especially the West, are now enmeshed in the long-term problems of political and economic balance defined in this chapter. Military aid thus implies a far more complex pattern of involvement than was entailed by economic aid, and as yet only tentative efforts have been made to define basic policy objectives.

Chapter 11

Conclusion

The magnitude of the subject becomes even more apparent in conclusion than at the outset. The cautionary words in the introductory chaper against viewing aid as an isolated factor in the Indian political scene seem more relevant than ever, and I am aware that some of the dimensions of the problem have only been indicated in a very limited way. Detailed knowledge of the political, economic, administrative and social structure of India is necessary for a proper understanding of the subject. In the international context the factor of conflicting ideologies must be recognised, but neither overestimated nor underestimated, while the relationship between domestic and international perspectives must be kept firmly in view. A complex series of interactions has been brought to light by this analysis. Within the limits indicated, I shall now attempt to draw together the main strands of the argument.

One primary impression that must emerge is that although areas of mutual interest clearly exist, there are substantial differences in emphasis and objectives between India and the major foreign donors. This is not simply a case of opposing tensions between supply and demand factors in a market situation. The gap is in fact much wider, in that many donors expect, or at least have expected, some political dividends from aid that in India's view are not legitimate. These differences in expectations have been widened by a failure in communication of ideas, while an all-round lack of perspective has led to much over-dramatisation of issues. The dialogue between India and the various aid-givers has been only partial and has in many respects moved along parallel lines.

It is clear that aid is a more identifiable issue in the donor countries than in India. Aid-givers have a variety of objectives, one of which may be a desire to assist in raising living standards, but include ideological, strategic, diplomatic, economic and trading objectives. All of these must be reconciled with domestic political pressures. For the larger donors in particular, India is only one of many recipients, albeit a major one. The Indian view of aid must therefore necessarily be cautious, balancing her need against the possible implications of involvement. As Mr Nehru frequently emphasised,[1] India is not over-concerned with external ideological struggles. Her attitude to aid is specific rather than general, being mainly concerned to fill Plan deficiencies and to obtain the best bargain possible. Particular policies may be modified in special instances where her bargaining position is weak, but basic policies are only altered by the internal balance of political forces and in accordance with India's own assessment of her interests, both of which must necessarily respond to rapidly changing circumstances. Concern with the various interests of the donor countries is only a by-product arising from her own priorities. Ideally, her policy-makers and administrators would prefer to view aid as an entirely technical, economic and non-political question. In view of India's massive dependence on aid it is a remarkable tribute to her skill and tenacity that the political temperature has been kept so relatively low, although particular issues have on occasions produced much heat. While India has its own conflicts, any possible idological or 'goodwill' impact which the donors might hope to achieve concerns her leaders not at all. In fact insofar as such objectives may be identified with a specific donor, they are likely to have the opposite effect. Gradual realisation of this fact has brought about a growing sophistication in the approach of aid-givers, especially the United States.

The debate in America on foreign aid to India was very soon influenced by the shibboleths of the Cold War and American policy has never entirely liberated itself from the distortions so produced. The concept of assistance to developing countries was in any case totally new and had to be developed cautiously; but the ideological suspicion felt towards India's policies reinforced this natural caution and as a result America's contribution to the Indian First Five Year Plan was limited to technical assistance, apart from the emergency Wheat Loan of 1951. The reaction to Soviet aid, however, was dramatic and there followed much serious re-thinking of the scale and form of assistance. The motivation, however, was still primarily ideological. The early years of the Second Plan in many ways marked the nadir of Indo-American relations. During this time differences were acute, but at the same time quite new demands were being made on the United States Congress for assistance. In retrospect this may be seen as a transition period, leading to a more balanced assessment of the American interest in India. During this third period there was less concern over 'non-alignment' and socialism and a greater concern that India should achieve growth, development and thereby stability, which would in turn reinforce the peace and security of the whole region. Although not stated in these terms, it would appear that America is prepared to invest

G*

substantially in Indian development in order to maintain an important component of the global status quo. However, this is proving a more complex strategy than had at first been anticipated. At its inception such an outlook assumed a continuous dialogue at top government level over broad economic priorities and the place of American aid in the Plans, the right of India to define and implement its own basic objectives being accepted. Under the Kennedy Administration, however, the ideological limits of American aid strategy were put to the test. Despite heavy pressure from the President and his advisers, the Congress proved unwilling to support public sector enterprises outside the sphere of 'infrastructure' projects. This has, of course, confirmed certain stereotypes in the Indian view of American aid. The rejection of the Bokaro steel mill project seems in retrospect to mark the beginning of a new trend towards sharper questioning of basic assumptions and a greater determination by the United States to demand results. If this trend was appearing under Kennedy, it has certainly characterised the Johnson Administration. The commitment to stability and growth is still substantial, but in return for aid the United States has demanded a major concentration of effort and resources on the problems of food production and population control and the elimination of administrative and institutional 'bottlenecks' to their solution. To say the least this indicates a less sensitive approach to the whole question of India's domestic sovereignty. In the short period, however, surplus food aid has been stepped up and in many cases has brought the accusation that the United States is using such aid to gain undue leverage over Indian policy-making, both domestic and foreign. American aid is on such a massive scale that such charges are inevitable and the United States will naturally expect some satisfaction in return for its investment. However, food aid carries with it certain specially invidious characteristics, and if the United States intends to sustain the new type of role I have described, some different styles must be evolved in order that her assistance may secure legitimacy. Perhaps this can never be achieved until India is clearly on the road to finding real economic strength and maturity; but the attempt must be made.

Although the Soviet Union has seemed generally content to explain its aid policy in ideological, or at least anti-Western polemical terms, on closer examination its objectives prove to have been influenced far more by diplomatic than by ideological considerations. This fact is demonstrated by its consistently cavalier treatment of the Communist Party of India. The forms of Soviet aid to India have proved mutually convenient, providing assistance to public sector development of heavy industry, oil exploration and refining. This has been of vital strategic importance in allowing India to pursue her own chosen pattern of development. The political impact of Soviet aid on India has for this reason been out of all proportion to its amount. The refusal of the United States to compete in these areas of the economy, except through the medium of the private sector, has given Russia ample opportunity to persuade India of the benefits of adopting the Soviet model of economic development, besides the chance to develop a mutually convenient pattern of trade. Nevertheless, the Indian private sector is now clearly growing at a more rapid rate than the public sector, while agriculture has been accorded a key role. The Soviet niche in heavy industrial development is secure and this sector may expect some continued and modest growth; but the original glamour is now somewhat dimmed in proportion to the general disenchantment with the concept of Five Year Plans. Nevertheless, this pattern of assistance has given Russia a continuing stake in India. Her basic diplomatic objective would appear to be the mitigation of Western influence in India, especially in the sphere of foreign policy. In this she has been generally successful. Possibly some ideological bonuses were expected at the outset in terms of domestic economic policies, but as these have not accrued and as Russia has not altered its pattern of aid, one may reasonably assume that she is content with diplomatic successes. The threat of China has given her a stake in the stability and security of'India, although she has not been willing to play the overall support role borne by the United States. This allows her to avoid the political embarrassments borne by the United States, maintain the prestige which her own style of aid attracts, and tolerate with equanimity the enjoyment by India of the economic fruits of 'non-alignment'. However, the new balance of international interests and pressures on the subcontinent built up since the Sino-Indian border war in 1962 and the ideological split in the Communist camp determine the limits of Indian bargaining power.

The degree to which India has been forced to yield to external pressure is difficult to determine due to the generally secret nature of aid negotiations. It is unlikely, in any case, that donors will make a direct connection between offers of aid and the adoption of a given political course by India, especially where foreign policy matters are concerned. More subtle diplomatic methods will be adopted. On the foreign policy front, while pressures have been extensive it is clear that aid has made no significant impact, though it may have encouraged some modification in certain instances.[2] Pressures have undoubtedly increased on this front since the Indo-Pakistan war in 1965, but the impact on India's foreign policy approach and military emphasis seems negligible. However, during the latter period the diplomatic atmosphere has been in no way comparable to the Dulles era and the United States appears to have shifted its major criteria to the economic sphere. It is in matters of detail that donors have been far more able to exert influence. Furthermore, important modifications of principle and emphasis have been effected in matters urged by donors, notably the World Bank and the United States, especially towards the end of the period covered, but the extent to which the Indian government was influenced by foreign opinion rather than by internal political factors and their own economic judgments is not certain. The possibility that donors may genuinely persuade India that a given course of action is in her own best interests should not be ignored. India has never displayed unwillingness to listen to foreign advice,[3] but the form in which such advice is given is extremely important. If influence linked to aid has been confined to the domestic front and advice presented in a strictly pragmatic and non-ideological manner, the effect on India's planning and development might have been far more widespread and beneficial. Present efforts to concentrate on the key problems of agriculture and population are weakened by past mistakes.

India's dependence on external aid has increased continuously. The proportion of external assistance to public sector investment on Plan projects rose from 10 per cent during the First Plan to 24 per cent in the Second Plan to an estimated 29.3 per cent in the Third Plan. The entire foreign exchange component of Plan projects during the Third Plan was financed by external assistance and indebtedness was expected to grow seriously during the Fourth Plan.[4] In this context, the extent to which India has maintained her political and administrative independence and the finesse with which she has neutralised aid issues with highly sensitive political connotations within a carefully defined technical and administrative framework is indeed remarkable.

Several contributing factors may be identified. First, despite numerous differences with the donor countries over domestic and foreign policy, she has maintained a generally clear idea of the purposes for which aid was required, related to detailed development plans. Despite numerous adjustments in accordance with changing circumstances, both external and internal, and despite numerous 'bottlenecks' in the economy and administrative system, this sense of clarity has been maintained. Together with rigid control over the private sector and the highly developed administrative machinery for processing foreign aid,[5] the defences against external influences over development and policy are considerable. A second factor is the large and growing number of donors, anxious to use aid as a means of trade. Despite India's dependence on a few large donors, above all the United States, this factor does increase her bargaining power. With experience, considerable expertise and knowledge of relative costs, technical ability, etc. in the various donor countries has been developed, and despite the factor of tied aid some choice is left open as to which country will be invited to take up particular projects within their overall financial commitment.[6] Corresponding influence by the small donor countries is very limited, as only the major donors carry significant weight.

Turning to broader policy questions, the major factor during the period under review has been East-West competition. This period has witnessed the transformation from Cold War to 'peaceful coexistence' and by the end of the period substantial areas of common interest had emerged. To this extent India's bargaining power has been marginally reduced, though the United States and the Soviet Union still retain both positive and negative reasons for maintaining the existing balance. As frequently emphasised, the willingness of the Soviet bloc to finance sectors of the Plan which the United States and the World Bank were unwilling to support has been a crucial factor in India's development strategy. At the same time the willingness of other Western donors, notably Britain and West Germany to undertake public sector industrial projects has further enhanced her bargaining power. Above all India's strategic position in world politics has always been too vital for the major countries to ultimately withold assistance from her, whatever the extent of disagreement.

In her negotiations with aid-giving countries, India has achieved some significant successes, of which the most important has been her persuasion of a wide range of donors that her economic development is worth substantial financial backing. Furthermore, despite grave doubts on particular aspects, the concept of planning has received broad approval. India has received progressively larger sums of aid while substantially protecting her political independence. On points of detail drastic improvement in terms of loans have been negotiated and during the latter part of the period important reductions in the practice of project-tying have been negotiated with some countries.[7] Against this, some failures must be recorded. Although India has received formal approval of her Plans, and substantial assistance, she has failed to evoke significant enthusiasm. Criticism and scepticism in the West have remained at a high level throughout this period, especially since the formulation of the Second Five Year Plan. This is reflected in the American failure to evoke from other Western donors the level of assistance for which she had hoped, despite moderate successes achieved through the medium of the Consortium. Western opinion has become progressively more concerned with the deficiencies of Indian agriculture, notwithstanding notable advances on the industrial front. Though India continues to be regarded as a test-case of an underdeveloped country attempting to achieve economic 'take-off' by relatively democratic means, there is now far less tendency to talk of Indian development in terms of 'demonstration' effect. A further notable failure for India, and a continued underlying source of friction, is her failure to persuade the United States and the World Bank to assist public sector projects outside the 'infrastructure' category. Though this has not blocked her chosen pattern of development, it has proved a most important inhibiting factor. In matters of detail the most important frustrations for her have been the failure to secure adequate advance commitments, the extent of 'project-tying' still in operation, and her inability to persuade Western countries to assist with the problem of repayment by offering generous tariff concessions.[8]

As well as identifying issues arising from aid negotiations of political significance, this work has concentrated on Indian attitudes. The difficulties of isolating aid from other related factors has been amply demonstrated, and only the broadest conclusions are possible. However, the overall judgment would be that the Indian reaction is generally negative, in the sense that aid only becomes a live issue when negotiations on some particular aspect reveal sharp differences of opinion. For policy-makers and administrators it constitutes an unpredictable variable to be integrated into the development plans, their foremost priority. Apart from occasional ministerial outbursts, official statements are formulated in the briefest and most general style. In answer to parliamentary and press questioning and polemics, ministers and officials are adamant against any suggestions that aid involves external interference in Indian affairs. The complexities involved in aid relationships are carefully avoided. Greatest hostility is displayed in Parliament and the press, but here again this varies greatly according to immediate issues and appears to be mainly a by-product of domestic political conflicts. From the evidence of opinion polls,[9] and in view of the high level of illiteracy, popular knowledge of the existence of foreign aid appears to be significant, though knowledge of the issues involved is probably slight. From being relatively unimportant in the earlier years, during the Third Plan period aid appears to have become at least an identifiable contributing factor in determining popular attitudes, though the precise extent cannot be measured. Nevertheless, foreign policy issues of immediate relevance to India's borders appear to be preeminent as opinion-formers. Otherwise there appears to be continued support for the concept of 'non-alignment' according to its broadest definition and aid would generally be viewed within this context. By extension, the general public seem less sensitive than the politicians and less concerned with the complexities of aid bargaining than their leaders, being generally content to accept assistance from any quarter, except where the crudest attempts to attach offensive conditions are plainly visible.

However, it is at the level of leadership and informed opinion that attitudes are most important and here, over and above the specific attitudes analysed, one is aware of an underlying duality. The more psychological aspects involved do not obviously admit of objective analysis, at least within the framework and methodology of this work. Equally, it would be unobjective to deny that such aspects exist. Basically, the main source of tension is to be found in the conflict between the desire for self-reliance and acute awareness of India's continued and growing dependence on aid. At the senior policy and planning levels this conflict is partially resolved in two ways. First, insistence on the objective of independence, or at least the significant reduction in foreign assistance within the foreseeable future, becomes progressively more emphatic. At the same time the pressure on the donor countries for more generous aid here and now becomes stronger, its temporary nature being continually emphasised. While the fate of the Fourth Plan was still in the balance, a concept generally referred to as the 'hump' was developed. According to this theory, large injections of aid will enable India to reach 'take-off' in five or ten years, and aid may then be tapered off. Despite the enthusiasm of many Indian planners and some American liberals, the Johnson Administration backed by an increasingly sceptical public opinion, has chosen to see the 'hump' as a mountain—with insufficient evidence that green pastures lie on the other side. Secondly, while perfunctory expressions of gratitude continue to be made where appropriate, the theme of mutual interest is increasingly stressed. As one commentator puts it, India 'has increasingly come to regard aid to underdeveloped countries as something in the enlightened self-interest of developed countries, as an act of faith rather than of grace, as a responsibility rather than as charity, however exotically labelled'.[10] At the same time India 'views herself as deserving of special consideration in the near future', on the grounds, explained by B. K. Nehru, of population, stability of government and administration, extent of technical and managerial expertise, and existence of real potential for achieving self-sustaining growth if the one seriously deficient factor of capital is adequately supplied. Above all, India was striving to maintain democracy and achieve development without serious restriction of individual liberty.[11] In this respect Indian planners and policy-makers would seem to have come partially to believe Western propaganda to the effect that they are indispensable in the ideological struggle between Communism and democracy. As a result, considerable complacency seems to exist that the West will always pour in sufficient funds to keep India afloat. The other aspect of the theme of mutual interest is the belief that the donor countries derive definite economic advantages from aid-giving. The practice of aid-tying guarantees them trade, and when country of origin-tying is supplemented by project-tying, India's bargaining power with suppliers is seriously reduced.[12] The latter may sometimes in effect determine their own price, their own fees for technical services, etc., the quality of goods supplied and the salaries of personnel sent to India. In India's view she is ultimately paying for these goods and services and resentment at loss of bargaining power amongst informed opinion should by no means be underestimated. The self-interest of both donor countries and India is therefore taken as axiomatic at the planning level and the question of gratitude does not arise. In this context it is not surprising that there is a growing desire among informed (and semi-informed) circles to be rid of aid as soon as possible. Many Indians would argue that aid props up inefficient political and bureaucratic systems and prevents a mood of realism from emerging. This approach naturally tends to express itself in terms of internal politics rather than through the mechanism of external diplomacy.

Since aid has been viewed as an aspect of international relations, the main weight of this study has naturally been given to the two most powerful rival donors, Russia and America. It is therefore appropriate to attempt a concluding assessment of the comparative political impact of their aid programmes in India. Here one must at once admit a general bias of opinion at the senior administrative level in favour of the Soviet Union. It is also clear that the balance of comment in Parliament and press is unfavourable to the United States, though according to opinion polls the balance would appear to be more even among the general public. The Soviet Union has several obvious points in its favour. First, its emphasis on heavy industry gives its aid clear prestige impact, industrialisation being viewed as the only means whereby an underdeveloped country could liberate itself from the shackles of colonialism, whereas America's constant emphasis on the need to give agriculture a far higher priority, while correct in retrospect, seemed until the latter part of the period to raise a question whether she really wanted India to escape from economic backwardness. The Soviet emphasis on public sector heavy industry has coincided perfectly with India's own concept of a 'socialist pattern of society'. As frequently emphasised, the importance of Soviet aid in India's development strategy has been out of all proportion to its quantum. Thus in the oil industry, Russian assistance has allowed India to establish public sector enterprises in all sections of the industry and so weaken the stranglehold of three dominant Western companies. This process has no doubt produced ideological rigidities and an 'uneconomic' use of scarce resources. In the long run, however, the improvement in bargaining power may bring the cost factor into a more favourable perspective. In the steel industry the prestige impact of Bhilai has been very great and by general consent its performance has been better than the two Western assisted steel mills of comparable size. The unwillingness of America to assist with the Bokaro project has further enhanced the value of Soviet Aid in the promotion of India's own chosen style of development. The means of repayment for these various projects is provided by the 'aid and trade' formula and in view of her heavy load of external debt, this system is very acceptable to India. A further important point in the Russians' favour is their policy of not concerning themselves with the overall economic viability of India's Plans. While close supervision is maintained over individual projects in the early stages, the advisory role is scrupulously maintained. Indians are rapidly trained and the project handed over as quickly as possible. While this is the general policy of Western donors, the Russians would appear to place more deliberate emphasis on these aspects. In general, the Soviet Union has the image in India of a country that has pulled itself up by its 'bootstraps' to a leading industrial power, from whom India could learn much. Perhaps the most important factor in Russia's favour has nothing to do with aid—her consistent support for India, at least up to the time of Tashkent, over Kashmir and all other foreign policy issues of immediate relevance to the Indian national interest. Had the Soviet line been different in this sphere, it is probable that her economic assistance would have been viewed in a rather different light.

Less favourable aspects of Soviet aid, from the Indian viewpoint, are the apparent lack of interest or capacity for provision of aid to agriculture.[13] Apart from one mechanised farm, the Soviet contribution in this increasingly vital sphere has been zero. Despite the crucial nature of Soviet aid, India's planners realise its limitations in size and scope. It is the United States and the World Bank which are relied on to provide the real overall support for her development. In some respects this fact constitutes a political advantage to Russia in that India does not experience the same sense of massive dependence as with the United States. Her investment in a crucial and prestige sector of the economy does not involve the same concern with overall viability, with its attendant frictions. In another sense, however, she cannot expect to carry the same weight in influencing the direction of the economy. Another weak point is that her loans are both project- and country-tied, and her normal repayment period of twelve years is relatively short. These last factors, however, are partially offset by the system of rupee repayments through 'aid and trade'.[14]

It should be noted that the growth of the Indian private sector may in time be expected to limit the role of Soviet aid in development, relatively if not absolutely. Foreign investment is developing at a steady rate and India has progressively extended the incentives for overseas capital, even though cumbersome bureaucratic procedures and residual attitudes of hostility limit this trend. The concentration of foreign capital in areas of most up-to-date technology must eventually weaken the public sector cum Russian assistance strategy, although the existence of such an alternative will continue to give Indian governments some leverage in their negotiations with foreign investors, the extent of such leverage depending on the capacity of the Soviet Union to diversify its investment pattern. For instance, lack of Soviet interest in the development of petrochemicals and fertiliser production in India would seem to weaken the value of future public sector Russian assisted oil refineries.

To view developments in a proper perspective, it is necessary to be aware of a several-pronged interaction between Indian and foreign investors, the Indian government and the various donor countries and institutions. The collaboration technique is becoming well established in the private sector and the configuration of interests entailed by such a line of development will increasingly affect future aid patterns. However, numerous permutations will be possible, since the interests of Indian and foreign investors both differ and coincide at various points. Indian businessmen are to some extent nationalistic, both by conviction and interest, in their attitudes to foreign capital. At the same time they use the question of incentives to overseas investors as a weapon against the advance of socialism on the domestic front, despite the fact that some basic development of the public sector is seen to be beneficial to private enterprise. Extension of these attitudes will be expressed towards various forms of foreign aid. At the same time, the Indian government's attitude towards the domestic private sector is ambivalent, being concerned both to eliminate inefficiencies and monopolies, if necessary by allowing the entry of foreign investment, and at the same time to build up national self-reliance and productive capacity. These contrary pressures are also reflected in aid bargaining.

America's predominance in the supply of aid to India is overwhelming,[15] yet her comparative failure in public relations impact is remarkable. The main points of criticism would appear to be: 1. The apparent connection at various periods between aid, military alliances, and other foreign policy issues; 2. The apparently ideological emphasis on the private sector and refusal to support public sector non-infrastructure industrial projects—an emphasis which was dramatically illustrated by the case of the Bokaro steel mill;[16] 3. The diffuse nature of American compared with Soviet aid; 4. Doubt as to whether the United States really approves of the objective of rapid industrialisation. These are all weighty factors, but probably the root cause of American unpopularity is the simple fact of dependence. Skilled diplomacy, which the United States has increasingly displayed, may reduce tensions but cannot in such a situation remove them. She is thus in a special position compared with every other donor. Dependence is aggravated by uncertainty and tensions are increased by the annual necessity to run the gauntlet of Congress. Lately, India's food crisis has increased the frequency of PL 480 negotiations, heightening American demands for policy adjustments and India's sense of dependence and resentment. By contrast, the Soviet system of aid carries far greater long-term certainty, though it should be noted that concentration on a few major projects necessarily involves long-term commitment.

Although from a goodwill aspect American aid has serious disadvantages compared with the Soviet Union, its political and economic impact, in the broadest sense, may eventually be more profound. Thus, while aid spread over a wide range of projects large and small may not have such a great public relations impact, it may still eventually improve the lot of a far greater number of people. The American concern for balanced development, although unpopular with Indian planners, may in the end contribute substantially to economic and therefore political stability. If this occurs, the United States will have achieved its main objective, whether it receives popularity or not. The growing emphasis on agriculture creates a situation where the type of aid America is better suited than Russia to give will now receive a very high priority. The high proportion of food aid to total American aid creates an image of generosity, but also of charity, and therefore President Johnson's concern for India to achieve self-reliance is at least equal to that expressed by Indian leaders. If self-sufficiency in agriculture were to be achieved, with maximum internal and external resources being allocated to this objective, the whole ethos surrounding American aid might change. However, there is a serious doubt as to how far the United States will back India's efforts. Aid to India is now being cut back as part of a general cut in the American foreign aid budget. Future prospects are uncertain and will depend not only on India's performance, but on the course of the Vietnam war and internal American pressures. From the evidence available it also appears probable that the process of bargaining will get far tougher and that there will be fewer inhibitions, on the part of the United States and the World Bank at least, in imposing conditions on future loans. The nature of these conditions will probably show a different emphasis compared with the greater part of the period analysed. Although disapproval of the public sector, outside a limited sphere, is likely to persist and although the United States will probably continue to show its concern over such matters as a Kasmir settlement, Indian defence spending, attitudes to Communism, etc. the real weight of pressure may be expected over questions of internal priorities. Though the Soviet bloc's stake in heavy industrial development is still crucial and may be expected to grow in absolute terms, India's own emphasis on agriculture makes the future American role decisive. Whereas the basic Kennedy style assumed a dialogue confined to formal questions of economics, a serious attack on India's agricultural problems must imply a far deeper involvement in basic social and administrative questions, necessarily entailing the charge of political interference.[17] Successful absorption of aid depends on many factors that only India can determine. Formal political and economic issues reach down to more fundamental features of the Indian scene—regional antagonisms, linguistic and caste politics, social taboos and institutional barriers.

In this context it may well be argued that aid can only act as a catalyst, in a rather marginal sense, in assisting the forces of modernisation within India. Even in a strictly economic context, therefore, one may doubt the wisdom of proceeding beyond the level of involvement obtaining under the Kennedy Administration, though very possibly Kennedy himself might have wished to move far more rapidly, However, should the imperative need for quick results impel the United States to take the risk, a clear definition of functional relationships must be established, involving major adjustments by all concerned. Unless aid can achieve some reasonable degree of legitimacy in this new context, all these efforts will prove self-defeating, whatever the level of expertise attained.

To these ends certain principles, simple in conception yet highly complex in application, need to be established. Had these been understood from the beginning many difficulties could have been avoided. I would therefore advocate the following basic approach as a means of reconciling the types of conflict I have described.

1. India must continue to be recognised as the final arbiter of her own destinies. With the possible abandonment of formal Five Year Plans this principle could become obscured. The donor countries must accept, not only in principle but in spirit, India's right to determine her own pattern of economic and social development and the values associated therewith.

2. Once this first principle has been accepted, aid-givers have a perfect right to express disagreement on all matters, general and particular. India must therefore accept that so long as she receives aid there will be a dialogue in which she can expect both her policies and methods of administration to be called into question. What counts is the quality of the dialogue, in which the functional roles of all concerned must be properly defined. Once it is established that India has the last word and so long as there is felt to be a genuine interest and spirit of cooperation by donors, she will accept questioning and advice, with proper discretion, on most matters related to development. In this context there can be a profitable interaction of ideas and experience.

3. Where consensus cannot be achieved on this basis with regard to specific projects and objectives, aid-givers are properly entitled to withold aid from the relevant area of the economy by the relevant amount. The really serious political difficulties arise when aid is witheld or unduly delayed with reference to general areas of policy, domestic or foreign, where the reasons for such occurrences are vague and undefined and where the quantities involved are subject to uncertainty. Indians are often aware of undefined pressures in

various directions, but the relationship of these pressures to each other is rarely measurable, even in retrospect. The powers concerned show tendencies to apply pressures on an *ad hoc* basis and perhaps do not even properly understand the process themselves. Where aid is witheld in a limited economic area for a specific reason the political consequences are manageable, but where specific disagreements are converted into generalised pressures or vice versa then confusion, despondency and bad blood are infused into the whole pattern of aid relationships.

Of course, these prescriptions are very much over-simplified, especially since a greater proportion of future aid may be expected to enter on a non-project basis. However, so far as possible, the areas both of agreement and disagreement should be carefully defined. Aid must be confined to areas of firm agreement, in recognition of the fact that only where Indian initiative is exercised both in planning and execution of programmes can foreign aid play its proper supplementary role in achieving worthwhile results. Perhaps the point of no return has already been passed but some definite formulation of principles on these lines would be a considerable improvement compared with the present state of drift.

The fundamentally political nature of aid has been established by this analysis. In India's case a variety of special circumstances, together with a certain degree of mythology, have combined to conceal this unpalatable truth. The harsher realities of foreign aid experienced by many smaller countries have been milder in their impact upon her. Her growing weaknesses now render her more vulnerable. Leadership and restraint by all concerned will be vitally necessary during the crisis period ahead. However, in such a rapidly changing situation, a more open recognition of political factors by all parties could well constitute the main pre-requisite for the evolution of more realistic and constructive aid relationships. In the context of a deteriorating political situation, it is essential that India spells out a legitimate role for foreign aid programmes and the associated personnel, making clear those forms of involvement that are acceptable and those that are not. She must also define her internal objectives clearly if she wishes to prevent foreign influence from taking advantage of her divisions. Once this is done, India must be prepared to shoulder squarely her administrative responsibilities and not to use alleged and undefined pressures from foreign aid-givers as a blanket defence to cover her own shortcomings. Without a consensus on basic objectives and respective roles, aid cannot function effectively. The atmosphere surrounding aid has deteriorated sharply during the last two or three years and if it is to continue at all the whole concept will need re-definition. On all sides, policy and attitudes are to far too great an extent the by-product of other pressures.

Appendix no. 1

Overall aid contributions may be assessed under the following categories: 1. Total contribution by Country/Institution; 2. Proportion of loan and grant contributions; 3. Interest rates and repayment periods. 4. Distribution according to purpose; 5. Allocation between public and private sectors; 6. The degree to which aid is tied to projects and to supplies from the country of origin.

Table 1 shows total aid to India in all forms from the beginning of the First Five Year Plan up to 31st March 1965.

Table 1
Foreign aid–sources

(crores of rupees)

country or institution	aid authorised	per cent of total	aid utilised	per cent of total
IBRD	403.4	7.7	358.6	9.6
IDA	230.9	4.4	110.7	3.0
United States	2,719.3	51.7	2,178.0	58.4
Soviet Union	485.4	9.2	245.2	6.6
West Germany	402.8	7.7	295.8	7.9
United Kingdom	330.7	6.3	250.0	6.7
Canada	181.5	3.5	138.2	3.7
Japan	145.0	2.8	82.1	2.2
Italy	64.1	1.2	9.0	0.2
Czechoslovakia	63.1	1.1	6.0	0.2
France	47.6	0.9	13.0	0.3
Poland	40.3	0.7	9.8	0.3
Yugoslavia	19.1	0.4	4.3	0.1
Netherlands	15.8	0.3	2.8	0.08
Switzerland	15.3	0.3	2.0	0.05
Australia	15.2	0.3	14.4	0.4
Belgium	9.6	0.2	1.2	0.03
Austria	6.1	0.1	2.5	0.07
Norway	4.6	0.09	4.0	0.1
New Zealand	4.1	0.08	3.6	0.1
Sweden	2.2	0.04	–	–
Denmark	2.4	0.05	0.4	0.01
United Nations	50.4	1.0	–*	–*
total	5,258.9	100.0	3,731.6	100.0

*Lack of data

Note: Source for all tables, *Report on Currency and Finance for the Year 1964-65*, Reserve Bank of India, Bombay, 1965, pp s 134-49

The dominating position of the United States is quite apparent, providing over five times the quantum of assistance compared with any single donor, and over half the total assistance. This is a fact of overwhelming political significance in considering Indian attitudes to American aid, on which her Plans are so obviously dependent. Concentration of aid-giving in a few hands is equally apparent. Five donors, the World Bank, the United States, the Soviet Union, West Germany and the United Kingdom provide 87 per cent of authorised and 92.2 per cent of utilised aid. The World Bank ranks second after the United States and in view of its provision of aid untied to purchases in specific countries, its role in development planning is of crucial importance in the context of India's chronic foreign exchange deficit. The Soviet Union is the third largest source in terms of aid authorised, with 9.2 per cent of the total, but in terms of aid actually utilised she ranks slightly behind West Germany and the United Kingdom–a somewhat remarkable fact in view of the prestige accorded to her aid. Communist countries combined provided 11.6 per cent of aid authorised and a mere 7.2 per cent of aid utilised. The political significance and impact of aid from Communist sources must therefore be presumed to lie in causes other than the mere quantum provided.

Table 2 shows that the loan component of total aid authorised up to 31st March 1965 constituted 65.8 per cent, the proportion growing steadily. Since PL 480 aid mostly materialises in loan form, the role of grant aid is clearly diminishing, a fact of qualitative as well as quantitative significance.

Table 3 shows that only Australia, New Zealand, Norway and the United Nations give aid in 100 per cent grant form. Canada is the only

Table 2
Aid distribution by type

Type of aid	aid authorised	per cent of total	aid utilised	per cent of total
loans repayable in foreign currency	3,168.3	60.2	2,008.9	53.8
loans repayable in rupees	294.7	5.6	263.0	7.0
grants	374.8	7.1	295.8*	7.9
other assistance–PL 480, 665 and 3rd country currency assistance from the United States	1,421.1	27.0	1,163.9	31.2
total	5,258.9	100.0	3,731.6	100.0

*UN aid utilisation not included

other nation to give the majority of its aid in this form. The United States provides the largest amount in absolute terms, though grant aid has constituted only a small proportion of its total aid.

Table 3
Distribution of aid by type and source (per cent)

country or institution	loans repayable in foreign currency		loans repayable in rupees		grants		PL 480, 665 etc.	
	authorised	utilised	authorised	utilised	authorised	utilised	authorised	utilised
IBRD	100.0	100.0	–	–	–	–	–	–
IDA	100.0	100.0	–	–	–	–	–	–
United States	31.0	27.4	10.8	12.1	5.9	7.1	52.3	53.4
Canada	25.7	16.2	–	–	74.3	83.8	–	–
Australia	–	–	–	–	100.0	100.0	–	–
United Kingdom	99.5	99.6	–	–	0.5	0.4	–	–
New Zealand	–	–	–	–	100.0	100.0	–	–
Poland	–	–	100.0	100.0	–	–	–	–
Yugoslavia	–	–	100.0	100.0	–	–	–	–
Czechoslovakia	–	–	100.0	100.0	–	–	–	–
Austria	100.0	100.0	–	–	–	–	–	–
Belgium	100.0	100.0	–	–	–	–	–	–
Netherlands	100.0	100.0	–	–	–	–	–	–
Norway	–	–	–	–	100.0	100.0	–	–
Sweden	100.0	–	–	–	–	–	–	–
Denmark	58.3	–	41.7	100.0	–	–	–	–
West Germany	99.5	99.4	–	–	0.5	0.6	–	–
Japan	100.0	100.0	–	–	–	–	–	–
Soviet Union	–	–	99.8	99.4	0.2	0.6	–	–
Switzerland	100.0	100.0	–	–	–	–	–	–
France	100.0	100.0	–	–	–	–	–	–
Italy	100.0	100.0	–	–	–	–	–	–
United Nations	–	–	–	–	100.0	100.0	–	–

Table 4 shows that far more aid has been devoted to industrial development (58.2 per cent of authorised aid up to 31st March 1965) than to any other purpose. This reflects India's own development bias during the Second and Third Plans, though the emphasis is now shifting to agriculture. It also reflects the bias of most donors, the majority of whom regard trade promotion as a prime motive for the provision of aid.

Table 4
Overall distribution of aid by purpose

(per cent)

purpose	loans authorised	loans utilised
railway development	10.3	14.1
power and irrigation	8.3	6.5
steel and iron ore	15.0	15.4
port development	1.2	1.0
transport and communications	2.9	3.0
industrial development	58.2	54.3
agricultural development	0.9	0.9
wheat loan (1st plan only)	3.1	4.8

From table 5 it is apparent that while aid for industrial development is widespread, assistance for the vital but less profitable 'infrastructure' section of the economy has been wholly carried by the World Bank, the United States and Canada.

Table 5
Percentage aid distribution by country to various purposes

(per cent)

	railway development	power and irrigation	steel and iron ore	port development	transport and communications	industrial development	agricultural development (including American wheat loan)
IBRD	44.6	10.8	20.7	7.4	0.7	14.9	0.8
IDA	26.7	11.5	–	3.7	27.8	18.6	11.7
United States	9.1	16.7	4.3	–	2.6	59.3	7.9
Canada	7.2	49.9	1.9	–	4.1	3.2	33.6
Soviet Union	–	–	34.1	–	–	65.9	–
France	–	–	–	–	–	58.5	–
United Kingdom	–	–	21.1	–	–	78.9	–
Italy	–	–	–	–	–	100.0	–
Czechoslovakia	–	–	–	–	–	100.0	–
Yugoslavia	–	–	–	–	–	100.0	–
Poland	–	–	–	–	–	100.0	–
Switzerland	–	–	–	–	–	100.0	–
Austria	–	–	–	–	–	100.0	–
Belgium	–	–	–	–	–	100.0	–
Netherlands	–	–	–	–	–	100.0	–
Sweden	–	–	–	–	–	100.0	–
Denmark	–	–	–	–	–	100.0	–
Japan	–	–	–	–	–	100.0	–

Table 6 shows the special World Bank interest in railways and other forms of transport and communication, while the United States has provided the bulk of assistance for power and agricultural development. Other countries have, of course, provided technical assistance for these purposes.

Table 6
Donors' share of aid for infrastructure purposes

(per cent)

country/ institution	railways	power	transport and communications	agriculture*	total
IDA	17.7	9.4	65.1	19.7	20.7
IBRD	51.6	15.4	2.7	2.5	26.5
United States	29.7	67.0	30.2	66.3	47.7
Canada	1.0	8.2	1.9	11.5	5.1
total	100.0	100.0	100.0	100.0	100.0

*Includes 1st Plan Wheat Loan.

The Soviet Union's lead in steel development is evident from table 7 and will become more apparent as the Bokaro scheme matures. West Germany, the United Kingdom and the World Bank (private sector only) have been the other main contributors. The United States has made no direct contribution to the construction of any steel plant, though it has been associated with Japan in the Bailadilla (Orissa) iron ore project. Its credits have been largely used for imports of steel products.

Table 7
Percentage share of loans by country for steel* and iron ore projects in India to 31st March 1965

country/institution	loans authorised	loans utilised
IBRD	16.4	22.3
United States	9.6	14.1
Canada	0.2	0.03
Soviet Union	32.4	19.0
West Germany	27.1	28.9
United Kingdom	13.6	15.1
Japan	0.7	0.6
total	100.0	100.0

*Includes imports.

Table 8 shows the contribution of various donors towards assistance in India's industrial development (other than steel and iron ore).

Table 8
Percentage share of loans by country for industrial development to 31st March 1965

donor	authorised	utilised
IBRD	3.0	2.8
IDA	2.2	1.1
United States	34.1	42.8
Canada	0.07	0.04
Soviet Union	16.1	15.0
West Germany	9.9	10.8
France	2.4	1.1
United Kingdom	13.1	16.5
Italy	3.2	0.8
Czechoslovakia	3.2	0.5
Yugoslavia	1.0	0.4
Poland	2.0	0.8
Switzerland	0.8	0.2
Austria	0.3	0.2
Belgium	0.5	0.1
Netherlands	0.8	0.2
Denmark	0.1	0.03
Sweden	0.1	–
Japan	7.1	6.7
total	100.0	100.0

It is a surprising fact that apart from steel development, America's contribution to India's industrial development was more than twice that of Russia, whose financial provision has generally been comparable to that of the United Kingdom. The popular association of Russia with industrial development is no doubt due to her concentration on a few heavy industrial projects in the public sector, whereas American aid is more widely distributed. West Germany and Japan have also made significant contributions. The low World Bank contribution may mean that industrialisation is accorded a low priority, but it is more likely that the Bank prefers to concentrate its limited funds on the key 'infrastructure' sectors neglected by the majority of donors.

The question of allocation of aid funds between public and private sectors is one of considerable political significance. Unfortunately, precise data cannot be obtained due to the large 'non-project' and 'semi-project' (i.e. aid fixed within broad categories) component of loan aid. These are classified as Public/Private in the official sources used. Data is also incomplete with regard to grants and technical assistance, though the majority of such aid may be assumed to go to the public sector.

Table 9 shows that while Soviet aid is 100 per cent in the public sector, the American contribution in that direction is nonetheless significant, especially when technical aid and projects financed from PL 480 counterpart funds are added. American propaganda fails to point out that her own overall contribution to the public sector is at least comparable to that of Russia, but it is for infrastructure rather than heavy industrial purposes. It is the American and World Bank abstention from public sector heavy industrial development that gives Soviet aid its special value in Indian eyes, though the British and West German contribution here has also been useful.

Table 9
Percentage donor distribution between public and private sectors/percentage donor contribution to public and private sectors (loans* authorised to 31st March 1965)

donor	public sector	private sector	mixed	public sector	private sector	mixed
IBRD	61.7	38.3	–	14.7	46.1	–
IDA	81.4	18.6	–	11.1	12.8	–
United States	40.8	9.4	49.7	27.4	32.0	41.5
Canada	96.8	3.2	–	2.7	0.4	–
Soviet Union	100.0	–	–	28.5	–	–
West Germany	41.6	–	58.4	8.2	–	14.3
France	–	10.1	89.9	–	1.4	3.1
United Kingdom	22.9	3.2	79.2	4.4	3.2	17.8
Italy	–	–	100.0	–	–	4.7
Czechoslavakia	36.7	–	63.3	1.4	–	2.9
Yugoslavia	–	–	100.0	–	–	1.4
Poland	64.5	–	35.5	1.5	–	1.0
Switzerland	–	–	100.0	–	–	1.1
Austria	–	–	100.0	–	–	0.5
Belgium	–	–	100.0	–	–	0.7
Netherlands	–	–	100.0	–	–	1.2
Denmark	–	–	100.0	–	–	0.2
Sweden	–	–	100.0	–	–	0.2
Japan	2.6	9.2	88.1	0.2	4.0	9.4
				100.0	100.0	100.0

*Excludes PL 480, 665.

Table 10 indicates the extent to which donors tie aid to projects.

Table 10
Project and non-project assistance–loans (excluding PL 480, 665 and United States third country currency assistance and commodity counterpart funds from Canada) and grants to 31st December 1964 (crores of rupees)

donor	project	semi-project	non-project	(per cent) non-project	total
Australia	15.29	–	–	–	15.29
Austria	6.11	–	–	–	6.11
Belgium	9.52	–	–	–	9.52
Britain	138.00	63.32	105.33	34.3	306.65
Canada	165.94	–	0.66	0.4	166.82
Czechoslovakia	63.70	–	–	–	63.70
Denmark	2.41	–	–	–	2.41
France	52.43	–	–	–	52.43
Italy	62.38	–	4.76	9.3	67.14
Japan	146.07	0.47	–	–	146.54
Netherlands	6.44	–	9.47	59.5	15.91
New Zealand	4.04	–	–	–	4.04
Norway	4.13	–	–	–	4.13
Poland	40.30	–	–	–	40.30
Rumania	5.59	–	–	–	5.59
Sweden	4.26	0.34	–	–	4.60
Switzerland	15.34	–	–	–	15.34
United States	475.50	28.57	459.52	47.7	963.59
Soviet Union	484.31	–	–	–	484.31
United Nations	50.44	–	–	–	50.44
West Germany	264.95	40.83	64.49	17.4	370.27
IBRD	403.81	–	–	–	403.81
IDA	230.86	–	–	–	230.86
Yugoslavia	19.74	–	–	–	19.74
total	2,671.56	133.53	644.23	18.7	3,449.34

The question of 'tied' aid is one that carries strong political overtones. Since 1959, when the United States made all its aid bilateral, no country has provided aid untied to its own supplies. The World Bank is the only source of multilateral loan aid. Only America, Britain and West Germany have provided aid untied to projects in any significant quantity.

Appendix no. 2

Extracts from industrial policy resolutions, 1956 [1]

. . . The adoption of the socialist pattern of society as the national objective, as well as the need for planned and rapid development, require that all industries of basic and strategic importance, or on the nature of public utility services, should be in the public sector. Other industries which are essential and require investment on a scale which only the State, in present circumstances, could provide, have also to be in the public sector. The State has therefore to assume direct responsibility for the future development of industries over a wider area. Nevertheless, there are limiting factors which make it necessary at this stage for the State to define the field in which it will undertake sole responsibility for further development, and to make a selection of industries in the development of which it will play a dominant role. After considering all aspects of the problem, in consultation with the Planning Commission, the Government of India have decided to classify industries into three categories, having regard to the part which the State would play in each of them. These categories will inevitably overlap to some extent and too great a rigidity might defeat the purpose in view. But the basic principles and objectives have always to be kept in view and the general directions hereafter referred to, be followed. It should also be remembered that it is always open to the State to undertake any type of industrial production.

In the first category will be industries, the future development of which will be the exclusive responsibility of the State. The second category will consist of industries, which will be progressively State-owned and in which the State will therefore generally take the initiative in establishing new undertakings, but in which private enterprise will also be expected to supplement the effort of the State. The third category will include all the remaining industries and their future development will, in general, be left to the initiative and enterprise of the private sector.

Industries in the first category have been listed in Schedule A of this Resolution. All new units in these industries save where their establishment in the private sector has already been approved, will be set up only by the State. This does not preclude the expansion of the existing privately owned units, or the possibility of the State securing the cooperation of private enterprise in the establishment of new units when the national interests so require. Railways and air transport, arms and ammunition and atomic energy will, however, be developed as Central Government monopolies. Whenever cooperation with private enterprise is necessary, the State will ensure, either through majority participation in the capital or otherwise, that it has the requisite powers to guide the policy and control the operations of the undertaking.

Industries in the second category will be those listed in Schedule B. With a view to accelerating their future development, the State will increasingly establish new undertakings in these industries. At the same time private enterprise will also have the opportunity to develop in this field, either on its own or with State participation.

All the remaining industries will fall in the third category, and it is expected that their development will be undertaken ordinarily through the initiative and enterprise of the private sector, though it will be open to the State to start any industry even in this category . . .

. . . The division of industries into separate cetegories does not imply that they are being placed in water-tight compartments. Inevitably, there will not only be an area of overlapping but also a great deal of dovetailing between industries in the private and the public sectors. It will be open to the State to start any industry not included in Schedule A and Schedule B. when the needs of planning so require or there are other important reasons for it . . .

Schedule A

1 Arms and ammunition and allied items of defence equipment.
2 Atomic energy.
3 Iron and steel
4 Heavy castings and forgings of iron and steel.
5 Heavy plant an machinery required for iron and steel production, for mining, for machine tool manufacture and for such other basic industries as may be specified by the Central Government.
6 Heavy electrical plant including large hydraulic and steam turbines.
7 Coal and lignite.
8 Mineral oils.
9 Mining of iron ore, manganese ore, chrome ore, gypsum, sulphur, gold and diamond.

10 Mining and processing of copper, lead, zinc, tin, molybdenum and wolfram.
11 Minerals specified in the Schedule to the Atomic Energy (Control of Production and Use) Order, 1953.
12 Aircraft.
13 Air transport.
14 Railway transport.
15 Ship-building.
16 Telephones and telephone cables, telegraph and wireless apparatus (excluding radio receiving sets).
17 Generation and distribution of electricity.

Schedule B

1 All other minerals except 'minor minerals' as defined in Section 3 of the Minerals Concession Rules, 1949.
2 Aluminium and other non-ferrous metals not included in Schedule 'A'.
3 Machine tools.
4 Ferro-alloys and tool steels.
5 Basic and intermediate products required by chemical industries such as the manufacture of drugs, dyestuffs and plastics.
6 Antibiotics and other essential drugs.
7 Fertilisers.
8 Synthetic rubber.
9 Carbonisation of coal.
10 Chemical pulp.
11 Road transport.
12 Sea transport.

Appendix no. 3

Foreign aid: administrative procedures

All foreign aid is integrated within the framework of India's Five Year Plans. The chief function of foreign aid is to provide plant, equipment, components and technical personnel not available in India. In particular, donor countries provide the necessary foreign exchange for the acquisition of these scarce factors. The bulk of foreign aid to India is provided for specific projects, and all the projects must first have been approved for inclusion in the current Five Year Plan.[1] In the case of foreign exchange assistance not tied to specific projects, all imports must nonetheless obtain sanction within the framework of India's total foreign exchange budget. Coordination of all requirements for and availabilities of foreign exchange, both long and short term, is effected by the Ministry of Finance, in conjunction with the Planning Commission and the Reserve Bank of India. Each project within the Plan passes through the Department of Economic Affairs of the Ministry of Finance, the Planning Commission and finally the cabinet. Liaison is maintained with the Development Wing of the Ministry of Commerce and Industry, which possesses information about equipment, personnel, etc. within the country, and sanction must be obtained from this department before expenditures are passed. In the case of technical assistance all requirements are scrutinised by a Technical Assistance Selection Committee on which the Department of Economic Affairs is represented, and for which it acts as secretariat. Its decisions are subject to approval by the Planning Commission. For every project the foreign exchange cost is estimated, and only when all these preliminary stages have been undergone is foreign assistance sought. Negotiations will be effected through the office of the Additional Secretary for Foreign Assistance Operations, Department of Economic Affairs, Ministry of Finance, though initiative in seeking assistance will also be taken through a variety of media, e.g. through diplomatic channels, United Nations forums, visits by ministers and delegations and through specific agencies such as the office of the Commissioner General for Economic Affairs, Washington, DC. Visits by heads of state, such as the visit of Kruschev and Bulganin to India in 1955, or the visit of Prime Minister Nehru to the United States in 1949, can greatly improve the climate for foreign assistance. Thus, the former visit preceded the substantial capital inflow from the Soviet Union, and the latter paved the way for the 1951 Wheat Loan[2] and speeded the flow of technical assistance under the Point Four programme.[3] The government of India has a variety of sources open to it, and will naturally select the country or agency best suited to assist the project. The procedure varies slightly in each case, but the basic procedure is as follows: First an agreement is negotiated. In most cases a technical and economic report will be prepared by the corporation concerned, in conjunction with the relevant ministry. The project will then be sponsored by the Ministry of Finance with the relevant agency of the donor country, the United Nations or with the World Bank. In the case of a large project, where the government feels that it has not sufficient technical experience to draw up the proposed project, a project report will be prepared by the donor country (e.g. the Bhilai steel mill, built by Russia) or by private consultants sponsored by the donor country (e.g. the Durgapur steel mill, built by a consortium of British steel and engineering firms). In either case, a detailed contract will finally be drawn up, stating such details as the amount loaned, the rate of interest, the period of repayment, the equipment and services to be supplied by both parties and other relevant details. The procedure for disbursement of funds varies slightly according to the donor country or agency concerned, but essentially the Reserve Bank of India is credited with the donor country's currency (or a currency mutually agreed in the case of the IBRD) against presentation of invoices or other suitable documents. The precise banking arrangements are mutually agreed, though the donor countries have established banking media to act as the source for initial disbursement and to accept ultimate repayment (e.g. the Export-Import Bank of the United States and the German Bank for Reconstruction and Development), whatever the intermediate stages. In the case of technical assistance, the procedure is very similar, negotiations and authorisations being channelled through the Department of Economic Affairs and the relevant agency of the donor country or international organisation. In this case, however, the donor country will be more active in finding suitable organisations, e.g. universities, to provide personnel, equipment, etc.[4] Responsibility for repayment is in the hands of the External Finance Division of the Department of Economic Affairs, which redeems promissory notes as they fall due.

Again, the precise banking arrangements are worked out by mutual agreement, and payments may be made either through accounts in India or in the donor country. In most cases repayment is made in the donor country's currency, but in the case of most Soviet bloc aid and a large part of American aid, repayment is made in rupees, paid to one of the donor country's accounts in India. In the case of loans made under PL 480 and PL 665, the proceeds from sale of foodstuffs or materials by the Indian government are paid into a special counterpart fund for the use of the AID in India, but mainly for mutually agreed development projects.

A continuous process of evaluation and review is maintained during the course of a project. Experts from the donor countries or the IBRD are in continuous contact with the government of India and the administering agency or corporation. Points of difference are ironed out by consultation, and in some cases the project may be revised during the course of operation; for example, the capacity of all three public sector steel mills was increased after the original project reports had been agreed. Annual reports are required under the Indo-American technical Co-operation Agreement. The IBRD and USAID make frequent technical and economic assessments of India's total requirements and utilisation of aid as well as requiring regular reports on particular projects. The Germans also maintain strict surveillance through the economic section of the German embassy in India. The British maintain surveillance through the economic commission of the United Kingdom High Commission in India, though in a somewhat more informal manner. All donor countries maintain control in one form or another. In the case of Soviet bloc countries, the contracting agencies themselves, being branches of government, bear the brunt of negotiation with the Indian government, the economic commissions of the Russian and other East European countries concerning themselves more with the promotion of trade. Foreign government agencies of Western countries, such as the French Petroleum Institute and ENI, the Italian government oil corporation, would be similarly placed to undertake negotiation and control.

Appendix no. 4

India's voting record at the United Nations (1958-62)

Summary of India's Voting Record from XIIIth to XVIIth Sessions of General Assembly (1958-62).
Source: *Foreign Operations Assistance Appropriations for 1964*, Hearings before A Subcommittee of the Committee on Appropriations, House of Representatives, U.S. Congress, 88th Congress, 2nd session, pp 238-45.

During the above period the American and Soviet voting was in direct opposition (i.e. ignoring abstentions by either country) on ninety-two resolutions. India's record on these occasions was:

Agreement with United States	19
Agreement with Soviet Union	38
Abstention	34
Not present	1

Excluding abstentions, India agreed with the United States on sixty occasions and disagreed on forty. The corresponding figures for the Soviet Union are eighty-three occasions agreed and twenty disagreed.

Breakdown of issues on which India voted with the United States where the latter was in direct opposition to the Soviet Union show the following results:

Constitutional, organisational and financial issues of the UN	7
Nuclear weapons and disarmament	4
Economic development	2
Congo	2
Korea	2
Hungary	1
Relief for Hong Kong refugees	1
total	19

Breakdown of issues where India voted with Russia where America was in direct opposition show the following results:

Colonial and trusteeship	14
African affairs and human rights	6
Congo	6

Chinese representation	5
Nuclear weapons and disarmament	4
Cuba	3
Constitutional and organisational	2
Property rights of Palestine Refugees	2
Korea	1
Establishment of commission on national rights over natural resources	1
total	38

Although the bias is in favour of the Soviet Union, the distribution of issues voted upon clearly establishes India's independence in voting according to her principles and national interest.

Appendix no. 5

Summary of the main provisions of three oil refinery agreements between the Government of India and Esso, Burmah-Shell and Caltex Ltd (November, December 1951 and March 1953)

(Source: *Establishment of Oil Refineries in India*, Text of agreement With the Oil Companies, Ministry of Production, Government of India, 1956.)

1 All three companies to be incorporated as Indian companies.
2 The Indian government to provide guarantees against nationalisation for a period of twenty-five years from the commencement of full-time refining operations.
3 Existing duty protection on oil products to be maintained for ten years from the commencement of full-time refining operations, or until 31st December 1965, whichever is the sooner.
4 Duty protection to be imposed on motor spirit of two annas per imperial gallon for a similar period.
5 Freedom to be guaranteed for the companies to purchase crude oil from any source they chose, though preference to be given to purchase in India (primarily to their own sources of supply). (The wording here is extremely vague, however, and the relevant clauses constitute no serious limitation on the companies' freedom of action.)
6 No import duty was to be imposed on crude oil until it was necessary for the protection of indigenous crude, in which case the government would take steps to ensure that the economic position of the companies was not altered to their disadvantage.
7 Import duty on all supplies, materials and equipment for the construction of the refinery and related facilities to be limited to 5¼ per cent ad valorem tax, full duty being imposed one year after the commencement of full-scale refining operations.
8 Guarantees to be given by government as to wharfage rates.
9 Foreign exchange to be guaranteed for all import requirements for

the purpose of construction and operation, freight charges, engineering and technical services, royalties, licence fees, contributions to Head Office expenses and remittance of dividends. SVOC and Caltex required a guarantee of dollars for the purchase of crude oil (presumably from themselves)–a somewhat harsh demand in view of the fact that they proposed to control 100 per cent of the ordinary shares and that the government's main objectives in sanctioning the refineries was to save foreign exchange.

10 Provision to be made by the Indian government of basic facilities such as power, water, land transport and harbour facilities. The companies agreed to assist substantially in the matter of housing for employees, either by direct building themselves or by financial contributions.

11 Tax guarantees designed to ensure that the companies lost no advantage by virtue of being incorporated as Indian companies.

An attempt was made by Burmah-Shell and Caltex to include an arbitration clause, but this was rejected. A formula was arrived at, however, as follows:

> . . . It was . . . agreed that should any difference between the Government of India and the Indian Companies arise in connection with the interpretation of the contents of the letters exchanged between the Government of India and Caltex (India) Ltd., the Government of India would in the event of failure to resolve the difference by mutual consultation and discussion, consider sympathetically any proposal that such difference should be referred to a single person to be agreed upon between the Government of India and the Indian Company or failing agreement, to be appointed by the Attorney-General of India.[1]

This clause is, in the ultimate analysis, definitely favourable to India.

With regard to the training of Indians, the companies gave guarantees in very general terms. For example the Caltex agreement reads:

> Caltex will take appropriate steps to ensure that the Indian Company will train an adequate number of Indian personnel in refinery operations for employment in the refinery and, subject to the right of the management to select personnel and to judge what is necessary for the efficient working of the refinery, will employ Indians in all capacities to the extent that qualified Indian personnel is available . . .[2]

The other agreements are similarly worded and clearly the companies are in an unassailable legal position with regard to the interpretation of this clause. The Indian Government has shown general satisfaction at the implementation of this aspect of the Agreements.

Appendix no. 6

Facilities and incentives offered to foreign private capital in India[1]

Government attitude to foreign capital

The policy of the government of India regarding foreign investment is to attract private foreign capital in those fields in which the country needs to develop in pursuance of the plan targets. Thus while government have been generally encouraging investment of private foreign capital in the country, it is on a selective basis. If any project is approved for development in the private sector and if imported plant and machinery are required, foreign investment is normally welcome as a means of financing the project.

The government of India welcome technical know-how from abroad in industrial undertakings in the public as well as in the private sector. At the present stage of India's technological research and experience, there are a number of industries in which foreign technical know-how is almost essential; in some it is indispensable.

Government consider that foreign investment has to play an important part in the schemes of economic development and it is receiving all the facilities that indigenous capital at present enjoys.

1. Once foreign capital is admitted into the country, there is no discrimination between Indian and foreign capital. Government, however, expect that all undertakings, Indian or foreign, conform to the general requirements of their industrial policy.

2. Government have continued the facilities for remittance of profits and no restrictions have been placed on withdrawal of foreign capital investments.

3. If and when foreign enterprises are acquired, compensation will be paid on a fair and equitable basis.

4. As a rule, the major interest in ownership and effective control of an undertaking should remain in Indian hands. There is however no rigid or doctrinaire insistence on this rule. Government do not object to foreign capital having control of a concern if this is found to be in the national interest. But each individual case is considered on its merits.

5. In the matter of employment of personnel, government do not

object to the employment of non-Indians in positions requiring technical skill and experience when Indians of requisite qualifications are not available. Vital importance is, however, attached to the training and employment of Indians even for such positions, in the quickest possible manner.

Taxation policy

Several tax incentives have been given by government in recent years to encourage industrial investment. Important ones are briefly indicated below:

1. Tax holiday for new industrial undertakings: Profits of a new industrial undertaking are exempt from tax up to 6 per cent of the capital employed for a period of five years. The dividends declared by such undertakings out of the exempted profits are also exempt from tax to the shareholders, who receive them.

2. Development rebate: In addition to depreciation allowances, which are liberal, a development rebate equal to 20 per cent of the cost of plant and machinery is allowed as a deduction from the taxable income in the year of installation, thus enabling the enterprise ultimately to charge to revenue 120 per cent of the cost of the asset.

3. Tax-free loans: Interest on loans obtained from approved foreign institutions or on moneys borrowed or debts incurred abroad for import of capital equipment.

4. Carry-forward of losses and allowances: If the profits of an enterprise in a year are not sufficient to absorb depreciation allowances due for that year, the unabsorbed depreciation is available for deduction from the profits of succeeding years for an unlimited period. Similarly, unabsorbed development rebate and business losses are available for carry-forward and deduction against profits for the succeeding eight years.

5. Expenditure on scientific research: In the computation of business profits, capital expenditure incurred on scientific research related to the business, is allowed to be spread over five years and charged to the revenue in addition to the current expenditure, which is allowed in full.

6. Royalties: The royalties received from an Indian concern by a foreign company in pursuance of an agreement made with it on or after 1st April 1961 which has been approved by government are charged to super-tax at a concessional rate. Thus the tax payable on such royalty is 50 per cent as against 63 per cent in the case of other income.

7. Technical personnel: Technicians of foreign nationality taking up

employment in India are exempt from tax on their remuneration for 365 days and where contracts of service are approved by government for 36 months. If the technicians continue to remain in employment in India after the 36 months and the employer pays tax on the technician's income chargeable under the head 'salaries' for a period not exceeding 24 months following the expiry of the 36 months, such tax shall not be treated as income of the technician. A 'technician' for this purpose is defined as a person (i) who has specialised knowledge and experience in constructional or manufacturing operations or in mining or generation or distribution of electricity or any form of power and (ii) who has been employed in a capacity in which such specialised knowledge and experience are actually utilised.

In the case of persons who have specialised knowledge and experience in industrial and business management techniques only, the exemption is for a period of six months from the date of their arrival in India, provided their service contracts have been approved by the central government before the commencement of their service.

8 Rebate on import earnings: A rebate of one-tenth of income tax and super-tax payable in respect of profits attributable to export earnings is allowed to an Indian company or any other company making prescribed arrangements for declaration and payment of dividends in India or any person other than a company.

9 Home leave passages: The value of periodical home leave passages provided to employees of foreign nationality is excluded from their taxable income.

10 Avoidance of double taxation: Agreements for the avoidance of double taxation exist with a number of countries, e.g. Pakistan, Ceylon, Sweden, Finland, Norway, Japan, the Federal Republic of Germany and Denmark. Agreements with the United States and France await ratification. Negotiations for the conclusion of such agreements with some other countries are also under way. Apart from securing a clear-cut demarcation of the zones of taxation between India and foreign countries concerned according to the nature and source of income, these agreements ensure that the benefit of tax concessions is actually retained by the foreign investor as far as possible.

11 Relief from double taxation: Agreements for double taxation relief are in force with the governments of some countries e.g., Kenya, Tanganyika, Uganda and Zanzibar. In respect of taxes paid in countries with which there are no specific agreements, provision exists for granting of unilateral relief to the tax payers resident in India.

Exchange policy

All transactions involving foreign exchange are controlled by the authorities. The general policy adopted in respect of foreign investments is briefly described below, though variations in individual cases on merits are permissible:

1 Entry of foreign investment: The inflow of foreign investments into India is encouraged. It is regulated so as to channel them into fields consistent with the national economic policy. Thus, foreign investment is encouraged in the field of manufacturing and in industries for which adequate capacity does not already exist in the country, but is not permitted, for instance, in purely trading or financial enterprises. It is desired that foreign investment should eventually contribute to strengthening the foreign exchange position of the country, through the production of commodities which would lead to a saving of foreign exchange on imports or to earning it through exports. Further, the investment should lead to increased efficiency in the fields concerned.

The usual forms of foreign financial participation in India are equity capital and long-term loans. Any Indian company may issue shares in consideration of cash or of plant and machinery or technical assistance. Technical collaboration against payment of fees or royalties on reasonable terms is also permitted.

2 Repatriation of foreign investment in India: Repatriation of investments from sterling area countries (except Pakistan, Norway, Sweden and Denmark) is allowed freely. In respect of investments from non-sterling countries, capital invested after 1st January 1950 in projects approved by government is allowed to be freely repatriated together with profits ploughed back and any capital appreciation in the value of investments.

3 Remittance of profits, dividends and interest: The income earned by non-resident investors on their investments in India is allowed to be remitted freely to their country. The subsidiaries of foreign companies in India are allowed to remit their profits and dividends in full to their parent offices after payment of all taxes due.

4 Remittances by foreigners employed in India: Persons of foreign domicile resident in India, are, in general, offered liberal remittance facilities for meeting all their current expenses including maintenance of their families abroad and for transfer of assets to their country at the time of retirement.

Currency convertibility agreement with the United States

Under the agreement signed in 1957 by India and the United States based on the American Investment Guarantee Programme, American private investors, on payment of a small premium, can obtain guarantee from their government for the reconvertibility into American dollars of the proceeds from the sale of their investments in India and/or earnings from investments in projects approved by the government of India. In 1959 this agreement was extended so as to provide for the payment of adequate compensation to American investors in the event of expropriation of their assets in India.

Appendix no. 7

Summary of the recommendations of the Swaminathan committee on industries development procedure [1]

1. Establishment of a speedy procedure for issuing 'Letters of Intent', i.e. a notification that a collaboration proposal is acceptable to the government in principle, pending a more detailed investigation. It was hoped that under the new procedure, 'Letters of Intent' would be issued within one month of the initial application, which would be considered by a smaller subcommittee,[2] in place of the original full licencing committee.

2. A special procedure for subsequent clearance of proposals related to certain industries designated as 'key' industries, whereby all applications relating to a given enterprise, such as capital issues, import licences, foreign exchange, etc. would be considered at a single meeting of the subcommittee referred to under 1, with the addition of the Chief Controller of Imports and Exports and, when necessary, the Controller of Capital Issues being co-opted as additional members.

3. Preferential treatment in foreign exchange allocation to be given to 'key' industries, special attention being given to this matter by the proposed subcommittee.

4. Establishment of a special cell in the Ministry of Industry to deal exclusively with all applications for licences under the Industries Act, and also applications for the subsequent clearances that may be required, and for their prompt distribution to other authorities concerned.

5. The special procedure recommended for 'key' industries should also be applied to enterprises which would be substantially import-saving or export-earning.

6. Other industries would still apply to the relevant authorities for clearances, but in each case, a decision should be reached within three months. A procedure whereby the Ministry of Industry could maintain close watch on progress of clearances was suggested. In addition, several

recommendations for speedier issue of import licences, together with several other proposals, were advanced by the committee.

The government accepted the recommendations, except that it envisaged a somewhat larger licencing subcommittee, and advanced some modifications to the proposed licencing procedure.[3]

Notes

Chapter 2

1 Except where otherwise stated all data in this chapter are computed from two sources: 1. *Report on Currency and Finance for the Year 1964-5*, Reserve Bank of India, Bombay, 1965, pp S 134-49. This source gives total figures up to 31 March 1965; 2. *External Assistance 1964*, Ministry of Finance, Department of Economic Affairs, Government of India, New Delhi, 1965.

2 See *India 1963–A Report of a visit to India by Sir Norman Kipping attended by M. Donelan*, Federation of British Industries, London, 1963. Although 'Kipping' loans are designed primarily to help Indo-British collaboration projects, they are not allotted exclusively in this way. The test is 'British orientation', i.e. the extent to which projects depend on imports from British sources.

3 A useful analysis of the development and philosophy of Japanese aid is provided by J. White, *Japanese Aid*, Overseas Development Institute, London, 1964.

4 For an excellent account of the social and political impact of these schemes, see the article by A. M. Klausen, 'Technical Assistance and Social Conflict–a Case Study from the Indo-Norwegian Fishing Project in Kerala, South India', *Journal of Peace Research*, 1964, Universitetsforlaget, Peace Research Institute, Oslo, 1964, pp 5-18.

5 For details of Indo-Soviet trade activities see K. Billerbeck, *Soviet Bloc Foreign Aid to the Underdeveloped Countries, An Analysis and a Prognosis*, Hamburg Archives of World Economy, Hamburg, 1960, pp 91-102; J. S. Berliner, *Soviet Economic Aid and Trade Policy in Underdeveloped Countries*, Praeger, New York, 1958, Chapter VII.

6 M. Kidron, *Foreign Investment in India,* Oxford UP, London, 1965, pp 115-6.

7 Cf pp 121, 123, 127-8.

8 See Annual Reports of the Ford Foundation, 32 Feroze Shah Road, New Delhi, and of the Rockefeller Foundation, 111 West 50th Street, New York.

9 For instance, the foundations have far more control over the selection of Indian students for overseas training than do individual governments.

10 The favourable comparison is most clearcut where 'infrastructure' projects are concerned.

11 Cf pp 92-111.

Chapter 3 The development of American aid policy in India

1 For full text see *Department of State Bulletin*, Superintendent of Documents, US Government Printing Office, Washington, DC, vol 20, no 500 (30 January 1949) p 123.

2 At this stage, awareness of Africa was virtually non-existent.

3 See elaboration of 'Point Four' concept by Dean Acheson at Press Conference in Washington, DC, on 30 January 1949, *Department of State Bulletin*, vol 30 no 501 6 February 1949), pp 155-6. Further elaboration was provided by G. McGhee, Assistant Secretary for Near-Eastern, South Asian and African Affairs in an address to the Far East-American Council of Commerce and Industry at New York on 31st January 1950, *Department of State Bulletin*, 17th February 1950, vol 22, no 556, pp 334-6, 343. This address, though moderately worded, foreshadowed American opposition to socialist patterns of development.

4 Malenbaum's views clearly developed rapidly. Contrast his article 'America's Role in Economic Development Abroad' in *Department of State Bulletin*, 17th March 1949, vol 20, no 508, pp 371-6, with his later publication, *East and West in India's Development*, Washington DC, National Planning Association, 1959. In the latter publication the scope of India's requirements, particularly for capital aid, and the extent of her problems is very clearly appreciated, and strong action advised.

5 It appears that the 'Point Four' programme was not included in the first draft of Truman's inaugural speech. The president

wanted his speech to be 'profound', important and of world-wide significance'. At this time Benjamin Hardy, working in the State Department, presented the idea of a low-cost technical assistance programme to developing countries to C. Clifford, the president's chief adviser and speech-maker, the idea being subsequently accepted by the president. Hardy's role was acknowledged by the president upon the death of the former in December 1951 in an air crash. See PhD thesis presented to the University of London in 1957 by B. Salomon, *Point Four–A Study in Political Motivation and Administrative Techniques*.

6 India's motives for joining the Commonwealth are well explained in a speech by J. Nehru in the Constituent Assembly, 16 May 1949, J. Nehru, *India's Foreign Policy–Selected Speeches September 1947-April 1961*, Ministry of Information and Broadcasting, Government of India, New Delhi, 1961, pp 134-46.

7 See for instance his address to a Joint Session of both Houses of the US Congress, Washington DC, 13 October 1949. J. Nehru, *India's Foreign Policy*, pp 589-92.

8 The death of Sardar Patel in 1950 partially accounts for a shift of emphasis on the Indian side, in that Nehru thereby gained complete control in the conduct of foreign policy.

9 *US Congressional Record*, Washington DC, appendix 14, July 1949 (legislative day of 2nd June 1949), p 4513, 81st session, vol 95. See also *US Congressional Record*, 81st Congress, 1st session, vol 95, 2, pp 14230-2 (11 October 1949).

10 This occurred under the terms of Public Law 48: India Emergency Food Act of 1951, published in *Department of State Bulletin*, vol 35, no 627 (2nd July 1951) p 38.

11 *US Congressional Record*, 82nd Congress, 1st session, vol 97, part 2 (5th March 1957), pp 1920-3362.

12 *Ibid.*, p 1920. Statement by Senator Maybank.

13 *Ibid.*, pp 1951-3. Statement by Representative Kersten.

14 *Indian Emergency Food Act of 1951*. Cf Chapter 3, note 10.

15 For full statement see *The Indo-US Technical Co-operation Programme–Report, 1963*, Ministry of Finance, Department

of Economic Affairs, Government of India, New Delhi, 1 December 1963.

16 See especially statement by Nehru in Lok Sabda on 1 March 1954: *Keesings' Contemporary Archives 1952-54*, Keesings Publications Ltd, Bristol, 1954, p 13462.

17 See Dulles-Cunha communique issued in Washington DC on 2 December 1955, referring to Portuguese provinces in the Far East, supported by a statement at a press conference also Washington on 6 December 1955, in which Mr Dulles said of Goa, ' . . . . As far as I know all the world regards it as a Portuguese province. It has been Portuguese for about 400 years'. *Keesings Contemporary Archives 1955-56*, p 14613.

18 *Report No. 9 Public International Development Financing in India* Research Project of the Columbia School of Law, New York, July 1964, pp 36-43.

19 *Clay Committee Report on Foreign Aid*, 25 March 1963. Official Text, United States Information Service, American Embassy, London, 1963.

20 *Ibid.*, p 4.

21 *The Hindu*, Madras, 23 August 1963.

22 Thus Nehru described the Kennedy Administration as 'the friendliest American Government that India has encountered'. Quoted in *Report No. 9, Public International Development Financing in India*, p 69.

23 E.g., at a press conference in New Delhi on 9 May 1963, Ambassador J. K. Galbraith expressed full confidence that the United States government would support the Bokaro project in these words ' . . . . In recent weeks a few people have predicted with something almost approaching pleasure that Americans never give support to publicly owned enterprise. I am not at all sorry to disappoint them'. *The Hindu*, Madras, 10 May 1963.

24 *Lok Sabha Debates*, 22 April 1963, vol 17, 4th session, starred question no 7, coll 1046-7, New Delhi. General Taylor's comments to the House Appropriations Committee that he did not know whether India or China had made the first move into the other's

territory and that the NEFA boundary was not properly marked, caused much offence to some members. Nehru insisted, however, that these remarks must be viewed in the context of a long speech.

25 Cf pp 164-5.

26 Cf pp 166-7.

27 Statement in TV interview, 9 December, quoted by P. C. Chakravarti in 'Indian Non-Alignment and United States Policy', *Current History*, vol 44, no 159 (March 1963), p 179.

28 P. J. Eldridge, 'India's Non-Alignment Policy Reviewed', *Australian Outlook*, vol 19, no 2 (August 1965), pp 146-57.

29 *Keesings Contemporary Archives*, vol 14, 7-14 December 1964, p 19785.

30 The Report is secret; however, the consensus of informed opinion in Delhi is that the main recommendations of the Report are for: 1. General liberalisation of controls on the private sector, particularly with regard to licensing procedures; 2. Devaluation of the rupee; if this was unacceptable, the control by balance of payments through import duties rather than physical controls; 3. Greater emphasis on agriculture and 'infrastructure' projects rather than heavy industrial projects. The Report was prepared by Mr David Bell, Administrator of the Agency for International Development, Washington DC.

31 Total outlay on agriculture in the public sector during the Fourth Five Year Plan was estimated at Rs 2,372 crores, compared with Rs 1,090 crores in the Third Plan. Percentage of total public sector outlay will increase from 13.3 per cent to 16.4 per cent. *Fourth Five Year Plan–Resources, Outlay and Programmes*, Twenty-Second Meeting of the National Development Council, 5 and 6 September 1965, Government of India Planning Commission, New Delhi, 1965, pp 4-6. The definition of 'agriculture' above excludes related outlays on irrigation and cooperative schemes, transportation, etc. Production of foodgrains per annum is targeted for 120 million tons in 1970-1, compared with estimated achievement in 1965-6 of 92 million tons. *Fourth Five Year Plan–Resources, Outlays and Programmes*, p 8.

32 *Ibid.*, pp 27-33 (especially pp 29-30).

33 From conversations with Soviet officials it appears that the approach to Indian agricultural problems is rigid and doctrinaire. The view is taken that substantial improvement is impossible without widespread land reform and intensive mechanisation of large units. Without such reforms aid to agriculture is regarded as ill-founded. The only case where such a concept has proved applicable is the large mechanised farm at Suratgarh, Rajasthan, based on the major desert irrigation scheme in that area. *External Assistance 1964*, Ministry of Finance, Department of Economic Affairs, Government of India, New Delhi, 1964, pp 70-1. This is in sharp contrast with the far more diversified and experimental 'micro' approach of the United States and other Western agencies.

34 Based on conversations with officials of the Government of India Planning Commission.

35 Cf pp 150-1.

36 *The Hindu Weekly Review*, Madras, 13 June 1966.

37 See for instance K. Rangaswami's article, 'US Pressure Shows no Abatement', in *The Hindu Weekly Review*, Madras, 5 September 1966, p 7. The notion of 3 per cent of G.N.P. limitation on defence expenditure by India and Pakistan has been widely mooted. See for instance *The Hindu Weekly Review*, 11 November 1965. This idea was explicitly denied by Mrs Gandhi on American television (date not stated); *Ibid.*, 11 April, p 3. As the first article quoted points out, there is a question whether Pakistan would accept the unequal military capacity such a concept would imply, and also involves external judgments as to what India may legitimately spend on defence against China.

38 It appears from a statement by Vice-President Humphrey accompanying his announcement of the $100m non-project loan in New Delhi on 17 February 1965, that the United States was thinking primarily in terms of humanitarian aid–*The Hindu Weekly Review*, Madras, 21 February 1966, p 3. President Johnson was quite emphatic, however, during Mrs Gandhi's visit to America that no *quid pro quos* were being demanded, *Ibid.*, 4 April 1966, p 3.

39 Mrs Gandhi indicated agreement in her report to Lok Sabha on 7th April 1956, and European visit. *The Hindu Weekly Review*, 11 April 1960.

40 As per chapter 3, note 1.

41 Address to the Indian Parliament, 10 December 1960, *Department of State Bulletin*, vol 42 no 1071 (11 January 1960), p 47.

42 S. Chandrasekhar, *American Aid and India's Economic Development*, Praeger, New York, 1965, p 54.

43 Major theme of Chester Bowles, *Ambassador's Report*, Harper New York, 1964.

44 A. Stevenson, 'Putting First Things First', *Foreign Affairs*, vol 38 no 2 (January 1960), pp 191-208; see especially part 7, pp 205-8.

45 E. Black, *The Diplomacy of Economic Development*, Harvard UP, 1960, pp 18, 23.

46 See *Hearings of House of Representatives Committee on Appropriations and Foreign Affairs, 1958-64*, 84th-89th Congresses. For full references see bibliography.

47 The common 'liberal' view is simply stated by Chester Bowles and Thomas K. Finletter in an article entitled 'Some Hard Decisions' in *New Republic*, New York, 22 February 1960: ' . . . . If India, with all her advantages of able leadership, a competent civil service, trained technicians, substantial resources and the great tradition of Gandhi fails in her attempt to bring widening economic opportunites to her people through democratic means, how could less well-endowed nations hope to succeed? And if they, in their frustration, throw in their lot with Communist totalitarianism, what will then happen to the global balance of power?'

48 For general statement, implicit or explicit, of these themes, see W. Malenbaum, *East and West in India's Development*; C. Bowles, *Ambassador's Report; US Congressional Record*, Speech by J. F. Kennedy, 85th Congress, 2nd session, vol 104, part 4 (25 March 1958), pp 5246-52, followed by speech by Senator Cooper (ex-ambassador to India), *Ibid.*, pp 5253-5

49 A useful analysis of American reactions to Soviet aid is provided by Hans Heymann Jnr, 'Soviet Foreign Aid as a problem for U.S. Policy', *World Politics*, vol 12 (July 1960), pp 525-40.

50 *Foreign Assistance Activities of the Communist Bloc and Their Implications*, a study prepared at the request of the Special Committee to Study the Foreign Aid Programme, US Senate, by the Council for Economic and Industry Research, Inc no 8. (pursuant to Special Resolution 285, 84th Congress, and Special Resolution 35, 85th Congress), Washington DC, March 1957, p 1.

51 *Ibid.*, pp 1-2.

52 *Ibid.*, pp 47-8.

53 *Ibid.*, p 48.

54 *Ibid.*, pp 48-51.

55 Black, *The Diplomacy of Economic Development*, p 23.

56 *Ibid.*, chapter 2.

57 G. A. Almond and J. Coleman (eds), *The Politics of Development Areas*, Princeton UP, 1960; G. A. Almond, 'A Developmental Approach to Political Systems', *World Politics*, vol 17 (January 1965), pp 183-214.

58 H. Morgenthau, 'The Immaturity of our Asian Policy', *New Republic*, New York, 26 March 1956.

59 Robert A. Packenham, 'Political Development Doctrines in the American Foreign Aid Program'. *World Politics*, vol 18, no 2 (January 1966), pp 194-235.

60 Cf pp 34-6, 183-7.

61 As per chapter 3, note 46.

62 *Special Report on U.S. Foreign Operations*, Senator A. J. Ellender, U.S. Government Printing Office, Washington DC, 1960.

63 *U.S. Congressional Record*, 84th Congress, 2nd session, vol 102, part 8 (29 June 1956), pp 11392-3.

64 Speech before the Economic Club of New York, 16 January 1956: See *Vital Speeches of the Day*, vol 22, no 9 (16 January 1956), pp 263-66.

65 M. Friedman, 'Foreign Economic Aid: Means and Objectives', *Yale Review*, vol 47 (June 1958), pp 500-16.

66 *U.S. Congressional Record*, 6 June 1958, 85th Congress, 2nd session, vol. 104, part 8, p 10396. Section 2 of Mutual Security Bill 1959 as originally introduced in the Senate read: 'The Congress recognises the importance of the economic development of the Republic of India to its people, its democratic values and institutions and to peace and stability in the world. Consequently it is the sense of the Congress that it is in the interest of the United States to join with other nations in providing support of the type, magnitude and duration adequate to assist India to complete successfully its current programme for economic development'.

67 As per chapter 3, note 27. See also *US Congressional Record*, 85th Congress, 2nd session, vol 104, part 8 (4 June 1958), p 10109 (speech by Senator H. Humphrey).

68 E. Bunker, 'Progress and Potential in South Asia–The Example of India', *U.S. Department of State Bulletin*, vol 42, no 1090 (16 May 1960), p 781.

69 See for instance *U.S. Congressional Record*, 84th Congress, 2nd session, vol 102, part 9 (11 July 1956), pp 12290-1 (speech by Senator E. Kefauver).

70 J. K. Galbraith, 'Rival Economic Theories in India', *Foreign Affairs*, vol 36, no 4, p 590 (July 1958).

71 *Ibid.*, p 593.

72 For one of the best statements of Kennedy's ideas in this context see his speech in the Senate, *U.S. Congressional Record*, 85th Congress, 2nd session, vol 104 (July 1958), p 590.

73 Speech to the Economic Club of Detroit, 9 May 1960: 'The Economic Challenge in India–Can Democracy Meet It?', *Vital Speeches of the Day*, vol 26, no 22 (1 September 1960), pp 686-9.

74 H. Cabot Lodge, 'Mutual Aid Through the U.N.': *U.S. Department of State Bulletin*, vol 42, no 1084 (4 April 1960), pp 524-7. See also A. Rubinstein, *The Soviets in International Organisations*, Princeton UP, 1964.

75 Senator A. J. Ellender, *Special Report on U.S. Foreign Operations.*

76 In view of the Indian tariffs and extensive physical controls over imports, as well as collaboration agreements and other forms of private investment, foreign aid provides a sound basis for private firms to sell in the Indian market.

77 John P. Lewis, *Quiet Crisis in India*, The Brookings Institution, Washington DC, 1962, pp 278-85.

78 Cf pp 31-2, 180.

79 An interesting proposal for a World Commodity Exchange system has been outlined by M. J. Kust, 'Economic Development and Agricultural Surpluses', *Foreign Affairs*, vol 35, no 1 (October 1966), pp 105-15.

80 *The Hindu Weekly Review*, Madras, p 3, E. Sagar 'Release of Non-Project Part of U.S. Aid'. *Ibid.*, 5 September 1966, p 7, K. Rangaswami, 'U.S. Pressure Shows No Abatement'.

81 Black, *The Diplomacy of Economic Development*, chapter 2.

Chapter 4 Objectives of Soviet aid policy in India

1 See J. S. Berliner, *Soviet Economic Aid, the New Aid and Trade Policy in Underdeveloped Countries*, Praeger, New York, 1958 (for the Council on Foreign Relations); K. Billerbeck, *Soviet Bloc Foreign Aid to the Underdeveloped Countries, An Analysis and a Prognosis*, Hamburg Archives of World Economy, Hamburg, 1960; D. S. Nag, *Foreign Economic Policy of Soviet Russia*, Lakshmi Narain Agarwal, Agra, India, 1964.

2 For a good critique of this approach see the statement 'Soviet Aid: Myths and Facts', by F. M. Coffin, Deputy Administrator for Programme, AID, *House of Representatives, Pt . II, Foreign Assistance Act of 1962–Hearings before the Committee on Foreign Affairs, House of Representatives–87th Congress, 2nd Session, on a Draft Bill to Amend Further the Foreign Assistance Act of 1961, As Amended and For Other Purposes,* 26 March 1962, pp 336-40, U.S. Government Printing Office, Washington DC, 1962.

3 L. Labedz, 'The U.S.S.R. and the Developing Countries', in

Walter Lacqueur and Leopold Labedz (eds), *Polycentrism–the New Factor in International Communism*, Praeger, New York, 1962, p 154.

4 *Ibid.*, pp 154-5.

5 Gene D. Overstreet and Marshall Windmiller, *Communism in India*, University of California Press, 1959, p 253.

6 *Ibid.*, pp 253-4.

7 *Ibid.*, pp 253-75

8 *Ibid.*, p 304.

9 *Ibid.*, pp 304-5.

10 *Ibid.*, Chapter 14. The Congress adopted a resolution to oppose the government but support specific acts.

11 *Ibid.*, pp 321-3.

12 See exchange of letters between Nehru, Stalin and Acheson, 13-19 July 1950, Royal Institute of International Affairs, *Documents on International Affairs, 1949-50*, selected and edited by Margaret Carlyle, Oxford UP, 1953, pp 705-8.

13 For a valuable account of Indian diplomacy with China over the Korea issue see K. M. Pannikar, *In Two Chinas, Memoirs of a Diplomat*, Allen and Unwin, London, 1955, chapter 9.

14 Congress held from 5th to 15th October 1952, *Keesing's Contemporary Archives 1952-4*, Keesings Publications Ltd, Bristol, pp 12709-10.

15 Malenkov gave estimates of percentage increase in production as follows: overall 130 per cent, pig iron 70 per cent, steel 90 per cent, rolled metals 100 per cent, coal 80 per cent, oil 140 per cent. The implications for future aid policy to India are clear. *Keesings Contemporary Archives 1952-4, 952-4* pp 12709-10.

16 In India's case, probably the best example is the oil industry; cf pp

17 Cf pp 18-19.

18 Berliner, *Soviet Economic Aid, the New Aid and Trade Policy in Underdeveloped Countries*, chapter 2. Billerbeck, *Soviet Bloc*

Foreign Aid to the Underdeveloped Countries, An Analysis and a Prognosis, p 53.

19 L. Fituni, *Economically Underdeveloped Countries and the West*, Progress Publishers, Moscow, 1963.

20 Cf pp 31-3.

21 See *Second Five Year Plan*, Government of India Planning Commission, New Delhi, 1956. *Papers Relating to the Formulation of Second Five Year Plan* (memorandum prepared by the Panel of Economists, Planning Commission), Government of Indian Planning Commission, New Delhi, 10 April 1955. See also appendix no 1.

22 Cf chapter 9.

23 *Foreign Assistance Activities of the Communist Bloc and Their Implications for the United States*, a Study prepared at the request of the Special Committee to Study the Foreign Aid Program, U.S. Senate, by the Council for Economic and Industry Research Inc., Washington DC (Pursuant to Senate Resolution 185, 84th Congress and Senate Resolution 35, 85th Congress), no 8 (March 1957), p 1.

24 *Ibid.*, pp 1-2.

25 Overstreet and Windmiller, *Communism in India*, p 318. M. Windmiller, 'The Andhra Election', *Far Eastern Survey*, vol 24 (April 1955), pp 57-64.

26 Overstreet and Windmiller, *Communism in India*, p 321.

27 *Monthly Public Opinion Surveys of the Indian Institute of Public Opinion*, vol 1, nos 7, 8 and 9 (February, March and April 1956), pp 7-75. Indian Institute of Public Opinion, New Delhi, 1956.

28 S. Harrison, *India, The Most Dangerous Decades,* Princeton UP, 1960, pp 178-273.

29 *Foreign Assistance Activities of the Communist Bloc and Their Implications for the United States*, pp 21-2.

30 See for instance Hans Heymann Jnr, 'Soviet Economic Aid to South-East Asia—Threat or Windfall?', *World Politics*, vol 10, no 1 (October 1957), pp 91-101.

31 Cf pp 43-4.

32 See for instance, *Appraisal and Prospects of the Second Five Year Plan*, Government of India Planning Commission, May 1958. Due to foreign exchange difficulties the Second Plan was drastically reduced. A 'hard core' of projects was retained, emphasising mainly heavy industry projects, in which all major Soviet financed projects were retained in their original form.

33 See for instance Berliner, *Soviet Economic Aid, the New Aid and Trade Policy in Underdeveloped Countries*, pp 152-6.

34 This view appears to be particularly strongly held in World Bank circles. This type of criticism is also fairly common amongst Indian businessmen and certain journalists and is naturally connected with the issue of socialism versus free enterprise.

35 Billerbeck, *Soviet Bloc Foreign Aid to the Underdeveloped Countries, An Analysis and a Prognosis*, pp 14-17. The contrast, from the Soviet viewpoint between the objectives of Soviet and Western aid (the former endeavouring to build independent economies as against the dependent economies created by the latter) is vividly portrayed by Fituni in *Economically Underdeveloped Countries and the West.*

36 E.g. J. Nehru, *India's Foreign Policy–Selected Speeches*, September 1946-April 1961, pp 578-80; M. Brecher, *Nehru, A Political Biography*, Oxford UP, London, 1959, p 586.

37 Lacqueur and Labedz (eds), *Polycentrism*, p 154.

38 Cf chapter 3, Note 33.

39 Malenkov quote from Stalin at 19th Party Congress, *Keesings Contemporary Archives*, p 12709.

40 Especially applicable to concepts of resource allocation and mobilisation, investment criteria, planning techniques, etc. For full discussion of these issues see *Papers Relating to the Formulation of the Second Five Year Plan*, Government of India Planning Commission, 1955.

41 Overstreet and Windmiller, *Communism in India*, p 236.

42 *Ibid.*, pp 326-7.

43 *Ibid.*, p 327.

44 For instance, on the occasion of the visit of a Soviet goodwill mission to India led by A. A. Andreyev, a member of the delegation, M. Mukhitdinov made a strong statement at a press conference (New Delhi, 19 March 1959) attacking meddling by 'monopolists' on Soviet borders through arms aid to Pakistan. He charged further that the West did not want Afro-Asians to develop heavy industry, citing the failure of Western oil search ventures as an example. This speech clearly caused embarrassment in that a goodwill mission had used a hospitable base in India to attack others 'equally friendly' to India. *The Hindu*, Madras, 20 March 1959.

45 *Soviet News*, Moscow, 26 May 1959, reprint of interview between N. Kruschev and P. K. Karanjia, editor of Indian newspaper *Blitz*, Bombay.

46 Berliner, *Soviet Economic Aid* . . . , pp 152-6.

47 Cf chapter 9 (*passim*).

48 Berliner, *Soviet Economic Aid* . . . , chapter 7; Billerbeck, *Soviet Bloc Foreign Aid* . . . . , pp 15-6.

49 Cf pp 125-6.

50 Perhaps the correct interpretation of Soviet economic strategy is that having accepted India's pattern of mixed economy, Moscow sees the issue as a question of whether India will develop a dependent or independent capitalist economy. However, while the assistance of industrial projects in the public sector undoubtedly assists the latter objective, this would also appear to entail some Soviet participation in the Indian private sector, which has been almost entirely lacking.

51 *Monthly Public Opinion Surveys of the Indian Institute of Public Opinion*, vol 1, nos 7, 8 and 9 (February, March and April 1956), pp 1-4.

Part two: The political impact of foreign aid in India

Chapter 5: The politics of aid: the Indian response

1 For example, see John P. Lewis, *Quiet Crisis in India*, The

Brookings Institution, Washington DC, 1962, p 251. The author characterises the United States-India aid relationship as one based on 'diffidence'. The United States is claimed to rate Indian sensitivities as very high; the former is said generally to behave 'as if treading on eggs'.

2 An exception here would seem to be the fact that India does not have direct diplomatic relations with East Germany; the West German government's policy of making aid conditional on non-recognition of the East German regime is well known.

3 See, for instance, V. K. R. V. Rao and Dharm Narain, *Foreign Aid and India's Development*, Asia Publishing House, London, for the Institute of Economic Growth, Delhi, 1963; W. Malenbaum, *East and West in India's Development*, Washington DC, 1959.

4 Cf pp 34-6.

5 Cf chapter 3, note 37.

6 Black, *The Diplomacy of Economic Development, op. cit.* (*passim*).

7 There is, however, some evidence to the contrary, though this is somewhat fragmentary, since neither Indian nor donor-country officials will admit that any form of interference with Indian economic decisions exists. The normally reliable economic correspondent of *The Hindu*, Madras, H. Venkatasubbiah, in an article entitled 'Planners Hamstrung by Political Pressures' (26 December 1963), argues that foreigners were increasingly taking the initiative in administrative action. Thus the West German Minister for Economic Cooperation was endeavouring to set up a committee of German industrialists, trade unionists and officials to consider ways for the more efficient working of the Rourkela steel mill. The article claims also that following the Kipping Report the British government increased their proportion of non-project aid, but made greater efforts to encourage business for British financed industries, for which purpose questionnaires were sent out to twenty-five firms in India (*The Hindu*, 26 December 1963). Perhaps the greatest measure of initiative is exercised by the World Bank, which undertakes the important function of coordinating the annual consortium meetings. Its recommendations carry considerable

weight at these meetings, but like the individual donor countries its powers are mainly negative or advisory. It has, however, a permanent representative in Delhi to deal with the Department of Economic Affairs. An important instance where World Bank initiative was exercised in the face of Indian indifference was when the Bank sent its own experts to study India's coal transport problems. In this case, India declines to pay the costs of the survey. See the statement by K. D. Malaviya, Minister of Fuel and Mines, *Lok Sabha Debates*, vol 8, no 21, 2nd session, 3 September 1962, starred question 746, cols 549-52.

8 In this year the agency for International Development replaced the Development Loan Fund and became the chief coordinating agency.

9 Cf p 32.

10 Cf pp 65-7.

11 Lewis, *Quiet Crisis in India*, p 251.

12 Rao and Narain, *Foreign Aid and India's Development*, p 37. This theme was frequently referred to by Indian officials in interviews. The point was nicely put by one official, who said impassively that every country had its 'sensitivities' and India tried to respect them. A general atmosphere of philosophical calm appears to prevail, even in the face of major fiascos like Bokaro, and great confidence that if one country did not approve of a particular project, aid would be forthcoming from other sources. This feeling is especially applicable to the question of public sector heavy industry projects, unacceptable to the United States, and financed by the Soviet Union. See chapters 3 and 8.

13 Report No 9–*Public International Development Financing in India*, A Research Project of the Columbia University School of Law, New York, 1964, pp 48-62.

14 Cf p 151.

15 Cf chapter 2.

16 Government of India, *Economic Survey 1966-67*, Manager of Publications, New Delhi, 1967, pp 51-2.

17 *Ibid.*

18 *Fourth Five Year Plan–Resources, Outlays and Programmes,* Twenty-second Meeting of the National Development Council, 5 and 6 September 1965, Government of India Planning Commission, pp 25-6.

19 E.g., T. T. Krishnamachari, Minister of Commerce and Industry, stated that it was better to receive all aid in the form of loans rather than grants. Mr Nehru has stated that with loans there was no feeling of accepting charity. Source for both statements, *The Hindu*, Madras, 3 November 1954. The late prime minister made a very similar statement at the AICC in 1957; *The Hindu*, Madras, 18 September 1957.

20 *The Hindu Weekly Review*, Madras, 25 January 1965, p 3.

21 *Third Five Year Plan*, pp 138-41.

22 One exception was an outburst by B. K. Nehru, Indian ambassador to the United States, at the 48th National Trade Convention, Waldorf-Astoria, New York, 30 June 1961 (reported in the *New York Times*, 1 July 1961), in which he argued that the West's trade with developing countries was badly unbalanced; in particular he attacked the 'cheap labour' argument in defence of protection, noting that the West had no objection to importing tea, coffee, bananas and other products not in competition with home production.

23 *Keesings Contemporary Archives*, vol 15, pp 20581-3. A related question is Britain's possible entry into the European Common Market. M. Desai (then Minister of Finance) is believed to have held important conversations on this issue during his tour of European capitals between 1 and 23 July 1962: see *The Hindu*, Madras, 7 and 20 July 1962, and *Daily Telegraph*, London, 7 July 1962. Tariffs, of course, are only one aspect of India's export problem. Other requirements include improved quality, efficiency, marketing arrangements, after sales service, etc. see *Third Five Year Plan*, pp 134-41.

24 Rao and Narain, *Foreign Aid and India's Development*, p 9.

25 *Ibid.*, p 8.

26 *Ibid.*, pp 8-9.

27 *Ibid.*, p 10.

28 *The Third Plan Mid-Term Appraisal*, pp 46-7.

29 Cf appendix no 1 table 10.

30 *Ibid.*

31 See *The Third Plan Mid-Term Appraisal*, pp 46-51; Rao and Narain, *Foreign Aid and India's Development*, p 88; Lewis, *Quiet Crisis in India*, pp 278-85.

32 Lewis, *Quiet Crisis in India*, pp 184-5.

33 *Ibid.*, pp 278-85

34 *Ibid.*, pp 278-85.

35 *Ibid.*, p 281.

36 *Ibid.*, pp 281-3

37 *Report on Currency and Finance for the Year 1964-5*, pp S.134-9.

38 Appendix no 1, table 3.

39 Appendix no 1, table 10.

40 Cf pp 20-3.

41 *The Third Plan Mid-Term Appraisal*, p 47.

42 Lewis, *Quiet Crisis in India*, pp 262-4.

43 A. Schonfield, *The attack on World Poverty*, Chatto and Windus, London, 1959, chapter 1.

44 Cf pp 46-7.

45 E.g. see Rao and Narain, *Foreign Aid and India's Development*, p 90.

46 *Ibid.*, pp 73-4, 94.

47 Rao and Narain, *Foreign Aid and India's Development*, p 74, advocate extension of 'quasi formal' commitments over a five-year period.

48 E.g. See Lewis, *Quiet Crisis in India*, pp 285-92.

49 *Ibid.*

50 Several interesting examples can be given from *Lok Sabha Debates*. E.g. part 1, vol 4, 4th session, 16 September 1963, starred

question 1322, cols 2042-6; on this occasion a proposal by the American Education Foundation to run advanced courses for Indian headmasters came under heavy fire, revealing in the process markedly dogmatic anti-American prejudices: part 1, vol 2, 6th session, 2 April 1954, starred question 1534, cols 1677-9; interchange on the functions of Ford Foundation technical assistance to the development of cottage industries, produced a witty supplementary from Shri Mohiuddin: 'May I know in what cottage industries they had experience in America?': See also part 2, vol 10, 11th session, 12 December 1955, cols 2300-29, in the course of a debate on foreign technical personnel, the question of whether Russian 'experts' were qualified to conduct a survey of India's diamond resources was raised, in the absence of any clear knowledge by the Minister for Natural Resources and Scientific Research as to whether any diamond mines existed in Russia.

51 *The Hindu*, Madras, 3 November 1954.

52 *Lok Sabha Debates*, vol 3, part 2, 12th session, cols 5149-56. 50 per cent of the consultancy fee for this project was stated by Shri Bansal to be exempt from Indian income tax. No doubt this criticism partly reflected a general discontent with the whole Rourkela project.

53 Rao and Narain, *Foreign Aid and India's Development*, pp 52-4.

54 *Ibid.*, p 96. An obvious objection to this proposal is that it entails a forced saving, not only on the employee, but on his family, should they desire to live in India; this disincentive effect would probably have to be offset by some additional financial advantages upon return.

55 Cf p 151.

56 *Financial Times*, London, 9 September 1958.

57 *The Observer*, London, 24 August 1958; article by A. Schonfield entitled 'India Crisis is Chance for West'.

58 *Ibid.*

59 E.g. see Rao and Narain, *Foreign Aid and India's Development*, p 73.

60 *Ibid.*

61 Especially relevant to this whole question is *Papers Relating to the Second Five Year Plan* (Symposium).

62 Government of India Planning Commission, 1955. Cf table 15.

63 *Daily Telegraph*, London, 23 July 1962.

64 Cf pp 181-2, 184, 189.

65 Conflicting reports appear with regard to this project. *New York Times*, 18 May 1958, traces its origin to casual conversations with Indian officials during the Bulganin-Kruschev visit in 1955. Inadequate preparation led to uncoordinated deliveries, lack of spare parts and inadequate site development. *The Hindu*, Madras, 3 April, 1959, however, claims success for the scheme with rapidly improved acreage use and yields. The whole scheme depends on the Bhakra-Nangal irrigation system which in turn depends on full implementation of the Indus Waters Treaty (see IBRD Press Release no 650, 19 September 1960, 1818 High Street, Washington DC). The full benefits of the project may not be expected until 1970 at least.

66 Cf pp 138-43.

67 Cf pp 138-43.

68 For fairly typical examples of the CPI's attitude to foreign aid, which is largely based on straightforward anti-Americanism, see speeches by C. R. Chowdary, *Lok Sabha Debates*, part 2, vol 3, 3rd session, cols 3826-30, 7 April 1953: '. . . what locust is to vegetation, what cancer is to the human body, the American dollar investment is to our national economy and to our body politic'; and by H. N. Mukerjee (Parliamentary Communist leader at that time), who described the Indo-U.S. Technical Cooperation Agreement as a 'slavery bond'. *Lok Sabha Debates*, part 2, vol 2, 6th session, 23 March 1954, cols 2807-18.

69 Speech to the Federation of Indian Chambers of Commerce, reported in *The Times*, London, 8 March 1954. In the same report the minister of finance, C. D. Deshmukh, is said to have attempted to have dissuaded the prime minister from making this speech on the grounds that '. . . the economy could not afford political tantrums'.

70 E.g., speech by Shrimati S. Kripalani, in a foreign affairs debate relating to aid issues, *Lok Sabha Debates*, part 2, vol 2, no 1, (12 June 1952), cols 1629-30 (whole debate, cols 1606-73).

71 E.g., *Lok Sabha Debates*, part 1, vol 4, 4th session, 16 September 1953, starred question no 1316, cols 2027-8. Question of visit of American physical education expert, Dr Jay B. Nash, part 1, vol 3, no 21, 2nd session, 4 December 1952, starred question no 918, cols 1088-90. Questions on the work of Dr Laubach, American adult education expert. Part 1, vol 6, no 12 (20 February 1951), col 1576. In a question to the minister of agriculture, K. M. Munshi, on the work of American agricultural experts, Dr R. S. Singh asked if corresponding Indian experts had been sent to the United States. The minister replied (one imagines with monumental impassivity) that no such request had been received. Part 1, vol 2, 6th session (2 April 1954), starred question 1534, cols 1677-9. Question by Shri Monhiuddin re Ford Foundation team to assist with the development of cottage industries ' . . . may I know in what cottage industries they had experience in America?'

72 *Lok Sabha Debates*, 4 October 1951, part 1, vol 10, no 8, question no 1363, col 1877. Question by Shri Sonavane.

73 *Lok Sabha Debates*, part 1, vol 5, 5th session, 7 December 1953, starred question no 686, cols 882-3.

74 E.g. by J. J. Singh, prominent Indian businessman; reported in *New York Times*, 18 January 1956.

75 E.g., see forceful letter in *Economic Weekly*, Bombay, 65 Apollo Street, Bombay, vol 15, no 22, pp 876-7, by A. Rudra, New Delhi, to the effect that Pakistan has given alliance in exchange for aid, but India is only giving lectures ' . . . We want something for nothing and we have got the extraordinary mental makeup of dictating precisely how much we want for nothing and expressing indignation if we do not get immediately all that we want'. If India must have aid and won't join NATO, she should at least refrain from haughty assumptions as to the West's moral obligations to help.

76 *The Christian Science Monitor*, Boston, 31 May 1955. A similar statement by Asoka Mehta, now deputy chairman of the Planning Commission, appears in this same report.

77 *Lok Sabha Debates*, part 2, vol 2, 12th session, 16 March 1956, cols 829-31. Speech by Shrimati Jayashri.

78 The literature on India's non-alignment policy is too extensive to list here and to compile an adequate analysis would constitute a major research topic in itself. The best primary source, however, is undoubtedly Nehru's speeches. For a good coverage of basic principles see J. Nehru, *India's Foreign Policy–Selected Speeches, September 1946-April 1961*, The Publications Division, Ministry of Information and Broadcasting, Government of India, 1961, pp 24-98.

79 For a useful study of Indo-U.S. relations see S. L. Poplai and P. Talbot, *India and America–A Study of Their Relations*, Harper New York, 1958.

80 For some general statements on 'socialistic pattern of society', see *Second Five Year Plan*, chapter 2, pp 10-20; *Third Five Year Plan*, chapter 1, pp 1-19; *Jawaharlal Nehru's Speeches, March 1953-August 1957*, vol 3, Publications Division, Ministry of Information and Broadcasting, Government of India, pp 15-20, (speech at Avadi conference (60th) of Indian National Congress, 22 January 1955). For a useful analysis of Nehru's thought on socialism see M. N. Das, *The Political Philosophy of Jawaharlal Nehru*, Allen and Unwin, London, 1961, pp 124-67. For a hostile view of socialism, see Bauer, *op. cit.* (especially chapter 6).

81 Speech by H. N. Mukerjee, *Lok Sabha Debates*, part 2, 6th session (23 March 1954), part 2, cols 2807-18. Refers to S. Kent, *Strategic Intelligence for American World Policy*, Princeton UP, 1949.

82 *The Christian Science Monitor*, Boston, 30 January 1956.

83 *Ibid.*

84 Syed M. S. Alvi in *The Christian Science Monitor*, Boston, 14 May 1959. This theme was best expressed in Barbara Ward, *India and the West*, Publications Division, Ministry of Information and Broadcasting, New Delhi, 1961. The fact that this book was published by the Indian government shows that this criticism carries no official weight.

85 Refers to a statement by Mr Nixon at a conference in Washington

DC on 'India and the U.S.–1959', reported in *The Economic Weekly*, Bombay, vol 11, no 3, 1 June 1959, pp 19-20. The conference was held under the auspices of a private organisation, the International Committee for Economic Growth.

86 M. Millikan and D. L. Blackner (eds.), *The Emerging Nations: Their Growth and United States Policy*, Asia Publishing House, 1963. Review appears in *The Economic Weekly*, Bombay, vol 15, no 23, p 923-4, under the title 'Forming Them in Uncle's Image'. It should be noted that *The Economic Weekly* is a reputable and moderate journal, by no means committed to the government's economic policies.

87 Speech to the Economic Club, Detroit, 9 May 1960, reported in *Vital Speeches of the Day*, 1 September 1960, vol 26, no 22, pp 686-9. See also speech at San Francisco, 13 January 1961, reported in *The Hindu*, Madras, 16 January 1961.

88 *The Christian Science Monitor,* Boston, 17 March 1959.

89 Speech to the Committee for Economic Growth, Washington DC, 4 May 1959. Reported in *The Hindu*, Madras, 5 May 1959.

90 *The Hindu*, Madras, 18 September 1957. This speech is reported from a 'closed session' of the All Indian Congress Committee, and therefore the source is in some doubt.

91 Cf pp 89-90.

92 *U.S. Congressional Record*, 81st Congress, 1st session, vol 95, part 2 (13 October 1949), col 14393-L.

93 *New York Times*, 5 May and 11 November 1957.

94 In a letter of thanks to the American ambassador, Ellsworth Bunker for a recently negotiated loan, T. T. Krishnamachari, minister of finance, wrote that it was not easy for one state to tax itself to help what appears to be a distant and alien people. The United States had acted as a pioneer in 'extending the concept of aid by richer communites to those less fortunately placed, from the narrow field of the nation-state to the community as a whole'. American assistance was especially appreciated, since there were no political or economic 'strings' attached. Reported in *New York Times*, 30 January 1958. See also the statement by

B. K. Nehru, Indian ambassador to the United States, who at the signing of an Import-Export Bank Agreement remarked that India hoped to repay, not only in cash, but in the more abiding currency of human friendship, '.... for we are not likely to forget those who helped us in our hours of need'. Reported in *New York Times*, 5 March 1958.

95 *The Christian Science Monitor* Boston, 11 September 1956 (leading article).

96 Cf p 90.

97 *The Hindu*, Madras, 4 July 1963.

98 *The Christian Science Monitor*, Boston, 11 September 1956 (leading article).

99 *New York Times*, 5 June 1954.

100 *Monthly Public Opinion Surveys of the Indian Institute of Public Opinion*, New Delhi, vol 3, no 8, May 1958, p 19.

101 Illiterates are seriously underrepresented in this sample, as in all polls subsequently cited. They were estimated at 84 per cent of total population in 1956, *Monthly Public Opinion Surveys of the Indian Institute of Public Opinion*, vol 1, nos 7, 8 and 9 (February, March and April, 1956, p 35), but subsequent educational programmes would presumably have reduced this figure somewhat.

102 *Monthly Public Opinion Surveys of the Indian Institute of Public Opinion*, vol 1, nos 7, 8 and 9 (February, March and April 1956), pp 26-7.

103 In the case of West Bengal the trend is unaccountably far more pronounced in district towns than in either Calcutta or rural areas.

104 Cf pp 141-3.

105 *Monthly Public Opinion Surveys of the Indian Institute of Public Opinion*, vol 1, nos 7, 8 and 9 (February, March and April 1956), p 27.

106 *Ibid.* Naturally, the percentage of both right and wrong answers is higher for Calcutta and district towns than for rural areas, though in the case of technical assistance, rural areas do show a slightly higher percentage of correct answers than district towns.

107 See article in *The Christian Science Monitor*, Boston, 4 February 1955, by Sharokh Sabavala, a regular contributor on Indian affairs, entitled 'Food and Friendship for India'. The article is based on a series of discussions with community extension workers, farmers, etc.

108 *Monthly Public Opinion Surveys of the Indian Institute of Public Opinion*, vol 12, nos 6 and 7 (March and April 1966), p 47. *Ibid.*, vol 11, no 11, (August 1966), p 26.

109 *Ibid.*, vol 1, nos 7, 8 and 9 (February, March and April 1956), pp 5-6.

110 Cf chapter 3, note 17.

111 *Monthly Public Opinion Surveys of the Indian Institute of Public Opinion*, vol 1, nos 7, 8 and 9 (February, March and April 1956), pp 5-6.

112 *Ibid.*, pp 12-9.

113 *Ibid.*, pp 20-2.

114 *Ibid.*, pp 22-4.

115 *Monthly Public Opinion Surveys of the Indian Institute of Public Opinion*, vol 8, no 10, (July 1963), pp 18-21; vol 10, nos 9 and 10 (June and July 1965), pp 10-36; vol 12, nos 6 and 7 (March and April 1966) pp 12-45; vol 11, no 11 (August 1966), pp 3-12.

116 *Ibid.*, vol 1, nos 7, 8 and 9 (February, March and April 1956), pp 30-2.

117 *Ibid.*, pp 55-7, 75 and 93.

118 *Ibid.*, pp 58-60, 76 and 94.

119 *Ibid.*, pp 61-3, 77 and 95.

120 *Ibid.*, vol 1, nos 7, 8 and 9 (February, March and April 1956) pp 28-30; vol 7, nos 5 and 6 (February and March 1962) pp 38-53; vol 8, no 10 (July 1963), pp 18, 22-28.

121 *Ibid.*, vol 1, nos 7, 8 and 9 (February, March and April 1956), pp 25-6; vol 3, no 8 (May 1958), pp 20-2.

122 *Ibid.*, vol 12, nos 6 and 7 (March and April 1966), pp 46-55; vol 11, no 11 (August 1966), pp 25-30.

123 *Ibid.*, vol 12, nos 6 and 7 (March and April 1966), pp 56-9; vol 11, no 11 (August 1966), pp 31-4.

124 A poll in 1956 on the question 'Which country in the world will be strongest ten years from now?' produced a result overwhelmingly in favour of Russia: *Ibid.*, vol 3, no 8 (May 1958), p 5.

125 *Ibid.*, vol 7, no 10 (July 1962), pp 13-4.

126 *Ibid.*, pp 11-2.

127 *Ibid.*, vol 10, nos 9 and 10 (June and July 1965), p 47; vol 11, no 11 (August 1966), p 24.

128 *Ibid.*, vol 11, no 11 (August 1966), p 23.

Chapter 6: Food aid

1 For a full description of the system see *The Annual Report Carried Out Under Public Law 480, As Amended, During the Period January 1 Through December 31, 1966*, US Government Printing Office, Washington DC, 1967.

2 *Report of the Foodgrains Policy Committee 1966*, Ministry of Food, Agriculture, Community Development and Cooperation (Department of Food), Government of India, New Delhi, 1967, p 19.

3 *Bulletin on Food Statistics, February 1967*, Directorate of Economics and Statistics, Ministry of Food, Agriculture, Community Development and Cooperation, Government of India, New Delhi, 1967, pp 133-4.

4 V. Venkatasubbiah, 'Emasculating Costs of P.L. 480 Imports', *The Hindu Weekly Review*, Madras, 6 December 1965.

5 *The Annual Report Carried Out Under Public Law 480, As Amended, During the Period January 1 Through December 31, 1966*, U.S. Government Printing Office, Washington DC, 1967, appendix table 2.

6 Cf p 11 (table 1).

7 *U.S. Overseas Loan and Grants–Fiscal Year 1966*, Statistics and Reports Division, Office of Program Coordination, AID, 22 August 1966.

8 *Lok Sabha Debates*, 1st session, vol 5, no 50 (21 June 1962), starred question 1594, cols 12114-6.

9 E.g., see Rao and Narain, *Foreign Aid and India's Development*, pp 85-6.

10 As per chapter 6, note 4.

11 Cf pp 34-6.

12 *Report on India's Food Crisis and the Steps to Meet It*, by the Agricultural Production Team Sponsored by the Ford Foundation. Issued by the Government of India, Ministry of Food and Agriculture and the Ministry of Community Development and Cooperation, April 1959.

13 *Ibid.*, p 12.

14 Figures supplied by the Ministry of Food and Agriculture, Government of India.

15 *Report on India's Food Crisis and the Steps to Meet It,* p 27.

16 *Report of the Foodgrains Policy Committee 1966*, p 4.

17 *World Wheat Statistics*, International Wheat Council, 1966, p 45.

18 *Food and Fiber for the Future*, Report of the National Advisory Committee for Food and Fiber, U.S. Government Printing Office, Washington DC, July 1967, p 132.

19 Information supplied by the Ministry of Food and Agriculture, Government of India.

20 Information supplied by the Ministry of Petroleum and Chemicals, Government of India.

21 *Ibid.*

Chapter 7: Foreign aid and investment in the Indian oil industry

1 See *Second Five Year Plan*, Planning Commission, Government of India, New Delhi, 1956, chapter 2; *Third Five Year Plan*, Planning Commission, Government of India, New Delhi, 1961, chapter 1; *Industrial Policy Resolution 1956* (appendix no 1).

2 A subsidiary company of the Burmah Oil Co Ltd.

3 To be precise, the agreement was signed between the government of India on the one hand, and Anglo-Saxon Petroleum Co Ltd (a member of the Shell Group of Companies) and Burmah Oil Co Ltd.

4 For full text of all three agreements see *Establishment of Oil Refinieries in India – Text of Agreements with the Oil Companies*, Ministry of Production, Government of India, New Delhi, 1956 (summary provided in appendix no 4).

5 *Ibid.*, pp 9-11, 22-3, 36-9.

6 *Ibid.*, pp 2, 14, 25.

7 Terms laid down in letters exchanged. *Ibid.*, pp 1-7, 13-9.

8 *Ibid.*, pp 24-31.

9 *Report of the Oil Price Enquiry Committee, July 1961*, (Damle Report), Ministry of Steel, Mines and Fuel, Department of Mines and Fuel, Government of India, July 1961, chapter 3, pp 4-12.

10 *The Times*, London, 22 October 1955.

11 There was, however, periodic press speculation on this question: E.g., *The Daily Telegraph*, London, 29 September 1961, firmly claimed that Shri Malaviya was preparing to invoke the Essential Commodities Act to seize the companies' assets. *Le Figaro*, Paris, 31 December 1957, quotes the *Times of India* (undated) as stating that the government was studying the question of nationalisation. No doubt rumours of this nature were useful for undermining the morale of the companies.

12 Figures supplied by Ministry of Petroleum and Chemicals, Department of Petroleum, Government of India.

13 *Third Five Year Plan*, pp 513-4.

14 *The Third Plan Mid-Term Appraisal*, p 136.

15 Main terms of Agreement stated in *The Times*, London, 7 December 1957. Company not finally incorporated until February 1959, *The Hindu*, Madras, 20 February 1959.

16 Cf pp 127-8.

17 The report in *The Times*, London, 4 November 1957, lends

some basis to this speculation. Burmah Oil Co. is reported to have insisted that it would only finance a pipeline with Assam.

18 *Financial Times*, London, 4 August 1956.

19 *The Hindu*, Madras, 8 April 1956.

20 *The Hindu*, Madras, 8 April 1957.

21 *Financial Times*, London, 15 July 1957.

22 *The Hindu*, Madras, 4 November 1957. K. D. Malaviya denied that deadlock had been reached, though he did hint at certain tensions. Burmah Oil Co. was reported as expressing the companies' unwillingness to invest further in India, due to the government's policies.

23 Announced at a press conference, New Delhi, 1st June 1961, by K. D. Malaviya. For main outline of the terms and issues involved, see *Financial Times*, London, 11 April 1961 and *The Hindu*, Madras, 2 June 1961.

24 *Financial Times*, London, 29 June 1961.

25 *The Times*, London, 10 January 1962.

26 See *Financial Times*, London 6 March 1962; *The Hindu*, Madras, 20th March 1962; *Financial Times*, London, 8 November 1962; *The Hindu*, Madras, 11 November 1962. The state finance minister of Assam threw in an additional issue by advocating joint nationalisation by the state and union governments. Press Conference, Shillong, 12 January 1962. Reported in *The Hindu*, Madras, 14 January 1962.

27 *The Third Plan Mid-Term Appraisal*, p 136. Estimated 2,200 tons daily by early 1964.

28 *External Assistance 1964*, Ministry of Finance, Department of Economic Affairs, Government of India, 1964, pp 68-9, 72-3.

29 *The Hindu*, Madras, 5 September 1955 and 3 October 1955. Countries visited included the Soviet Union primarily, but also Rumania, the United Kingdom, France, Holland and Switzerland.

30 *The Hindu*, Madras, 27 November 1955.

31 *New York Times*, 20 March 1956.

32 *Ibid.*, The Oil and Natural Gas Commission was later converted into a statutory body and given substantial powers for the overall control of industry.

33 The first strike was at Cambay in September 1958. See *Daily Telegraph*, London, 23 September 1958. The Minister of Steel, Mines and Fuel, S. S. Singh, while acknowledging Soviet aid, claimed that Indian geologists selected the site and must therefore be given the credit. See *Financial Times*, London, 18 September 1958. The first consignment of crude oil was delivered to the Bombay refineries in September 1961. *The Hindu*, Madras, 3 September 1961.

34 *Third Five Year Plan*, p 514.

35 Agreement signed 11 March 1955, reported in *New York Times*, 12 March 1955. The Agreement provided for extensive participation and training of Indians, both in India and the United States. The Venture was abandoned in October 1960. Reported in *Financial Times*, London, 24 October 1960. Cost to government was $3.51m. (Rs. 67 crores). *Third Five Year Plan*, p 514.

36 *The Hindu*, Madras, 13 September 1961 and *The Guardian*, London, 12 August 1961.

37 *New York Times* 13 May and 13 August 1961; *The Hindu*, Madras, 13 September 1961. The first of these reports suggested undertones of suspicion as to whether the oil companies really wanted to find oil.

38 Reports of negotiations with ENI, a state owned Italian corporation, appeared in *Financial Times*, London, 24 October 1960 and 29 November 1960 and 23 August 1962; *The Hindu*, Madras, 30 August 1961.

39 *The Hindu*, Madras, 29 July 1962.

40 Cf table 36, p 120.

41 Information supplied by the Ministry of Petroleum and Chemicals, Department of Petroleum, Government of India.

42 Cf table 37, p 127.

43 *The Hindu*, Madras 30 September 1959.

44 *External Assistance 1964*, p 73.

45 *The Hindu*, Madras, 11 May 1963.

46 *External Assistance 1964*, p 60.

47 *The Hindu*, Madras 8 May 1963, reporting detailed statement by K. D. Malaviya to both Houses of Parliament on 7 May 1963.

48 *Financial Times*, London, 22 January 1964; *The Hindu*, Madras, 28 December 1963; *The Times*, London, 31 December 1963.

49 *Formation Agreement between Government of India and National Iranian Oil Co and Amoco India Incorporated of U.S.A. for Establishment of an Oil Refinery at Madras–November 18, 1965*, Government of India, Ministry of Petroleum and Chemicals. Printed in India by Government of India Press, Minto Road, New Delhi, 1966.

50 Information supplied by Ministry of Petroleum and Chemicals, Department of Petroleum, Government of India.

51 *Ibid.*

52 *Third Five Year Plan*, p 529.

53 *The Guardian*, London, 25 October 1960 and *Financial Times*, London, 18 March 1961.

54 *Third Five Year Plan*, p 529.

55 Supply contract was probably included in the 2nd Russian credit, allotted to the Third Plan, of Rs. 59.53; see *External Assistance 1964*, pp 72-3.

56 *Financial Times*, London, 18 March 1961.

57 Report by Stephen Barber in *Daily Telegraph*, London, 27 September 1962.

58 *Third Five Year Plan*, p 529. See also the statement by K. D. Malaviya at a press conference, New Delhi, 25 September 1962, that a condition of refinery expansion was that the companies should accept payment for imports in rupees, reported in

Financial Times, London 26 September 1962. Such a condition could not be demanded if Russia were not accepting rupee payments.

59 Reports claiming this to be common Soviet practice appear periodically in the press, e.g. *Daily Telegraph*, London, 27 September 1962, report by Stephen Barber. However, supporting evidence is not supplied by these reports, *The Hindu*, Madras, 31 January 1964, reports that with oil sales rising in Europe, Russia is already bargaining much harder with India over oil prices.

60 *Financial Times*, London 1 August 1963. Information also supplied by Ministry of Petroleum and Chemicals, Department of Petroleum, Government of India.

61 *Financial Times*, London, 1 August 1963.

62 Information supplied by Ministry of Petroleum and Chemicals, Department of Petroleum, Government of India.

63 *The Observer*, London, 16 April 1961. Unfortunately no sources are given for these calculations.

64 *Christian Science Monitor*, Boston, 12 August 1960; see also *Third Plan Mid-Term Appraisal*, p 136.

65 Information supplied by Ministry of Petroleum and Chemicals, Department of Petroleum, Government of India.

66 *Ibid.*

67 *The Observer*, London, 16 April 1961; see also *The Hindu*, Madras, 29 April 1961, for a vigorous but somewhat unconvincing denial of this charge by the minister, who stated that India's policy was for each sector to use its own sources of crude oil. He further denied that there was any shortage of capacity.

68 Based on conversations with officials of the government of India.

69 *Establishment of Oil Refineries in India.*

70 This is admitted by the companies; see *Report of the Working Group on Oil Prices–August 1965* (Talukdar Report), Government of India, Ministry of Petroleum and Chemicals, Department of Petroleum, p 26.

71 See *Report of the Oil Price Enquiry Committee, July 1961* (Damle Report), pp 13-5; see also *New York Times*, 29 July 1959 and 24 October 1959; *New York Herald Tribune*, 29 July 1960.

72 *Report of the Oil Price Enquiry Committee–July 1961.*

73 *Ibid.*, chapter 6.

74 *Ibid.*, chapter 22.

75 *Ibid.*, p 92.

76 *The Hindu*, Madras, 28 September and 1 October 1961; *Daily Telegraph*, London, 29 September and 16 November 1961.

77 *Report of the Working Group on Oil Prices–August 1965, op. cit.*

78 *Ibid.*, pp 3-4.

79 *Ibid., pp 1-4.*

80 *Ibid.*, pp 107-12.

81 *Ibid.*, chapters 4 and 6.

82 *Ibid.*, pp 39-40.

83 *Ibid.*, p 76.

84 *Ibid.*, p 40.

85 See *ibid.*, p 31. Statement based mainly on information supplied by Ministry of Petroleum and Chemicals, Department of Petroleum, Government of India.

86 *Report of the Working Group on Oil Prices–August 1965*, p 31.

87 Based on conversations with representatives of the oil companies in India.

88 *The Hindu*, Madras, 16 February 1962. Statement by K. D. Malaviya, inaugurating the first trainload of Ankleshwar oil to the Bombay refineries, 15 February 1962.

89 This statement ignores the contribution of Oil India Ltd, whose major discoveries were made before 1958 by Assam Oil Co Ltd, whilst still a 100 per cent private company.

90 *External Assistance 1964*, pp 45-6.

91 *Ibid.*, p 43.

92 *Ibid.*, pp 68-9, 72-3.

Chapter 8: Foreign aid in the steel industry

1 Information supplied by the Government of India Planning Commission.

2 The private sector contribution may in fact be understated, as secondary producers and rerollers are not included; see *Report 1964-65*, Ministry of Steel and Mines, Department of Iron and Steel, Government of India, 1965, p 2. Most of these producers would be in the private sector. Figures quoted, in this source, however, do not relate to the full year.

3 Figures supplied by the Government of India Planning Commission.

4 *External Assistance 1964*, Ministry of Finance, Department of Economic Affairs, Government of India, New Delhi, pp 15-6, 36-40, 72-3, 126-7.

5 Cf pp 12-13, 20-23.

6 Selig S. Harrison, *India – The Most Dangerous Decades*, Princeton UP, 1960, p 201.

7 *External Assistance 1964*, pp 36-40.

8 Total capacity targets envisaged in the expansion were: Bhilai 2.5m. tons, Durgapur 1.5m. tons, Rourkela 1.8m. tons, expanded in each case from an original capacity of 1m tons: *External Assistance 1963*, pp 11, 24, 51. The targets were expected to be completed by the end of the Third Plan, but to date only Bhilai is even within sight of completion.

9 *External Assistance 1963*, p 50.

10 *Lok Sabha Debates*, vol 14, 4th session, no 36 (1 April 1958), cols 7755-64; part 2, vol 3, 12th session (12 April 1956), cols 5149-56.

11 *Review of the First Five Year Plan*, Government of India Planning Commission, New Delhi, May 1957, p 185.

12 *Ibid.*

13 *Ibid.*

14 *Financial Times* London, 20 November 1956.

15 *Lok Sabha Debates*, vol 14, 4th session, no 36 (1 April 1958), cols 7755-64; *The Hindu*, Madras, 27 May 1962, based on conversations in Delhi in 1964 and 1966.

16 *Lok Sabha Debates*, part 2, vol 2, 12th session (12 April 1956), cols 5149-56.

17 *Financial Times*, London, 23 November 1956.

18 *The Times*, London, 1 September 1954.

19 *The Times*, London, 11 September 1954.

20 *The Hindu*, Madras, 3 February 1955.

21 *The Times*, London, 14 September 1954; *The Hindu*, Madras, 14 September 1954.

22 *The Guardian*, London, 18 November 1959 (report by Taya Zinkin).

23 *Christian Science Monitor*, Boston, 14 December 1954, reports a damning appraisal of Russian steel-making capacity by K. Lalbhai, leader of a returning Indian trade delegation, who stated that some of the steel plants were 'housed in crumbling over-age buildings which would be condemned even in my country'. However, a report on this delegation's view in *The Hindu*, Madras, 10 December 1954, although critical in many respects, does not contain this particular emphasis. *The Christian Science Monitor*, Boston, 14 December 1954, also contains an uncorroborated report that the steel mill offered to India was one of six offered to China, only five having been accepted. See also *The Times*, London, 11 September 1954.

24 *The Times*, London, 14 September 1954.

25 *Financial Times*, London, 3 and 7th January 1955; *The Hindu*, Madras, 26 and 28 November, 1954.

26 *Ibid.*, See also *The Times*, London, 4 January 1955 and *Financial Times*, London, 12 and 18 January 1955. The latter report indicates that Britain had a potential interest in the proposed Rourkela expansion.

27 *The Times*, London, 31 December 1954.

28 *The Hindu*, Madras, 17 December 1954.

29 *External Assistance 1963*, pp 96-7; *The Times*, London, 22 November 1955.

30 *New York Times*, 3 January 1955.

31 *The York Times*, 5 June 1955.

32 *The Times*, London, 14 September 1954.

33 *The Times*, London, 20 December 1954 (leading article).

34 Overstreet and Windmiller, *Communism in India*, pp 252-308.

35 *Manchester Guardian*, 25 September 1954; *quoting Hindustan Times*, New Delhi (undated).

36 *Hindustan Steel Ltd: 9th Annual Report 1962-63*, Ranchi (Bihar), 1 November 1963, p 7; *Hindustan Steel Ltd: 10th Annual Report, 1963-64*, Ranchi (Bihar), 10 December 1964, pp 7, 62, 78, 94.

37 *Ibid.*

38 Cf tables 40 and 41.

39 *Hindustan Steel Ltd: 9th Annual Report, 1962-3*, p 9; *Report, 1964-65*, Ministry of Steel and Mines, Department of Iron and Steel, pp 6, 8, 10.

40 The range of products from Durgapur would appear to be somewhat more complex than those from Bhilai. See *Hindustan Steel Ltd: 10th Annual Report, 1963-64*, p 19.

41 Department of Iron and Steel, *Report, 1962-63*, p 10; *Report, 1963-64*, p 19.

42 The Durgapur and Rourkela expansion projects are not so far advanced and will presumably need increases in foreign personnel, through the capacity expansion involved in both cases is smaller and India may be expected to use a greater proportion of her own personnel at an earlier stage.

43 *The Hindu*, Madras, 6 August 1961, 27 June 1961, 8 April 1962; 10 and 17 December 1961, 27 May 1962, 18 July 1962. One serious strike at Bhilai is reported in *The New York Times*, 19, 20 and 21 February 1960 and *The Hindu*, Madras, 13 and 29 January 1954.

44 *The Hindu*, Madras, 15 May 1959 and 12 and 14 June 1959, describes troubles caused by the weakness of the foundation piles. Management spokesmen admitted the error and agreed to make good the loss at the contractors' expense; *The Times*, London, 30 March 1959, reported that a Communist weekly, *New Age*, 22 March 1959, charged that foundation work at Durgapur was defective. On this occasion the contractors played the issue down, maintaining that the defect was confined to the melting shop. A Colombo Plan team, led by Sir Eric Coates (who was a prime mover in the original negotiations) condemned guerilla warfare between departments and stated that ISCON (the consortium of contracting forms) certification of the technical standard of products was 'far from satisfactory'.

45 Indeed it seems that the Germans had first choice of site and chose Rourkela, see *The Hindu*, Madras, 13 and 19 January 1954.

46 *The Hindu*, Madras, 18 July 1962.

47 The minister for steel, mines and fuel, S. S. Singh, on two occasions stated that Rourkela was below standard in efficiency compared with the other two public sector mills. Press conference, New Delhi, 5 August 1961, reported in *The Hindu*, Madras, 6 August 1961; statement to Iron and Steel Advisory Council, 30 March 1962; *The Hindu*, Madras, 31 March 1962. This view is generally confirmed by Indian officials.

48 Hindustan Steel Ltd proposed a consortium of steel engineers to deal with technical difficulties. This scheme did not come to fruition, but shortly afterwards some sixty German engineers

arrived to deal with breakdowns; *The Hindu*, Madras, 9 August 1961.

49 *The Times*, London, 28 January 1958; *Manchester Guardian*, 15 February 1958.

50 *Observer Foreign News Service*, London, no 14334, 12 February 1959: C. Dunn, 'Why Bhilai is Different'.

51 *The Observer*, London 8 February 1959.

52 *The Guardian*, London, 6 November 1959 (article by Taya Zinkin); an article by the financial editor in *The Guardian*, 12 December 1958, argues that the British at Durgapur have the best relations with Indians, by comparison with the general 'uncommunicative' nature of Indo-Russian relations.

53 As per chapter 8, notes 49, 50, 51.

54 *The Guardian*, London, 6 November 1959 (article by Taya Zinkin).

55 *The Guardian*, London, 26 November 1959 (article by Taya Zinkin).

56 *Ibid.* The official German explanation is that use of these facilities is in the contract of German technicians; however, British subcontractors, with no such contract, are admitted.

57 Mrs Renu Chakravarty, a Communist MP in West Bengal is reported to have stated that ' . . . the entire atmosphere in Durgapur is vitiated with the stinking atmosphere of white man's superiority', *The Hindu*, Madras, 1 April 1959; C. Dunn in *The Observer*, London, 8 February 1959, refers to Communist press sources as commenting in a similar vein.

58 *The Guardian*, London, 18 November 1959.

59 *The Guardian*, London, 24 September 1959 (leading article).

60 *Ibid.*

61 *Lok Sabha Debates*, vol 14, 4th session, no 36 (1 April 1958), cols 7110-2.

62 *Ibid.*

63 *Third Five Year Plan*, pp 466-7.

64 *External Assistances 1964*, pp 70, 73. Department of Iron and Steel, *Report, 1964-65*, pp 15-7.

65 *The Hindu*, Madras, 26 October 1958, reports visit of Sir Peter Robertson MP, chairman of the Newton Chambers Co. to Delhi to discuss the proposed projects for a fourth public sector steel mill; see also *Daily Express*, London, 15 May 1959, which indicates strong British and Russian competition for the Bokaro contract.

66 *Daily Express*, London, 15 May 1959; *New York Times*, 21 September 1961.

67 *The Hindu*, Madras, 4 May 1961; *The Hindu*, Madras, 24 October 1963.

68 *The Hindu*, Madras, 24 October 1963.

69 Ambassador J. K. Galbraith made a clear statement of this theme at New Delhi on 12 April 1963, reported in *The Hindu*, Madras, 13 April 1963, '. . . [the right course] is to have an American firm build the plant on behalf of the Indian government and then run it for a considerable period of time. This will give the United States a chance to show what we can do. It will assure that India gets an efficient, low cost source of steel'.

70 Report of U.S. Steel Mission, see *New York Herald Tribune*, 4 May 1963; *Eastern Economist*, Delhi, 10 May 1963.

71 *The Hindu*, Madras, 18 July 1962; *The Times*, London, 2 March 1962.

72 Cf chapter 8, note 69.

73 *The Times*, London, 2 March 1961. C. Subramaniam, minister of steel, mines and fuel, stated in Parliament on 1 May 1963 that it was the government's intention ' . . . . to associate fully Indian resources and skills in design and engineering of steel plants with the further stages of the project'; reported in *The Hindu*, Madras, 2 May 1962.

74 *The Hindu*, Madras, 28 March 1962.

75 *The Guardian*, London, 15 August 1961, article by Sudhir

Ghosh MP. Officials reported to regard Hindustan Steel Ltd as 'overloaded', in *The Hindu*, Madras, 16 February 1962

76 Based on conversations with Indian officials.

77 *The Hindu*, Madras, 30 April 1962.

78 *The Hindu*, Madras, 4 and 14 May 1962.

79 *The Hindu*, Madras, 16 May 1962.

80 *New York Times*, 25 April 1963.

81 Official Text of Clay Committee Report was released by the U.S. Information Service, 25 March 1963. Cf pp 32-3.

82 *New York Times*, 25 April 1963.

83 Statement in New Delhi on 12 April 1962, reported in *The Hindu*, Madras, 13 April 1963. Galbraith argues that by building the mill in the public sector ' . . . . [the United States] will not arouse suspicions now happily stilled, that we are seeking to mould Indian economic policy to our own image. That was suspected in the past. It did everyone a disservice. We should not feel impelled to repeat our mistakes'. This statement is obviously a criticism of the Clay Report.

84 *New York Times*, 15 August 1963.

85 Letter to *New York Times*, 9 June 1963, by Shri Bharat Ram, president of Federation of Indian Chambers of Commerce and Industry; statement by J. D. Tata, *New York Times*, 25 May 1963.

86 *Clay Committee Report*, p 4.

87 *New York Times*, 23 August 1963.

88 *New York Times*, 4 September 1963.

89 *New York Times*, 8 September 1963. In the same report Galbraith is said to have discussed the issue with some forty or fifty congressmen and found them more concerned with the scale of the project than with the question of private or public enterprise.

90 *The Hindu*, Madras, 12 September 1963.

91 See particularly a report by H. Venkatasubbiah in *The Hindu*, Madras, 8 September 1963.

92 *Ibid.*

93 *The Hindu*, Madras, 12 December 1963. The Report estimated the proportion of plant and equipment for various purposes that could be manufactured in India as follows: stocking and handling of raw materials 75 per cent, coke ovens 66 per cent, byproduct plants 60 per cent, blast furnaces 60 per cent, steel melting shops 20 per cent, mills 10-20 per cent.

94 *The Hindu*, Madras, 30 January 1964.

95 *The Times*, London, 31 January 1964.

96 *The Hindu*, Madras, 25 February 1964.

97 *New York Times*, 2 May 1964.

98 *Financial Times*, London, 5 June 1964.

99 *New York Times*, 4 May 1964 (leading article).

100 Statement at New Delhi, 9 May 1963: *The Hindu*, Madras, 10 May 1963.

Chapter 9: Foreign private capital: some political aspects

1 *India–Pocket Book of Economic Information 1963*, Government of India, Ministry of Finance, Department of Economic Affairs, 1963, p 78.

2 M. Kidron, *Foreign Investments in India*, Oxford UP, London, 1963, p 242.

3 *Ibid.*, p 243.

4 *Ibid.*, pp 224-5, 268, 281ff, 289ff.

5 *Ibid.*, pp 258-74.

6 *Lok Sabha Debates*, 14th session (1961), appendix 2, annexure no 27, (*vide* starred question no 521 (a) dated 16 August 1961, col 2252). Press note issued by Government of India Press Information Bureau on 'Role of Foreign Private Investment'.

7 For a good overall statement of government policy towards the private sector see M. Shah, minister of commerce and industry,

in *Economic Review* (Weekly Journal of All India Congress Committee), vol 15, no 3, 1 July 1963, pp 11-4.

8 See appendix no 2.

9 See appendix no 6. See also Kidron, *Foreign Investment in India,* pp 286-97.

10 *Lok Sabha Debates*, vol 12, no 14 (30 March 1962) pp 2578-84, starred question 305. Answer by M. Shah, minister for commerce and industry, to Shri A. M. Tariq. In a supplementary, Shri Indrajit Gupta charged that these fourteen exceptions contravened the 1956 Industrial Policy Resolution, whlch charge the minister denied.

11 *Spotlight on Investment Opportunity: Steel Forgings*, Industrial Fact Sheet No. 3, Indian Investment Centre, New Delhi; reports that foreign capital might be admitted into steel production itself (e.g. in *Financial Times*, London, 26 February 1964) were denied by C. Subramaniam, minister for steel, mines and heavy engineering, in Lok Sabha, 24 April 1964; reported in *The Hindu*, Madras, 25 April 1964.

12 Kidron, *Foreign Investment in India*, pp 285-96. The Reserve Bank of India officially regards 40 per cent as a controlling interest (p 286).

13 M. Shah, minister for commerce and industry, in Lok Sabha, 25 April 1959 (reported in *The Hindu*, Madras, 26 April 1959), declared himself well satisfied with the pace of 'Indianisation' and absence of discrimination against Indians. He also paid warm tribute to foreign firms for keeping Indian national sentiment so well in view.

14 Compiled from information in *The Hindu*, Madras, 28 December 1956 and 24 February 1964. Unfortunately different income categories are given in each report.

15 In an excellent article in *The Manchester Guardian*, London, 2 December 1958, the financial editor argues that although there was no doubt as to the ability of the new generation of Indian scientists, technologists and managers, foreigners were being moved out a little too fast. The article also quotes an elderly Birmingham (England) engineer who described his

Indian toolroom workers as rather like English workers fifty years ago—fine craftsment with their hands, but not so much at home with elaborate machinery. A similar theme is advanced in an article by Richard Fry in *The Guardian*, London 24 January 1961.

16 *Keesings Contemporary Archives, 1955-56*, Keesings Publications Ltd, Bristol, pp 14714, 14943.

17 *Financial Times*, London, 30 November 1955.

18 Jawaharlal Nehru frequently attacked the concept of socialism as largely static and irrelevant; e.g. his speech at Ajmer All India Congress Committee, 25 July 1954, where nationalisation is described as 'neither Socialism nor Communism nor sense nor logic'; quoted in a hostile context, by A. Mehta, *Lok Sabha Debates*, 27 September 1954, 7th session, part 2, vol 7, cols 3392-9.

19 E.g. speech by J. D. Tata at a shareholders meeting of the Indian Iron and Steel Co., 27 August 1957 (reported in *The Hindu*, Madras, 30 August 1957); see also article by D. Duxbury, 'Investment Opportunities in India'. *Financial Times*, London, 21 March 1956. The article is based on surveys by the Federation of British Industries.

20 E.g. see *The Times*, London, 11 January 1961 and *The Hindu*, Madras, 15 May 1964. Report of US delegation of businessmen.

21 Donald Kennedy, United States Chargé d'Affaires, New Delhi expressed the view that India's welcome to foreign capital was more apparent than real. The combination of socialism and nationalisation gave foreign businessmen the feeling that they were only being used so long as they were needed; *Christian Science Monitor*, Boston, 14 January 1955.

22 Cf p 86. On a somewhat lighthearted note, anti-Americanism at one stage even took the form of neurosis over Coca-Cola manufacturing in India. Presumably this represented imperialism, alien culture, etc. *Lok Sabha Debates*, part 1, vol 9, no 5, starred question 184, 13 August 1951, cols 228-30; part 1, vol 2, no 19, starred question 831, 2 December 1952, cols 967-70.

23 *Lok Sabha Debates*, vol 62, no 14, 16th session, starred question

305, 30 March 1962, cols 2578-84. Question on foreign controlled firms. *Lok Sabha Debates*, part 2, vol 3, 12th session, 12 April 1956, cols 5149-94. Wide ranging debate on foreign investment and technical aid, especially in the steel industry. *Lok Sabha Debates*, part 2, vol 7, 7th session (27 September 1954), cols 3388-435. Debate on American participation in the Industrial Finance Corporation reveals fears of American domination of a wide range of firms even through minority shareholdings.

24 *Lok Sabha Debates*, part 2, vol 8, 10th session (27 September 1955), cols 15390-401. During the course of a debate on the Industrial Finance Corporation, Shri N. B. Shoudhury (cols 15391-4) objected to the need for providing assurances against nationalisation and points to trouble in Argentina and Iran. His general conclusion is that it was better to accept loans at higher interest rates than to depend on equity capital.

25 *Economic Weekly*, Bombay, vol 15, no 7, 16 February 1963, pp 304-5.

26 Kidron, *Foreign Investment in India*, chapter 7.

27 See statement by G. L. Mehta, chairman of Indian Investment Centre at the annual general meeting, 9 July 1964 (obtainable from Indian Investment Centre, New Delhi), p 2, giving figures for number of enquiries by Indians and foreigners for joint ventures, as follows: 1961-2, 1272; 1962-3, 1050; 1963-4, 750. However, other factors, such as the tendency to licence a large part of required capacity early in a Plan period, play a part.

28 *New York Times*, 18 April 1963; *The Hindu*, Madras, 21 April 1963 and 22 April 1964. For details of the new tax proposals in 1963 see *Supplement to Taxation*.

29 Indian Investment Centre, *Investing in India. Basic Facts of the Indian Economy*, New Delhi, 1962, pp 29-34.

30 Described fully in *Objects and Functions*, Investing in India series, Indian Investment Centre, New Delhi, 1961.

31 Mehta (see note 27).

32 *Ibid.*, p 9.

33 The report of the United States delegates visiting India in 1964

(see *The Hindu*, Madras, 15 May 1964) for the purpose of increasing American capital participation, stated that one application took three years before a decision was taken.

34 *Report on Currency and Finance for the Year 1964-65*, pp 144, 146-7. *External Assistance 1964*, pp 36-9, 85.

35 Hearings before the subcommittee of the Committee of Appropriations, House of Representatives (USA), Mutual Security Appropriations for 1961, 86th Congress, 2nd session, pp 280-1, Hearings on US aid to IFC, ICICI, and National Small Industries Corporation Ltd.

36 *The Hindu*, Madras, 28 May 1959.

37 *Ibid.*

38 *Report on the Indo-U.S. Technical Cooperation Programme for 1962-3*, Department of Economic Affairs, Ministry of Finance, Government of India, New Delhi, Agreement no 97, pp 82-3, December 1963.

39 *Exchange Control*, Investing in India series, Indian Investment Centre, New Delhi, 1961, p 10 and appendix 4, pp 36-9.

40 *The Scotsman*, Edinburgh, 20 May 1955 and *Financial Times*, London, 22 July 1955.

41 Statement by G. L. Mehta, 9 July 1964, *The Hindu*, Madras, 19 and 20 April 1964. The delegation, however, reported that substantial deterrents to foreign capital still remained: see *The Hindu*, Madras, 15 May 1964.

42 E.g., statement by N. Knowles, deputy director of Bureau of Foreign Commerce of the US Department of Commerce and leader of a trade mission then touring India, reported in *The Hindu*, Madras, 7 January 1959; see also US Department of Commerce report on this mission; *The Hindu*, Madras, 22 January 1959; *The Hindu*, Madras, 24 and 26 May 1959. One highly favourable statement (quoted in a hostile context by the *Daily Worker*, London, 11 June 1959), was made by Ralph Binney, vice-president of the First National Bank of Boston '..... Now is the time for American firms to move in. There is ample opportunity for making money there. You get virtually

a free ride on your capital for the first five years of a company's operation'.

43 Cf chapter 8, note 20.

44 E.g., see report of US delegation to India, April 1964, *The Hindu*, Madras, 15 May 1964; see also statement by Averell Harriman at a press conference at Madras on 28 February 1959, reported in *The Hindu*, Madras, 1 March 1959, to the effect that greater tax reliefs should be provided as incentives to foreign investors.

45 Cf pp 40-47.

46 *India 1963*; a report of a visit made by Sir Norman Kipping, attended by Michael Donovan, January 1963.

47 *India 1963*, p 19. Quotation from an (unnamed) American commentator: 'Anyone who invests in India is a sucker; but anybody who does not invest in India is a bigger sucker'.

48 Cf pp 13-14.

49 *India 1963*, chapters 1 and 5.

50 E.g. article by Daniel Duxbury in *Financial Times*, London, 21 March 1956, entitled 'Survey of Investment Opportunities in India', based on surveys by the Federation of British Industries. However, the writer argues that British capital is far too unadventurous. See also statement by G. Cole, vice-chairman of Unilever Ltd of New Delhi, 15 March 1959, reported in *The Hindu*, Madras, 16 March 1959.

51 *Financial Times*, London, 14 October 1958.

52 Based on information supplied by the Indian Investment Centre and the Federation of Indian Chambers of Commerce.

53 Quoted by Asoka Mehta in a hostile context (original source unstated), *Lok Sabha Debates*, part 2, vol 7, 7th session (27 September 1954), col 3396.

54 E.g. speech by G. D. Birla to Management Association, New York, 26 April 1960, reported in *The Hindu*, Madras, 30 April 1960; article (highly optimistic) by G. D. Birla in *The Guardian*, London, 5 August 1962; speech by Shri Bharat Ram, textile industrialist, at Indian Investment Centre, New York, 17 April 1963; reported in *New York Times*, 18 April 1963.

55 Cf pp 143-6.

56 *New York Times*, 25 May 1963.

57 Letter to *New York Times*, 9 June 1963.

58 Speeches in Boston by Ambassador C. Chagla reported in *Christian Science Monitor*, Boston, 17 March 1959; see also speech of B. K. Nehru to the Economic Club, Detroit, *Vital Speeches of the Day*, vol 26, no 22, 1 September 1960, pp 686-9, 'The Economic Challenge In India—Can Democracy Meet It'?

59 E.g. *The Hindu*, Madras, 9 October 1962; *Financial Times*, London, 12 July 1962.

60 E.g. *Financial Times*, London, 26 February 1964; *The Hindu*, Madras, 19 February 1964; statement by J. R. Galloway, leader of a delegation of American businessmen which visited India in April 1964 to the effect that T. T. Krishnamachari was seeking a fivefold increase in foreign investment, *The Hindu*, Madras, 20 April 1964. The main fields of interest to India, according to Mr Galloway, were heavy machinery, toolmaking, chemicals, fertilisers and electrical equipment.

61 *The Hindu*, Madras, 8 May 1964.

62 Cf pp 123-4.

63 *The Hindu*, Madras, 28 April 1964.

64 *The Hindu Weekly Review*, Madras, 14 February 1966, p 4.

65 Based on conversations in Delhi, Calcutta, Bombay. Official reasons stated in *The Hindu Weekly Review*, Madras, 10 January 1966, p 5.

Chapter 10: Military aid

1 *India* (1960-1967). Reference Annuals compiled by the Research and Reference Division of the Ministry of Information and Broadcasting, Government of India, pp 86 and 108 respectively. The figures in the last two publications show some minor discrepancies: the 1961 figures are used except for the year 1951-2, which is based on the 1960 publication.

2 *The Hindu*, Madras, 19 June 1964.

3 *Ibid.*

4 See Easwar Sagar in *The Hindu*, Madras, 19 April and 23 May 1963; K. Rangaswami in *The Hindu*, Madras, 12 May 1963; see also *New York Times*, 15 June 1964.

5 Speech in Rajya Sabha, 23 August 1961; see *Foreign Affairs Record 1961*, Government of India, Ministry of External Affairs, New Delhi, pp 236-46.

6 Cf pp 1-2.

7 Report by R. Trumbull in *New York Times*, 17 March 1954; quoted by H. Mukerjee in a hostile context: *Lok Sabha Debates*, 23 March 1954, vol 2, part 2, 6th session, col 2812.

8 *Ibid.*

9 *The Hindu*, Madras, 21 February 1957.

10 Article by Thomas Brady, *New York Times*, 13 May 1964.

11 *New York Times*, 5 October 1960, estimates that these items constituted a value of $31.5m.

12 *New York Times*, 5 October 1960; *The Hindu*, Madras, 18 August 1961.

13 In addition, an unknown number of Ilyushin-14 jets had been purchased in 1961: *Financial Times*, London 14 March 1961.

14 *The Hindu*, Madras, 7 October 1961.

15 *New York Times*, 13 May 1964 and 7 June 1964.

16 *Dawn*, Karachi, 28 April 1963, claimed that total aid was for the purpose of equipping six mountain divisions.

17 *The Hindu Weekly Review*, Madras, 28 September 1964.

18 Value estimated at $50m. in *New York Times*, 7 June 1964.

19 Some information may be gleaned from the following sources; 1. Report on naval assistance issued as part of a communique issued following Y. B. Chavan's defence talks in London during November 1964: *The Hindu Weekly Review*, Madras, 30 November 1964. 2. *Lok Sabha Debates*, 19 August 1963, vol 19, 5th session, cols 1213-8, gives information on supply of radar equipment for

the United Kingdom. 3. *Lok Sabha Debates*, vol 13, 4th session, no 7, question 139 (14 August 1963), col 398: information provided on UK assistance towards Civil Defence services. Evidently a British adviser, General Irwin, recommended the construction of 100,000 shelters and large-scale removal of windows and ventilators in some northern states. Instructions on these lines were issued and later withdrawn. The prime minister stated that the measures were useless and would merely create panic.

20 *The Hindu*, Madras, 18 August 1963.

21 This would have included thirty-six Harvard trainer aircraft: see Y. B. Chavan in Lok Sabha, 22 April 1963, reported in *The Hindu*, Madras, 23 April 1963.

22 *Dawn*, Karachi, 28 April 1963.

23 *Ibid.* However, for a more modest view of Australian defence capacity, see statement by Shri Raghuramaiah, minister of defence production in the Ministry of Defence: *Lok Sabha Debates*, vol 12, 6th session, no 1, starred question no 3 (18 November 1963), cols 18-20.

24 Y. B. Chavan in *Rajya Sabha*, 18 August 1963, reported in *The Hindu*, Madras, 23 April 1963.

25 *External Assistance, 1964*, pp 17-21.

26 *New York Times,* 2 July 1963.

27 *Ibid.*

28 P. J. Eldridge, 'India's Non-Alignment Policy Reviewed', *Australian Outlook*, August 1965.

29 E.g. speech at Bangalore on 2 January 1954, reported in *The Hindu*, Madras, 4 January 1954.

30 *Ibid.,* and speech in Lok Sabha, 19 March 1963: *Foreign Affairs Record, 1963*, pp 77-85.

31 As per chapter 10, note 28.

32 Cf pp 39-46.

33 *New York Times*, 5 October 1960; *Daily Telegraph*, London, 16 September 1961.

34 *The Hindu*, Madras, 4 October 1961: *The Guardian*, London, 26 October 1961; *Lok Sabha Debates*, vol 4, no 35, 1st session, starred question no 1209 (31 May 1962), col 7993 (question to and statement by K. Menon, minister of defence).

35 *The Hindu*, Madras, 14 May 1962.

36 *The Hindu Weekly Review*, Madras, 28 September 1964, statement by Y. B. Chavan; *The Hindu Weekly Review*, Madras, 19 October 1964, report on visit of three-man defence team from the United States to Delhi.

37 *The Hindu*, Madras, 3 August 1963.

38 *Ibid.*

39 Strong statement by C. Rajagopalachari in Madras, 2 April 1961, reported in *The Hindu*, Madras, 3 April 1961; article by K. Rangaswami in *The Hindu*, Madras, 17 October 1960; J. Nehru, however, denied any such danger existed when the question was raised in Parliament on 30 March 1961; reported in *The Hindu*, Madras, 31 March 1961.

40 Cf pp 39-46.

41 *U.S. Congressional Record*, 87th Congress, 2nd session, vol 108, part 8, 15 June 1963, col 10663.

42 *Hearings before the Committee on Foreign Assistance, House of Representatives*, 88th Congress, 1st session on H.R. 5490, 30 April 1963: Foreign Assistance Act of 1963 (To Amend further The Foreign Assistance Act of 1961, As Amended and for Other Purposes), part 3; U.S. Government Printing Office, Washington DC, pp 415-9. During testimony of J. P. Grant, deputy-assistant secretary of state for north-east and south-Asian affairs, Chairman Morgan advocated strong diplomatic pressure on India and Pakistan: ' . . . . I think somebody ought to do some arm-twisting and get this settled'.

43 E.g. *Hindustan Times*, New Delhi, 13 April 1963.

44 *Lok Sabha Debates*, vol 17, 4th session, short notice question no 7, 22 April 1963, cols 11043-8.

45 This pro-Indian line has not always been consistent. It is interesting

to note that the Communist Party of India supported the formation of Pakistan, following the Stalinist line for India during this period: Selig S. Harrison, *India: The Most Dangerous Decades*, Princeton UP, 1960, pp 150ff.

46 B. K. Nehru stated that India receives less aid per capita from combined sources than American allies receive from one source: *Lok Sabha Debates*, 1st session 1962, appendix 3, annexure no 48, pp 381-3. Text of television interview on 23 May 1962 in Washington DC on NBC network.

47 A striking aspect of this entente is the growing tendency of the Pakistani press to draw on the *New China News Agency*, Peking, for anti-Indian propaganda: e.g. *Dawn*, Karachi, 19 April 1963, quotes an attack on the 'hypocrisy' of Indian non-alignment policy; *Dawn*, 5 June 1963, repeats a Chinese analysis of deteriorating (Indian) relations with south-east Asia. However, Pakistan has not yet withdrawn from SEATO and CENTO, and presumably this is an indication that she wishes to maintain some links with the West: A. Lamb, 'The Sino-Pakistan Boundary Agreement of 2 March 1963', *Australian Quarterly*, vol 18, no 3, December 1964, pp 299-312, denies that any substantial concessions were made to China in this border agreement.

48 *Lok Sabha Debates*, vol 17, 4th session, short notice question no 7, 22 April 1963, cols 11046-7.

49 *Ibid.*

50 A full description of the defence work of ordnance factories and public sector undertakings is given in *Defence Report, 1963-64*, pp 57-71.

51 Foreign collaboration is being invited in some defence projects, though the scope of such collaboration has not been disclosed for security reasons. Production includes electronic equipment, explosives, jeeps and tanks: *Lok Sabha Debates*, 5 June 1962, vol 5, no 38, question 1587, col 8859. Reply of K. Menon (minister of defence) to Shri Basumatri.

52 Russian military aid started to figure prominently a year or two earlier.

Chapter 11: Conclusion

1 See especially Nehru, *India's Foreign Policy*, pp 37-41 (speech in the Constituent Assembly, 8 March 1949), in which the basic ideological conflicts threatening peace are viewed as basically '..... derived from the background of Europe' (p 39). Although Europe's experience was not divorced from that of India, '.... there is absolutely no reason why we should be asked to choose between this ideology or the other in toto' (p 39).

2 India's failure to officially recognise East Germany is generally assumed to be the result of the West German policy of making aid conditional on non-recognition. There has never been any significant public debate on this issue and one may therefore assume that Indian leaders do not feel that any important point of principle is at stake.

3 Thus advice of noted economists such as W. Rostow, M. Millikan and J. K. Galbraith was frequently sought. When these men became key advisers of President Kennedy, they were in a good position to act in a liaison capacity and clearly had some influence on the shape and size of the Third Plan, particularly with regard to estimating its foreign exchange component. See *Report No. 9: Public International Development Financing in India*, A Research Project of the Columbia University School of Law, New York, 1964, pp 42-68.

4 Cf pp 72-3.

5 Cf pp 69-72. See also appendix no 3.

6 The practical limitations on bargaining are still substantial: see *Report No. 9: Public International Development Financing in India*, pp 54-6. A senior Indian official, much concerned with aid negotiations, estimated during an interview that a combination of country-tying and project-tying can increase the cost to India anywhere up to 60 per cent above what would apply if she received free foreign exchange.

7 Notably the United States, Britain and West Germany. See appendix no 1, table 10.

8 Cf pp 73-80, 82-4.

9 Cf pp 92-111.

10 *Report No. 9: Public International Development Financing In India*, p 43.

11 *Ibid.*, pp 43-4.

12 Cf pp 73-80.

13 Cf pp 56-7. See also chapter 3, note 33.

14 Cf pp 18-19.

15 Cf appendix no 1, table 1.

16 Cf pp 143-6.

17 Cf pp 34-6. Intimately related to agricultural development is the problem of land-ownership. Considerations of efficiency seem likely to involve channelling of aid to the better of farmers; Rao and Narain, *Foreign Aid and India's Economic Development*, pp 79-80. Basically these must be Indian decisions, but foreign donors cannot easily avoid being involved.

Appendix no 2

1 Indian Investment Centre, *Objects and Functions*, Investing in India Series, New Delhi, 1962, pp 77-8, 81-2.

Appendix no 3

1 Minor exceptions are sometimes made in the case of (relatively) small aid-giving institutions such as the Ford and Rockefeller Foundations.

2 Cf chapter 3, note 10.

3 Cf pp 27-9.

4 See Rao and Narain, *Foreign Aid and India's Economic Development*, pp 26-7. Concrete examples given of collaboration agreement for establishment of Uttar Pradesh Agricultural University.

Appendix no 5

1 *Establishment of Oil Refineries in India*, p 34.

2 *Ibid.*, p 26.

Appendix no 6

1 Indian Investment Centre, *Objects and Functions*, Investing in India Series, New Delhi, 1962, pp 12-7.

Appendix no 7

1 Summary of Interim and Final Reports in Government of India Resolutions (no 13 (2) /Lic. pol. /64 dated 13 January 1964 and no 13 (4) /Lic. pol. /64 dated 10 June 1964). Official announcement of government policy arising from Reports published in *Gazette Extraordinary of India*, Government of India, New Delhi, part 1, section 1, 10 June 1964.

2 To consist of: 1. Secretary, Ministry of Industry; 2. Secretary Department of Economic Affairs, or his representative; 3. Secretary, Department of Technical Development or his representative; 4. A representative of the Company Law Division of the Ministry of Finance; 5. Secretaries of the Administrative Ministries concerned or their representatives; 6. A representative of the Planning Commission.

3 Proposed cell for the coordination of licence applications subsequently established as the Department of Technical Development, Ministry of Industry.

Select bibliography

Public documents

External Assistance 1963, Department of Economic Affairs, Ministry of Finance, Government of India, 1964

External Assistance 1964, Ministry of Finance, Department of Economic Affairs, Government of India, 1964.

Report On Currency And Finance For The Year, 1964-65. Reserve Bank of India, Bombay, 1965.

Review of the First Five Year Plan, Government of India Planning Commission, May 1957.

Second Five Year Plan (Summary), Government of India Planning Commission, 1956.

Third Five Year Plan, Government of India Planning Commission, 1961.

The Third Plan Mid-Term Appraisal, Government of India Planning Commission, November, 1963.

Appraisal and Prospects of the Second Five Year Plan, Government of India Planning Commission, 1958.

Fourth Five Year Plan–Resources, Outlays and Programmes, Twenty-Second Meeting of the National Development Council, 5 and 6 September 1965, Government of India Planning Commission, 1965.

Lok Sabha Debates (1951-1964), Lok Sabha Secretariat, New Delhi.

Foreign Assistance Act of 1962, Hearings before the Committee on Foreign Affairs, House of Representatives, 87th Congress, 2nd session, on a Draft Bill to Amend Further the Foreign Assistance Act of 1961, As Amended, And For Other Purposes, U.S. Government Printing Office, Washington, DC.

Foreign Assistance Act of 1963, Hearings before the Committee on Foreign Affairs, House of Representatives, 88th Congress, 1st session on H.R. 5490 To Amend Further the Foreign Assistance Act of 1962, As Amended, And For Other Purposes, U.S. Government Printing Office, Washington, DC, 1963.

Foreign Assistance Act of 1964, Hearings before the Committee on Foreign

Affairs, House of Representatives, 88th Congress, 2nd session, on H.R. 10502 To Amend Further the Foreign Assistance Act of 1963, As Amended, And For Other Purposes, U.S. Government Printing Office, Washington, DC, 1964.

Foreign Operations Assistance (for 1961, 1962, 1963, 1964), Hearings before a Subcommittee of the Committee on Appropriations, House of Representatives, 86th Congress, 2nd session, 87th Congress, 88th Congress, 1st session, U.S. Government Printing Office, Washington, DC.

Mutual Security Appropriations (for 1957, 1958, 1959, 1960), Hearings before A Subcommittee of the Committee on Appropriations, House of Representatives, 84th Congress, 85th Congress, 2nd session, 86th Congress, 1st session, U.S. Government Printing Office, Washington, DC.

United States Congressional Record, 81st, 82nd, 83rd, 84th, 85th, 86th, 87th, 88th Congresses (1949-1964), Washington, DC.

Department of State Bulletin, 30 January 1949, vol 20, no 500, Publication 3,413, p 125. Inaugural address of President Truman (includes Point Four Programme).

Department of State Bulletin, 6 February 1949, vol 20, no 501, Publication 3,421, pp 155-6. Explanatory statement of 'Point Four' principles by Dean Acheson, U.S. Secretary of State.

Department of State Bulletin, 2 July 1951, vol 25, no 627, p 38. Public Law 48, India Emergency Food Act of 1951.

Department of State Bulletin, 11 January 1960, vol 42, no 1,072, p 47, Address to the Indian Parliament by President Eisenhower, 10 December 1960.

Foreign Affairs Record (1961 and 1963), Government of India, Ministry of External Affairs, New Delhi.

Government of India, *Economic Survey 1966-67*, Manager of Publications, New Delhi, 1967.

The Annual Report Carried Out Under Public Law 480, As Amended, During the Period 1 January Through 31 December 1966, U.S. Government Printing Office, Washington, DC, 1967.

U.S. Overseas Loans and Grants–Fiscal Year 1966, Statistics and Reports Division, Office of Program Coordination, AID, 22 August 1966.

Books

Allen, R. L., *Soviet Economic Warfare*, Public Affairs Press, Washington DC, 1960.

Almond, G. A., and J. Coleman (eds), *The Politics of Developing Areas*, Princeton, U.P., New Jersey, 1960.

Bauer, P. T., *Indian Economic Policy and Development*, Allen and Unwin, London, 1961.

Berliner, J. S., *Soviet Economic Aid, The New Aid and Trade Policy in Underdeveloped Countries*, Praeger, New York for the Council on Foreign Relations, 1958.

Billerbeck, K., *Soviet Foreign Aid to the Underdeveloped Countries. An Analysis and a Prognosis*, Archives of World Economy, Hamburg, 1960.

Black, Eugene R., *The Diplomacy of Economic Development*, Harvard U.P., 1960.

Bowles, C., *Ambassador's Report*, Harper, New York, 1964.

Brecher, M., *Nehru–A Political Biography,* Oxford U.P., London 1959.

Chandrasekhar, S., *American Aid and India's Economic Development*, Praeger, New York, 1965.

Documents on International Affairs, 1949-50, selected and edited by Margaret Carlyle, Oxford U.P., London, 1952, pp 705-8. (Exchange of Letters between Nehru, Stalin and Acheson on the Korean issue, 13, 15, 16, 18 and 19 July 1950).

Fituni, L., *Economically Underdeveloped Countries and the West*, Progress Publishers, Moscow, 1963.

Harrison, Selig (ed.), *India and the United States,* Macmillan, New York, 1961.

Harrison, S., *India The Most Dangerous Decades,* Princeton U.P., New Jersey, 1960.

Hunck, J. M., *India's Silent Revolution*, A Survey of Indo-German Cooperation, Verlag Handelsblatt, 1958.

Jackson, B. Ward, *India and The West*, Hamish Hamilton, London, 1961.

Jackson, B. Ward, *The Plan Under Pressure, An Observer's View*, Council for Economic Education, Asia Publishing House, Bombay, 1963.

Jackson, B. Ward, and Zinkin M., *Why Help India?,* Pergamon Press, Oxford, 1963.

Kenen, P. B., *Giant Among Nations: Problems in United States' Foreign Economic Policy*, Harcourt, Brace, New York, 1960.

Kidron, M., *Foreign Investment in India*, Oxford U.P., London 1963.

Labedz, L., 'The U.S.S.R and the Developing Countries' in W. Lacqueur and L. Labedz (eds.), *Polycentrism–The New Factor in International Communism*, Praeger, New York, 1962.

Lakdawala, D. T., *International Aspects of Indian Economic Development*, Oxford U.P., London, 1951.

Lewis, John P., *Quiet Crisis in India*, The Brookings Institution, Washington, DC, 1962.

Malenbaum, W., *East and West in India's Development*, National Planning Association, Washington, DC, 1959.

Malenbaum, W., *Prospects for Indian Development*, Macmillan, New York, 1962.

Millikan, M. and Blackner, D. L. (eds.), *The Emerging Nations: Their Growth and United States Policy*, A study from Center of International Studies, Massachussetts Insitute of Technology, Little Brown, Boston, 1961.

Nag, D. S., *Foreign Economic Policy of Soviet Russia*, Lakshmi Narain Agarwal, Agra, India, 1963.

Nehru, J., *India's Foreign Policy–Selected Speeches, September 1946-April 1961*, Publications Division, Ministry of Information and Broadcasting, Government of India, August 1961.

Overstreet, Gene D. and Windmiller, M., *Communism in India*, University of California Press, 1959.

Pannikar, K. M., *In Two Chinas, Memoirs of a Diplomat*, Allen and Unwin, London, 1955.

Papers Relating to the Second Five Year Plan, Government of India Planning Commission, 1955.

Poplai, S. L. and Talbot, P., *India and America–A Study of Their Relations*, Harper, New York, 1958.

Raj, K. N., *Indian Economic Growth–Performances and Prospects* (text of two lectures delivered at Patna, 24 and 25 January 1965), Allied Publishers, New Delhi, 1965.

Rao, V. K. R. V. and Narain, D., *Foreign Aid and India's Economic Development*, Asia Publishing House, London, for the Institute of Economic Growth, Delhi, 1963.

Report No. 9. Public International Development Financing in India, a Research Project of the Columbia School of Law, New York, July 1964.

Schonfeld, A., *The Attack on World Poverty*, Chatto and Windus, London, 1959.

Staley, E., *Future of Underdeveloped Countries*, Praeger, New York, 1965.

Weiner, M., *The Politics of Scarcity: Public Pressure and Political Response in India*, University of Chicago Press, 1962.

White, J., *Japanese Aid*, Overseas Development Institute, London, 1964.

Wolf, C., *Foreign Aid, Theory and Practice in Southern Asia*, a Rand Corporation Research Study, Princeton U.P., New Jersey, 1966.

Zinkin, M., *Development for Free Asia* (revised edition), Oxford U.P., London, 1963.

Articles

Almond, G. A., 'A Developmental Approach to Political Systems', *World Politics*, vol 17, no 2 (January 1965), pp 183-214.

Arnold, G. L., 'The Dilemmas of Western Aid to Free Asia', *Commentary*, vol 20, no 2, (August 1955), pp 116-24.

Bhargava, 'The Secret of Soviet Success in India', *New Republic* (New York), 26 December 1956.

Brzezinski, Z., 'The Politics of Underdevelopment', *World Politics*, vol 9, no 1, (October 1956), pp 55-75.

Bunker, E., 'Progress and Potential in South Asia–The example of India', *Department of State Bulletin*, vol 42, no 1090 (16 May 1960), p 781.

Chakravarti, P. C., 'Indian Non-Alignment and United States Policy', *Current History*, vol 44, no 259 (March 1963), pp 129-34.

Costa, E. P. W. da., 'India's New Five Year Plan', *Foreign Affairs*, vol 34, no 4 (July 1956), pp 665-72.

Edwardes, M., 'Illusion and Reality in Indian Foreign Policy', *International Affairs*, vol 41, no 1 (January 1965), pp 48-58.

Eldridge, P. J., 'India's Non-Alignment Policy Reviewed', *Australian Outlook*, vol 19, no 3 (August 1965), pp 146-57.

Friedman, M., 'Foreign Economic Aid: Means and Objectives', *Yale Review*, vol 47, no 4 (June 1958), pp 500-16.

Galbraith, J. K., 'A Positive Approach to Aid', *Foreign Affairs*, vol 39, no 3 (April 1961), pp 444-57.

Galbraith, J. K., 'Rival Economic Theories in India', *Foreign Affairs*, vol 36, no 4, pp 587-96.

Gardner, R. N., 'Aid and Trade–Party Views', *Foreign Policy Bulletin*, 15 September 1960.

Gupta, R., 'All About Aid', *The Economic Weekly*, vol 14, no 32 (2 June 1962).

Heymann, H. (jnr), 'Soviet Economic Aid in South-East Asia–Threat of Windfall?', *World Politics*, vol 10, no 1 (October 1957), pp 91-101.

'I.M.F. Must Change', (editorial), *The Economic Weekly*, vol 14, no 1 (6 January 1962).

Heymann, H. (jnr), 'Soviet Foreign Aid as a Problem for U.S. Policy', *World Politics*, vol 12, (July 1960), pp 525-40.

'International Economic Scene' (describes Conference in Washington, DC, under auspices of Committee for Internation Economic Growth headed by Mr Eric Johnston), *The Economic Weekly*, vol 11, no 3 (1 June 1959), pp 19-20.

Kamath, M. V., 'India's Dynamic Neutralism', *Current History*, vol 36, no 211 (March 1959), pp 135.

Klausen, A. M., 'Technical Assistance and Social Conflict–A Case Study from Indo-Norwegian Fishing Project in Kerala, South India', *Journal of Peace Research*, no 1 (1964), pp 5-18.

Knowland, Senator W. F., Speech before the Economic Club of New York, 16 January 1956, *Vital Speeches of the Day*, 15 February,1956, pp 263-66.

Kripalani, A. J. B., 'For Principled Neutrality', *Foreign Affairs,* vol 38, no 1 (October 1959), pp 46-60.

Kust, M. J., 'Economic Development and Agricultural Surpluses', *Foreign Affairs*, vol 35, no 1 (October 1956), pp 105-15.

Lamb, A., 'The Sino-Pakistan Boundary Agreement of March 2, 1963', *Australian Quarterly*, vol 18, no 3 (December 1964), pp 299-312.

Lodge, Cabot H., 'Mutual Aid Through the U.N.', *Department of State Bulletin*, vol 42, no 1,084 (4 April 1960), pp 524-7.

Department of State Bulletin, vol 556, Publication 3,777 (27 February 1950), pp 334-6, 343. Address by George G. MacGhee, Assistant Secretary for Near East, South Asian and African Affairs, to Far East-America Council of Commerce and Industry at New York, on 31 January 1950.

Malebaum, W., 'America's Role in Economic Development Abroad', Department of State Bulletin, vol 20, no 506 (27 March 1949) pp 371-6.

Master, M. A., 'External Assistance for Five Year Plans', *The Asian Economic Review*, vol 3, no 3 (May 1961), pp 213-33.

Mehta, G. L., 'As Others See us–An Indian View', *Foreign Affairs*, vol 37, no 1 (October 1958), pp 107-16.

Morgenthau, H., 'The Immaturity of our Asian Policy', *New Republic*, (New York), 26 March 1956.

Nehru, B. K., 'The Economic Challenge in Indian–Can Democracy Meet It?', *Vital Speeches of the Day*, vol 42, no 1084 (1 September 1956), pp 686-9.

Nove, A., 'The Soviet Model and Underdeveloped Countries', *International Affairs*, vol 37, no 1 (January 1961), pp 29-38.

Packenham, R. A., 'Political Development Doctrines in the American Foreign Aid Program', *World Politics*, vol 18, no 2 (January 1966) pp 194-235.

Palmer, N. D., 'India and the U.S.: Maturing Relations', *Current History*, vol 36, no 211 (March 1959), pp 129-34.

Pauker, G. J., 'South-East Asia as a Problem Area in the Next Decade', *World Politics*, vol 11, no 3 (April 1959), pp 325-45.

Pye, L., 'Soviet and American Styles in Foreign Aid', *Orbis*, vol 4, no 4 (July 1960), pp 159-73.

Rubinstein, A. Z., 'Soviet Policy Towards Under-Developed Areas in the Economic and Social Council', *International Organisation*, vol 9, no 2 (May 1955) pp 232-43.

Rudolph, S. H., 'Consensus and Conflict in Indian Politics', *World Politics*, vol 13, no 4 (April 1961), pp 385-99.

Rusett, A. de, 'On Understanding Indian Foreign Policy', *International Relations*, April 1959, pp 543-56.

Singh, S. L., 'Economic Assistance and Indian Foreign Policy', *Modern Review* (Calcutta), vol 113, no 3 (March 1963), pp 193-201.

Stern, R. E., 'Agricultural Surplus Disposal and U.S. Economic Policies', *World Politics*, vol 12, no 3 (April 1960) pp 422-33.

Sheean, V., 'The Case for India', *Foreign Affairs*, vol 30, no 1 (October 1951), pp 77-90.

Steuber, F., 'Development Assistance–A Growing Concern for Small Nations', *The Economic Weekly* (special number), vols 28, 29 and 30 (July 1962), pp 1,189-92; 'Foreign Exchange Prospects–A Reassessment', *Ibid*., pp 1,079ff.

Stevenson, A., 'Putting First Things First', *Foreign Affairs*, vol 38, no 2 (January 1960), pp 191-208.

Thornton, T. P., 'Peking, Moscow and the Underdeveloped Areas', *World Politics*, vol 13, no 4 (July 1961), pp 491-504.

Viner, J., 'Economic Foreign Policy on the New Frontier', *Foreign Affairs*, vol 39, no 4 (July 1961), pp 560-77.

Wood Tyler C., 'The Role and Character of Foreign Aid: Problems of Foreign Aid Viewed from the Inside', *The American Economic Review*, vol 49, no 2 (May 1959), pp 203-15.

Surveys and reports

Agreement between Government of India and M/S Phillips Petroleum Co. of U.S.A./Duncan Brothers and Co. Ltd. of Calcutta for Establishment of an Oil Refinery–27th April, 1963 (Cochin, Kerala), Government of India, Ministry of Mines and Fuel, Printed in India by the General Manager, Government of India Press, New Delhi, 1963.

Annual Report(s), Rockefeller Foundation, 111 West 50th Street, New York.

Annual Report(s), Ford Foundation, 32 Ferozeshah Road, New Delhi.

British Aid–1: Survey and Comment, Overseas Development Institute, London, W.1, 1963.

British Aid–2: Government Finance, Overseas Development Institute, London, W.1, 1964.

Bulletin on Food Statistics, February 1967, Directorate of Economics and Statistics, Ministry of Food, Agriculture, Community Development and Co-operation (Department of Food), Government of India, New Delhi, 1967.

Clay Committee Report on Foreign Aid, 25 March 1963, Official Text, United States Information Service, American Embassy, London, 1963.

The Colombo Plan, Prepared by Reference Division, Central Office of Information, London, July 1964; Quote No. RF.P. 5583/64, Classification II.5.

Compilation of Studies and Surveys by the Special Committee to Study the Foreign Aid Programme, U.S. Senate, 1957–No. 1. The Objectives of U.S. Economic Assistance Programs, Center of International Studies, Massachusetts Institute of Technology; *Ibid.*, Survey No. 8, Dr Lewis Webster Jones, *South Asia*.

Ellender, Hon., A. J. (U.S. Senator), *A Report on U.S. Foreign Operations*, U.S. Government Printing Office, Washington DC, 1960.

Establishment of Oil Refineries in India–Text of Agreements with the Oil Companies, Ministry of Production, Government of India, New Delhi, 1956.

The Ford Foundation and Foundation-Supported Activities in India. (Summary of Grants from 1951 to 15 January 1964), The Ford Foundation, 32 Ferozeshah Road, New Delhi 1, India.

Food and Fiber for the Future, Report of the National Advisory Committee for Food and Fiber, U.S. Government Printing Office, Washington, DC, July 1967.

Formation Agreement between Government of India and National Iranian Oil Co. and Amoco India Incorporated of U.S.A. for Establishment of an Oil Refinery at Madras–November 18, 1965, Government of India, Ministry of Petroleum and Chemicals. Printed in India by Government of India Press, Minto Road, New Delhi, 1966.

French Aid–The Jeanneney Report, Overseas Development Institute.

Government of India Resolutions Nos 13(2) and 13(4) /Lic. Pol./64 dated January 13 and June 10, 1964 (Reports deal with Government of India Licensing procedures; obtainable from Indian Investment Centre, New Delhi).

Hearn, B. J., *India: A Growing Market for U.S. Products and Investment*, Department of Commerce, Washington, DC, 1963.

Hindustan Steel Ltd.–9th Annual Report 1962-3, Ranchi, Bihar, 1 November 1963.

Hindustan Steel Ltd.–10th Annual Report 1963-4, Ranchi, Bihar, 10 November 1964.

India 1960 . . . India 1961: Reference Annuals compiled by the Research and Reference Division of the Ministry of Information and Broadcasting, Government of India.

Indian Institute of Public Opinion, *Monthly Public Opinion Surveys*, vol 1, nos 7, 8 and 9, February, March and April 1956; vol 2, nos 20 and 21, May and June 1957; vol 3, no 8, May 1958; vol 4, nos 1 and 2, October and November 1958; vol 6, no 3, December 1960; vol 7, nos 5 and 6, February and March 1965; vol 8, no 10, July 1963; vol 10, nos 9 and 10, June and July 1965; vol 11, nos 6 and 7, March-April 1966; vol 11, no 11, August 1966.

India Pocket Book of Economic Information (Annual) Ministry of Finance, Department of Economic Affairs, Manager of Publications, Government of India Press, Delhi.

India 1963, A Report made by Sir Norman Kipping attended by Michael Donovan, Federation of British Industries, 21 Tothill Street, London, S.W.1.

Indian Investment Centre, *Basic Facts of the Indian Economy*, New Delhi, 1962.

Indian Investment Centre, *Objects and Functions*, New Delhi, 1961.

Indian Investment Centre, *Exchange Control*, New Delhi, 1961.

Indian Investment Centre, *Taxation*, New Delhi, 1961.

Indian Investment Centre, *Supplement to Taxation*, New Delhi, 1963.

The Indo-U.S. Technical Cooperation Programme–Report 1963, Ministry of Finance, Department of Economic Affairs, Government of India, December, 1963.

IBRD Press Release No. 650, 19 September 1960, Subject–*Indus Waters Treaty Signed.*

Report 1963-4. Ministry of Defence, Government of India, 1964.

Report of the Oil Price Enquiry Committee (Damle Report), Ministry of Steel, Mines and Fuel, Department of Mines and Fuel, Government of India, July 1961.

Report of the Working Group on Oil Prices–August 1965 (Talukdar Report), Government of India, Ministry of Petroleum and Chemicals, Department of Petroleum, 1965.

Report 1962-3 . . . Report 1963-4 . . . Report 1964-5, Ministry of Steel and Mines, Department of Iron and Steel, Government of India, 1963, 1964 and 1965.

Report of the Foodgrains Policy Committee 1966, Ministry of Food and Agriculture, Community Development and Cooperation (Department of Food), New Delhi, 1967.

Report on India's Food Crisis and the Steps to Meet It, by the Agricultural Production Team Sponsored by the Ford Foundation. Issued by the Government of India, Ministry of Food and Agriculture and the Ministry of Community Development and Cooperation, April 1959.

Statement by G. L. Mehta, Chairman of Indian Investment Centre at the Annual General Meeting, 9 July 1964.

Swaminathan Report (deals with Licensing Procedures), Published in Gazette Extraordinary of India, Government of India, part I, section 1, 10 June 1964.

World Wheat Statistics 1966, International Wheat Council, London, 1967.

Newspapers and magazines

Blitz (New Delhi).

Eastern Economist (New Delhi).

Economic Times (Bombay).

The Economic Weekly (Bombay).

The Hindu (Madras).

The Hindu Weekly Review (Madras).

Hindustan Times (New Delhi).

Indian Express (Delhi).

Link (New Delhi).

The Statesman (Calcutta).

Times of India (New Delhi).

Dawn (Karachi).

Daily Express (London).

Daily Telegraph (London).

Daily Worker (London)

Financial Times (London).

The Guardian (London), formerly *Manchester Guardian*.

The Observer (London).

Observer Foreign News Service (London).

The Scotsman (Edinburgh).

The Times (London).

America (N.Y.).

Business Weekly (N.Y.).

Christian Century (Chicago, Ill.).

Christian Science Monitor (Boston).

Nation (N.Y.).

Newsweek (N.Y.).

New York Herald Tribune (N.Y.).

New York Times (N.Y.).

Time (Chicago, Ill.).

U.S. News and World Report (Washington, D.C.).

Le Figaro (Paris).

Japan Times (Tokyo).

South China Morning Post (Hong Kong).

Soviet News (Moscow).

Other sources

Federation of Indian Chambers of Commerce and Industry: Federation submission to Rao Committee on Utilisation of Foreign Aid (File No. Fin/14 (4) II). Other data on licensing difficulties and collaboration agreements.

B. Salomon, Point Four—*A Study in Political Motivation and Administration Techniques*, Ph.D. thesis presented to the University of London, 1957.

Index